OCCUPATIONAL SUBCULTURES IN THE WORKPLACE

Cornell Studies in Industrial and Labor Relations
Number 26

OCCUPATIONAL SUBCULTURES IN THE WORKPLACE

Harrison M. Trice

ILR Press
Ithaca, New York

Library of Congress Cataloging-in-Publication Data

Trice, Harrison Miller, 1920–
Occupational subcultures in the workplace / Harrison M. Trice.
p. cm.—(Cornell studies in industrial and labor relations:
no. 26)
Includes bibliographical references and index.
ISBN 0-87546-302-9 (cloth).—ISBN 0-87546-303-7
1. Occupations—Sociological aspects. 2. Professions—
Sociological aspects. 3. Corporate culture. 4. Industrial
sociology. 5. Business anthropology. I. Title. II. Series.
HD6955.T75 1993
302.3'5—dc20   92-39034

Copies of this book may be ordered through bookstores or directly
from

ILR Press
School of Industrial and Labor Relations
Cornell University
Ithaca, NY 14853-3901

Printed in the United States of America

5   4   3   2

A Song for Occupations

A song for occupations!
In the labor of engines and trades and the labor of fields
I find the developments,
And find the eternal meanings.

—Walt Whitman, *Leaves of Grass*

CONTENTS

ACKNOWLEDGMENTS   *ix*

INTRODUCTION   *xi*

PART I. AN EMPHASIS ON OCCUPATIONS AND
    THEIR CULTURES   *1*

1. The Nature of Occupational Life   *3*

2. Occupational Cultures   *20*

3. Ideologies in Occupational Life   *46*

4. Cultural Forms in Occupations   *82*

5. Rites of Passage in Occupational Cultures: Learning to
    Be an Insider   *112*

PART II. OCCUPATIONAL CULTURES INSIDE WORK
    ORGANIZATIONS   *139*

6. Occupational Subcultures and Countercultures   *141*

7. Adaptations between Occupational and
    Administrative Subcultures   *160*

8. Adaptations between Occupational Cultures   *186*

9. Conclusions and Implications: Toward a
   Subcultural Analysis of Organizational Culture   212

REFERENCES   229

INDEX   275

ACKNOWLEDGMENTS

THIS BOOK builds upon two previous publications with two different colleagues. *The Cultures of Work Organizations* (Trice and Beyer 1992) contains a chapter on occupational subcultures as well as a detailed examination of the concept of culture as it applied to other dimensions of work organizations. I have drawn repeatedly from the concepts and, at times, the empirical examples in that book. Professor Janice Beyer, of the College of Business Administration at the University of Texas at Austin, made many significant and essential contributions to that volume, including the refinement of concepts and their clear presentation. Without her input that work would probably have remained unpublished. The rather vague term "acknowledgments" for her work seems too weak, for without it I would not have gone on to this one. She deserves my deep appreciation, or said somewhat differently, my eternal gratitude.

Some years ago, in 1983 or 1984, a stroke of good fortune brought me into close collaboration with William Sonnenstuhl, an assistant professor at Cornell University's School of Industrial and Labor Relations. For some four years his keen intellect and critical assessments, combined with his emotional support, were of inestimable value in pulling together the relevant concepts and literature. His contributions were many and his support unwavering. Fortunately, he and I found the opportunity to collaborate on a piece about the interplay between occupations and organizations that has influenced this monograph, both directly and indirectly (Sonnenstuhl and Trice 1991).

Shirley Foster and her "library task force" of undergraduates deserve high praise for going well beyond the call of duty. They assiduously searched out relevant materials, making the phrase "library research" a palpable reality. Moreover, I owe acknowledgments to the Cornell University library system, a repository of knowledge I believe to be unsurpassed.

Also, more than routine recognition should be extended to ILR Press editor Erica Fox; to ILR Press managing editor Patty Peltekos; and to its director, Frances Benson. In my younger years I not only feared editors of any sort, but often held them in awe. The work of these three competent editors has strengthened and reaffirmed what I have slowly learned: Editors are empathetic persons; also they are valuable, even essential, to the process of preparing manuscripts. My appreciation for their help with this one will be a cherished memory for me.

Frances Viggiani, who was a graduate student when I was completing the manuscript, and advanced undergraduates in the course "The Study of Occupational Cultures" in the School of Industrial and Labor Relations at Cornell, have read and critiqued numerous of the chapters. They cannot all be named here, but during their field work they sharpened, challenged, and aided in revamping many of my main points. They have my heartfelt gratitude.

Introduction

INCREASINGLY, STUDENTS OF organizational behavior are maintaining that workplaces are cultures. Although different versions of this concept currently prevail, basic notions are common to all. There is agreement, for instance, that organizations develop distinctive sets of emotionalized, collectively held beliefs that impel members of these organizations to act in certain ways. These beliefs are, in essence, ideologies. Although ideologies are general sets of abstract ideas, they are necessarily expressed concretely through symbols, ceremonies, myths, rituals, stories, special languages, sagas, taboos and rites. These symbols and so on are, in effect, cultural forms that together with ideologies constitute the major ingredients of a culture. Studies of IBM (Deal and Kennedy 1982), colleges (Clark 1970), Jaguar Cars (Whipp, Rosenfeld, and Pettigrew 1989), Cadbury Limited (Child and Smith 1987; Dellheim 1987), and predivestiture AT&T (Tunstall 1983) strongly suggest that many work organizations develop a core culture that contains elements embraced by almost all the employees.

Organizational Subcultures

In addition to a distinctive core culture, organizations usually contain subcultures. "They have the same elements that cultures have: distinctive patterns of shared ideologies and distinct sets of cultural forms" (Trice and Beyer 1992), yet they differ noticeably from the core culture in which they are embedded. These ideologies and cultural forms will either enhance, or deviate from, the core ideologies and forms.

Subcultures are likely to form within informal groups, such as cabals and coalitions, and in formal groups, such as departments and management bureaucracies. Groups defined by demographic characteristics—age, sex, and ethnicity—also have a high potential for becoming significant subcultures.

One of the most powerful subcultures is made up of the higher echelons of management. One set of beliefs among members is that they dictate how to organize work and arrange the division of labor among employees. They believe that they should decide how tasks are divided, who will do them, and who should control the selection and training of employees. Further, they insist on a hierarchy of offices in which they are at or near the top and on a system of administrative rules and regulations. They constitute the "quintessential bureaucratic work group in our society" (Jackall 1988:12).

OCCUPATIONAL SUBCULTURES: A NEGLECTED DIMENSION OF ORGANIZATIONAL CULTURES

Another distinctive and organized source of subcultures in work life is occupational groups. Each such group tends vigorously to embrace, even attempt to create, a core culture. Such groups include persons who have mastered and applied specialized knowledge about the performance of a set of specialized tasks. Because of this esoteric capacity, they believe that certain workers have rights to perform certain work, to control training for the access to doing such work, and to control the way it is performed and evaluated (Freidson 1973). There is a clear-cut possibility that these ideologies will clash with the upper-management subculture and, in effect, deviate significantly at times from the organizational culture.

Although typically practiced within an organizational culture, occupations tend to be cultures in and of themselves. But despite this basic point, they have been largely overlooked by students of organizational cultures. One of the underlying themes of this book is that occupations are often very prominent subcultures in organizations but that they have been largely overlooked by scholars who attempt to understand organizational cultures. That understanding will be expanded and refined if the concept of culture is also applied to occupations. Part I of this book addresses this oversight by defining the cultural elements present in many occupations and showing how members socialize newcomers into the practices of a given occupation. Because the materials about occupational cultures are in a wide variety of books and journals and the concept is very much neglected, the majority of this book will be devoted to occupational cultures.

Members of occupations do not apply their knowledge and skills in a vacuum. To get their work done, they often must interrelate with members of other occupations, both within a specific organization and in the surrounding community. And, of course, they must also relate to the administrative hierarchy within the work organization itself. Part II examines occupations as subcultures and their modes of adaptation within these relationships. The implications for other relationships are also explored in part II, especially in chapter 9. Chapter 1 focuses on the inherently conflictual and dynamic nature of occupational life, against which occupations develop their cultures and interrelate with other cultures.

THEMES OF THIS BOOK

Three themes guide this study. The first theme is that occupations are distinct cultures in and of themselves; when practiced within organizations—as they usually are—they can be potent subcultures. Since the concept of culture has only infrequently been directly applied to occupations, it is necessary to develop this concept first before the role of occupations as subcultures in organizational cultures can be explored. Repeatedly, occupations have been left out of cultural analysis. The need to include them is a major theme of this book.

The second theme is that the inclusion of occupations as subcultures makes for a shift in emphasis in the study of organizational cultures. The change is from the study of a single, overall organizational culture to the interrelationships and adaptations of the multiplicity of subcultures that typically reside within an organization's boundaries. Occupations are only one example of this condition—a classical and prominent instance, but only one of the many subcultures that populate organizations.

The third theme—one that is closely related to the other two—is that occupations are dynamic, not static, collectivities. Control over their unique body of task knowledge will ebb and flow over time—very suddenly in some cases, gradually in others, and over a decade or so in still others. But change they will.

HISTORICAL BACKGROUND

A brief history of the cultural approach to the study of organizations reveals the neglect of occupations. Despite some modest attention in the early period, occupational cultures have been largely absent.

The use of the cultural approach is not recent. Its earliest use appears to be in the well-known bank-wiring room segment of the famous Hawthorne studies in late 1931 through the spring of 1932. This segment revealed the presence of an overall culture among the employees in the bank-wiring assembly room. Fairness, a living wage, and a right to work were the main ideology, giving rise to a emotionalized justification for the restriction of production. But even here a difference in task clusters (potential occupations) distinguished selector wiremen and soldermen. These two subgroups differed in status and in their intensity of feelings about the restriction of output.

The bank-wiring room study was set up by a specialist in human cultures—an anthropologist, W. Lloyd Warner. He introduced the research methods of cultural anthropology: observation and interviewing. Using these methods, his group focused on the changed set of beliefs about work among the employees in the bank-wiring assembly room.

During the mid-1940s, the Committee on Human Relations in Industry carried forward the interest in culture. Anthropologist Warner was its chairperson, and one of his students, Burleigh B. Gardner, was its executive secretary. The committee sponsored numerous culturally oriented research projects from 1942 until 1947. One of the most prominent was an ethnographic study of restaurants by William F. Whyte (1948). He focused on the culture of informal groups in restaurants and on the symbols that carried explicit meanings. In the process, he paid considerable attention to cooks, chefs, waiters, and waitresses. Except for this notice of occupations, they were given only scant attention during this period. "In five short years," however, "there was an unusual flourishing of anthropological and sociological research . . . a unique combination of circumstances involving academia, business, a great industrial city and the times" (Moore 1982:121).

DECLINE OF INTEREST IN THE CULTURAL APPROACH

Unfortunately, this strong beginning for the cultural study of work organizations did not last, and "very few anthropologists joined these pioneers" (Whyte 1978:130). Members of the Committee on Human Relations in Industry scattered. The rational, bureaucratic model of how organizations behave came to dominate the thinking of organizational scholars (Thompson 1967). This model was reinforced by the rise of high-speed computers. Through the 1960s and well into the 1970s, the model prevailed despite the scattered efforts of a few American and British researchers to continue the anthropological tradition begun by Warner and his students (e.g., Roy 1952, 1953, 1954, 1960; Turner 1971; Trice, Belasco, and Alluto 1969). Neither the cultures of organizations nor the culture of occupations received much attention during this period, although the approach did not die out completely.

RECENT REVIVAL OF INTEREST

Within the last decade a rather robust revival of interest in the cultural study of organizations has occurred. But, again, the focus has been largely on the study of organizational, not occupational, cultures. Numerous researchers had become disillusioned with the quantitative methods and quasi-experimental designs used with the bureaucratic model (Ouchi and Wilkins 1985) because of the rather trivial amounts of variance they explained and their failure to produce much prediction. Also, the structural/rational (bureaucratic) approach failed to include crucial aspects of how organizations actually functioned and how they affected the lives of their members. Thus, for this and other reasons, a search began for alternatives and a revival of the cultural approach.

In the early 1980s, three best-selling books argued that the cultural approach was an important alternative for understanding and managing organizations. These books were *In Search of Excellence* (Peters and Waterman 1982), *Theory Z* (Ouchi 1981), and *Corporate Cultures: The Rites and Rituals of Corporate Life* (Deal and Kennedy 1982). Business and trade magazines such as *Fortune* and *Business Week* published articles on the subject, while major newspapers such as the *Wall Street Journal* and the *New York Times* carried stories on it. Between 1983 and 1985, five business schools in major universities held at least five conferences on corporate culture or organizational symbolism. Three of these were published as books (Pondy et al. 1983; Frost et al. 1985; Kilmann, Saxton, and Serpa 1985). Since the mid-1980s, the Academy of Management, the professional association of teachers of management subjects in colleges and universities, has included a section of papers on organizational cultures at its annual program. Courses, both graduate and undergraduate, in business schools and departments of psychology, sociology, and anthropology are given in increasing numbers of universities. And for many consultants the approach has become an appealing "quick fix" (Kilmann 1984). Finally, academic journals continue to accept and publish research efforts to refine and explore the basic notion that work organizations are cultures.

But even in the midst of all this ferment, examination, and elaboration of the cultural approach to work organizations, one of the major modes for the organization of work—occupations—has remained largely ignored. Similarly, that occupations might themselves constitute cultures has been, with a few exceptions, downplayed and bypassed. At the same time, a recognition of the multiplicity of cultures in work organizations has become somewhat commonplace (Wuthnow and Witten 1988). That occupations are probably a significant source of that multiplicity has, ironically, escaped systematic attention. One group of researchers recently wrote that "occupational cultures have received considerably less attention in the literature than either national or organizational cultures, with a few exceptions" (Hofstede et al. 1990: 312).

Another group (Barley and Tolbert 1991:3) went even further, declaring that "organizational theorists, in particular, have almost completely ignored occupational phenomena, even though the interplay between occupation and organization clearly constitutes a central dynamic in the work lives of many individuals."

Equally unnoticed has been the impact the notion of cultural multiplicity will have on the concept of organizational cultures. That notion is bringing about a rethinking of the entire cultural approach. An exception is Joanne Martin and Debra Meyerson's formulation of three basic models of organizational cultures. One, known as differentiation, "emphasizes subcultures and usually does not even acknowledge sources of organization-wide agreements" (1988:110). A focus on the interrelation between subcultures will come to the fore along with a dynamic assessment of the ongoing adjustments that characterize those relationships. One way to commence this examination is to set forth an application of the cultural approach to occupations. With this in hand, the various adaptations between occupational subcultures, including those between subcultures, and a second largely unexamined subculture—that composed of high-status managerial employees—can be explored. This is the second theme of this book.

Such an exploration sets the stage for the perusal of other forms of subcultures and the mapping of their interrelationships. Here again a dynamic theme—the third one—emerges, for not only are occupations in and between themselves conflictual and dynamic in nature, but so too are their interrelations with other subcultures within organizations.

PART I. AN EMPHASIS ON OCCUPATIONS AND THEIR CULTURES

THE PURPOSE OF Part I is to underscore the cogency of occupations as cultures and as a distinctive part of work life. When they are disregarded, as they often are by students of work organizations, one side of a major dynamic in many work lives is missing, that is, the interplay between occupations and organizations. Efforts to understand organizations are thereby impaired. Consequently, this part focuses exclusively on occupations and their cultures in an effort to correct this imbalance. Following a close examination of occupational cultures in Part I, Part II will examine them as subcultures *inside* organizations in an effort to focus on the interplay between them and the numerous other subcultures with which they must interact, especially managerial subcultures.

Chapter 1 sets forth some of the unique features of occupations that distinguish them from organizations. It recognizes that organizations have come to be a potent force in work life. Nevertheless, occupations, in some form, continue to be a basic mechanism for organizing work. Chapter 2 examines the cultural dimensions of occupations and the factors in work life that encourage them.

Chapters 3, 4, and 5 focus upon three major cultural dimensions of occupations: ideologies, cultural forms, and the rites of passage that socialize members into an occupation. Although these are abstract concepts, Part I includes numerous empirical examples that add real life to the cultural framework presented.

1. THE NATURE OF
OCCUPATIONAL LIFE

*Occupations offer us an extreme and lighted instance of a
general aspect of all human societies. For society, by its
very nature, consists of both allowing and expecting some
people to do things which other people are not allowed to
do. All occupations include as part of their very being a
license to deviate in some measure from common modes of
behavior.*

—Everett C. Hughes

H ISTORICALLY, INSTITUTIONS such as the family, church, and community have dominated American life, but their influence has
waned as people have turned to the world of work as a primary source of economic rewards, interpersonal relations, recognition,
and emotional support. Some observers (Turnbull 1984) even conclude
that Americans have substituted competitive career success at any price
for traditional values. Although research data are not available to support these observations fully, it seems reasonable to believe that work
may provide "the single most important source of identity for individuals living in modern industrial societies" (Van Maanen 1977:176).
Thus, in a highly pluralistic society—the United States—citizens apparently are focusing almost exclusively on only one of its institutions—the workplace.

Accordingly, Americans today seem more preoccupied with work
than at any other time in their history. Work and the idea that time is
money are central themes for many segments of the work force (Triandis 1973:43). Even workers for whom leisure is the most affordable and
available "work many hours, week after week—sometimes reaching a
truly startling lifetime total" (Wilensky 1964b:139). Rosabeth M. Kanter
(1989:268) cites a *Wall Street Journal* survey that found that 88 percent
of top management worked ten or more hours a day, 18 percent worked
twelve or more hours, and 94 percent worked at least an hour every
weekend. The working time of average nonmanagerial employees has
also increased steadily since 1970, to the point that today they work an
estimated 164 extra hours of paid labor a year. One careful study concludes that this is an overall reversal of a previous decline in hours

worked and constitutes a "shrinkage of leisure," making leisure time less and less relevant (Schor 1991). A contrast with preindustrial cultures makes this point truly cogent. People in these societies worked on average no more than eight hundred hours a year, whereas high achievers in industrialized societies work several thousand hours a year (Sahlins 1972).

OCCUPATIONS WITHIN ORGANIZATIONS

Much of this work life has been organized around occupations. The eminent sociologist Émile Durkheim (1964a) put great emphasis on occupational life, suggesting that in modern society, nation states and work organizations were too distant from individuals to provide them with a sense of place and that the institutions of traditional society, such as family and religion, had become too weak to do so. Consequently, he foresaw modern life as revolving around occupations. Durkheim's focus on occupations influenced the Chicago school of sociology, whose early practitioners studied members of a variety of occupations, including waitresses (Donovan 1920), salesladies (Donovan 1931), public school teachers (Donovan 1938), thieves (Sutherland 1937), and taxi-dancers (Cressey 1932). This scholarly interest in occupations continues to the present through the work of writers such as George Ritzer and David Walczak (1986), Robert A. Rothman (1987), and Ronald M. Pavalko (1988). In addition, the JAI Press of Greenwich, Connecticut, inaugurated two series of annual research monographs that focus on occupations (Simpson and Simpson 1981–; Lopata 1990–).[1]

Other analysts, however, have pointed to the emergence and proliferation of organizations, as opposed to occupations, as one of the great social transformations that distinguishes the modern from the premodern world (Scott 1981). According to this view, there has been a "waning of occupational solidarity" as organizations wield "increasing supremacy in the work world" (Abbott 1989:276). This view dominates much of the recent scholarly attention given to studies of the workplace. In two sophisticated books on organizational behavior, for ex-

1. The position and prestige of occupations in the general social order have also provided indexes to status attainment and social stratification (Blau and Duncan 1967; Duncan and Hodge 1963; Hall 1969). Furthermore, the insightful work of John Van Maanen and Stephen R. Barley (1984) has been a turning point. Their seminal work pointed clearly to the need for the careful inclusion of occupational cultures in the study of work organizations.

ample, occupations as such are addressed only briefly (Perrow 1986; Scott 1987). Furthermore, content analysis of six sociological journals— two specialized and four general—published during 1976 and 1982 indicated the "inattention paid to unions and collective action by American scholars who deal with occupations," but a French specialized journal was quite the opposite (Hall 1983:9). Since unions can reflect an occupational base, these findings suggest that students of work life tend to ignore occupations. It seems fair to conclude that most current teaching and research about organizational behavior focus almost exclusively on organizations, rather than occupations, as the mode for organizing work life.

Despite this academic trend, it seems likely that occupations will continue to play a prominent role in work life. At the same time, work organizations obviously play a very potent role indeed. In short, occupations, with a few exceptions, have, in the past century, come to apply their knowledge and skills within the framework of organizations. This fact clearly changed the nature of occupational life but did not necessarily eliminate it. The long and influential history of occupations, reaching from ancient times to the present, suggests that to dismiss them summarily would be unfortunate. Consider the following examples.

In the ancient world the emergence of copper miners helped humankind move into the Bronze Age. The written symbols needed to transact the sale and exchange of merchandise required much skill and precision, and complex and lengthy training was necessary to prepare scribes for laborious recordkeeping. In a history of Egypt written in Greek around 300 B.C., Imhotep was specifically designated as an engineer and credited with building the first Egyptian pyramid for King Joser (DeCamp 1960). Engineers and architects also built the aqueducts of ancient Rome, Solomon's temple, and the Tower of Babel. There were also many famous coaches in ancient Greece, and, in the second century A.D. Philostratus wrote a sophisticated handbook for athletic coaches describing in detail how they differed from teachers of gymnastics (Ball and Loy 1975). Blacksmithing was a common and essential occupation anywhere horses were basic to transportation and war. Plumbing became an occupational specialty as housing developed over the past two centuries. Accountants first appeared as a clear-cut occupation in colonial America in 1718 when a Mr. Tymms began to maintain the financial records of merchants and shopkeepers in Boston (Previtz and Merino 1979).

Occupations have also played crucial roles in more recent American history. For example, General Dwight D. Eisenhower's decision during World War II to launch the invasion of Europe on June 5–6, 1944, was "one of the truly great decisions in military history," and he based it on the "strength of a weather forecast." The meteorologists who had made the forecast were right: a fair-weather interval did follow the night's turbulence, permitting a surprise landing (Eisenhower 1986:251). Similarly, the cryptographers who broke the Japanese naval codes just before the crucial battle of Midway produced the basic intelligence essential to an American surprise attack and victory in this crucial engagement (Prange 1982). And, although they were often laughed at, stereotyped, and the butt of oil drillers' jokes, geologists nevertheless "had led to the finding of three-fourths of the oil discovered from 1920 to 1929" in American oil fields (Boatright 1963:89).

Moreover, occupations have provided Americans with heroes and heroines: Edward R. Murrow and Mike Wallace for journalists, Clarence Darrow for lawyers, Frank Lloyd Wright for architects, Florence Nightingale for nurses, Jane Addams for social workers, Vince Lombardi for coaches, Benjamin Franklin for printers, Herbert Hoover for engineers, and Julia Child for chefs. These heroes and heroines are rarely associated with a given organization, as Pierre S. DuPont of the DuPont Company, Thomas Watson of IBM, or David Packard of Hewlett-Packard would be. This point is highlighted in a cross-cultural comparison of Western occupations with those in Japan. Citing William G. Ouchi (1981) and R. E. Cole and K. Tominaga (1976), James R. Lincoln and Kerry McBride (1987:297) write as follows:

> In Western—especially American—organizations, job titles proliferate, and individuals generally pursue careers within occupational specialties. One oft-noted reason is the attempt by American unions to preserve control over task assignments and labor supply by insisting on detailed job classification and work rules. More generally, however, a case could be made that occupational consciousness and organization play an unusually central role in American culture and social structure, owing to a variety of institutional processes, such as the strength of the professions, the vocational emphasis of American education, and relatively weak attachment to employing organizations and local communities.

Even though occupations continue to be a force in American work life, they unquestionably are less so than in past decades. Increasingly, members of occupations have come to practice within the boundaries of large, bureaucratic firms. These organizations themselves create new occupations to meet their needs or train internal employees not only in how to perform certain traditional tasks but also in how to do them within the organizational framework. Further, management frequently has been successful in deskilling occupations, regardless of their origins. Nevertheless, occupations continue to be a prominent feature of work life even though their incorporation into organizational structures is a distinct trend. As we shall see, occupations are prominent subcultures within organizations.

FEATURES OF OCCUPATIONS

DISTINCTIVE SET OF TASKS

Members of an occupation claim the right to perform a distinctive set of tasks, and an occupation cannot be said to exist until there is a consensus that certain individuals are expected to perform these tasks and to exercise degrees of control over how they are done (Hughes 1958; Child and Fulk 1982). The occupational right to perform a particular kind of work is enhanced through the possession of a relatively distinct and unique knowledge base, which members must master and be able to put into practice. The distinctiveness of an occupation resides in its unique body of knowledge, often combined with an unusual trait of those occupying it. Architects, for example, see themselves as artistic and creative as well as possessing knowledge about planning and supervising the construction of buildings (Blau 1984).

Occupations tend to be the result of conflict in which groups of workers struggle to win a social mandate to perform a set of tasks. Journalists emerged, especially during the 1920s, partly as a result of conflict with salaried publicity agents. Efforts to generate "objectivity" were encouraged as journalists consistently encountered the publicity agents' distorted versions of the truth (Abbott 1988). Considerable controversy erupted between lawyers and accountants, particularly in the 1940s and 1950s, over which occupation was legally constituted to perform certain areas of tax work and related management consulting (Montagna 1974). And, most recently, midwives have been increasingly challenging doctors for the legal right to assist women in giving birth. Even in highly stratified work organizations, "occupations struggle to divide skill, authority, earnings, work control, status, and privileges" (Form 1987:45).

Thus, occupations reflect divisions of labor that come about through dynamic social interactions "in the course of which the participants are continually engaged in attempting to define, establish, maintain, and renew the tasks they perform and the relationship with others which their tasks presuppose" (Freidson 1976:311). Rothman (1979:495) reviewed research on occupations and reported that it contained a "view of occupational roles as dynamic and shifting, responding to external groups."

Occupations are opportunistic, taking root and developing in niches created by new technology, new functions, new concepts, or scarcity in the labor market. Today's engineering occupations, for instance, grew out of the older occupations of civil engineering and metalworking during the mid-nineteenth century when large-scale chemical and electrical companies such as DuPont and General Electric required many technicians for their new processes (Noble 1979; Zussman 1985). Similarly, the occupations comprising rehabilitation therapy took root during the two world wars when medicine and nursing failed to supply the necessary personnel to care for and rehabilitate wounded soldiers (Gritzer and Arluke 1985).

Occupations also develop around very different kinds of knowledge. Crafts such as carpentry, plumbing, electrical work, and baking developed around the mastery of specific techniques and strategies for performing tasks, while professions such as medicine and law developed around more abstract bodies of knowledge. In these occupations members' "practical skills grow out of an abstract system of knowledge, and control of the occupation lies in the control of abstractions that generate the practical techniques" (Abbott 1988:8).

Andrew Abbott suggests that occupations "make up an interacting system, an ecology" (1988:33) and that their development is quite idiosyncratic, with events accumulating in "fits and starts." In developing a unique identity and consolidating control over distinctive tasks, members of all occupations must overcome a series of obstacles that vary depending on the historical time and social context (Larson 1977). Generally, members must construct an occupational association to press claims for exclusive control over their distinctive tasks, establish educational processes for socializing newcomers, resolve conflict about what actually constitutes their unique work, and create a social consensus that they have the legitimate right to perform the distinctive tasks that they claim for themselves. According to Abbott (1988:18), the "next event after an occupational association may be licensing, examinations, or a code of ethics." Members of occupations may also try to secure governmentally sponsored licensing legislation. While there is no predictable series of stages that all occupations go through (Abbott 1988), I will use Harold L. Wilensky's (1964a) broad outline of the typical processes as a starting point for describing how occupations become identified with a set of distinctive tasks.

First, workers begin to perform certain specific and relatively complex sets of work tasks on a full-time basis and, in the process, accumulate either a body of abstract knowledge or task-related strategies and techniques. Next, workers begin to set up and attempt to control programs for teaching newcomers the accumulating body of knowledge and techniques. Although informal techniques for socializing newcomers may already be in existence, it is the establishment of formal training that characterizes the developing occupation. In craft occupations, formal education may take the form of apprentice programs; in applied occupations, it generally takes the form of college education.

Those workers pushing for formal training, and the first ones to go through it, usually then combine to form an occupational association directed toward taking collegial control via the education of newcomers and the designation of peers who are qualified to review the practice and performance of their work. At this point the occupational association will often seek to accredit via its own examinations those newcomers who have completed the prescribed training.

In forming an occupational association, members struggle among themselves to define and control the performance of their distinctive tasks and the strategies used to perform them. The association must also mediate between the "old guard," those who have not been through the formal training, and the newcomers. During this period, the association also attempts to exclude from performing their distinctive tasks those workers who have not gone through formal training. It is here that the major boundaries of an occupation become tentatively defined. As the emerging occupation competes and negotiates with other workers who also claim control of the disputed tasks, their tentative "jurisdiction" (Abbott 1988:20) over those tasks begins to prevail.

Members of an occupational association typically agitate politically to win legal support for their claim to the exclusive right to perform certain tasks. Such recognition often comes in the form of state licensure, certification, or unionization. And, having attempted to erect boundaries around their right, associations also press for the adoption of a formal code of ethics proclaiming a commitment to scrupulous service for clients and to the responsibility of individual practitioners rather than the organization within which they practice. In some instances, an occupation may emerge full blown, skipping practically all of the stages. Psychiatry, for example, began with the formation of a group of "medical reformers," mostly asylum administrators and a few neurologists, who declared that the mad were sick. They quickly created a formal association, a code of ethics, and a journal (Abbott 1988).

Even though members of craft occupations possess less complex skills and require less training than do those in the applied occupations, the development processes described above apply to them as well. Indeed, Wilensky's (1964a) major point is that workers seek to be called "professionals," even though there may be an enormous discrepancy in the degree of complexity in their skills and training time. As complexity and preparation time decline, so does the degree of control that the occupation can expect to exercise over the performance of its tasks. Nevertheless, occupations tend to have similar developmental elements. Occupational associations may be less clearly formed in craft occupations than in the applied occupations, but often the main outlines can be discerned.

CONTROL OVER TASKS

Another distinguishing feature of an occupation is that it has control over its specific set of tasks and the distinct body of knowledge about how those tasks are to be performed. In dynamic terms, these tasks and who performs them can and often do change: other occupations may claim a right to do some of them, new occupations may emerge via a recombination of some of them, or the tasks themselves may become obsolete or transformed through the ever-present efforts of managers and employers to deskill them.

Members of occupations tend to insist that they, rather than administrators, are the ones qualified to decide if a mistake has been made in the performance of their tasks. Everett C. Hughes (1958:93) is insistent on this point: "A colleague-group (the people who consider themselves subject to the same work risks) will stubbornly defend its own right to define mistakes, and to say in a given case when one has been made." Such a group claims that it understands the requirements of its work and insists on the right to decide that a mistake has indeed been made. Lawyers, doctors, and accountants, for example, are vehement in their insistence that only their occupational peers are qualified to review and pass on performance. Thus, even in large, specialized law firms, promotion decisions are under the control of one's colleagues, not in the hands of those lawyers that make up the firm's formal hierarchy (Tolbert and Stern 1988). Mistakes occur frequently among skilled construction workers, but they "learn the techniques of mistake management along with installation techniques" (Riemer 1979:131). Jazz musicians firmly deny the layperson's ability to judge whether or not they are playing badly (Becker 1951). Baseball players, by contrast, are unable to escape the judgment of their audience.

> The audience has a degree of expertise rarely found in most practitioner-client relationships and, in one way or another, the client has paid for the privilege of voicing his opinion in the form of cheering or booing. [For the baseball player] mistakes at work are closely watched by fans, judged by an outsider and computer and published regularly in the mass media and official record books (Haerle 1975:465).

Falling between these two extremes are those members of occupations who exercise considerable control over their tasks but have no agreed-upon criteria for evaluating their performance. Thus, among public school teachers "there has been no consensus within the teaching profession as to what constitutes competent teaching performance" (Gross 1988:58). This may be due, in part, to the unique history of public school teaching in America. George Baron and Asher Tropp (1970:89) contrasted English and American teachers, concluding that in England "the content of what is taught in the schools is virtually never discussed save in professional gatherings of educators, whereas in America constant efforts, through citizen committees and parent-teacher associations, to insure that what is done in the schools is done with the 'authority' of lay opinion." When charged with incompetence and inefficiency, American teachers are at the mercy of school boards, hearing officers and special panels, and arbitrators (Gross 1988). Richard L. Warren (1975:147), in his case study of teaching experiences in a metropolitan area of the western United States, characterized teachers as isolated from the milieu in which they work—"a lonely accommodation with the organizational and cultural context."

Somewhat similarly, the specific knowledge needed to be a librarian is not clear: "Lay opinion does not recognize any special talent for librarianship even among those about to graduate, nor is there any commonly accepted criterion by which one might judge good or poor performance by a librarian" (Goode 1961:312). Despite these handicaps, both librarians and teachers exercise considerable control over how their tasks are performed. For instance, "egg crate school structures" (Lortie 1975) have developed in most American schools. In each of their separate niches, "teachers have considerable autonomy over instruction and classroom management" (Peterson 1987:137).

Although the accumulation of distinctive, unique knowledge is most advanced, integrated, and controlled among the high-status occupations where abstract knowledge tends to prevail, it also exists in the crafts. Here knowledge consists of folklore, experiences, and techniques. Thus, funeral directors, plumbers, electricians, miners, and journalists all possess distinctive bodies of craft knowledge. Access and exposure to this corpus of knowledge is, in large part, controlled by the occupation. Members teach newcomers either informally on the job or in a formal setting (e.g., apprentice programs), and the length of training can vary from a few months to several years. As newcomers progress through the socialization process, they come to identify with, and become committed to, the tasks of the occupation, even though the conditions surrounding their performance may be controlled by an organization. This commitment deepens as the newcomers make sacrifices to enter and remain in the occupation and renounce other options for making a living.

Studies of occupations have tended to focus almost exclusively on such high-status fields as law and medicine. This study develops a framework for the analysis of many occupations, rather than exclusively those often referred to as "the professions." I concur with Frederick C. Gamst (1977:2), who admonished anthropologists interested in the workplace "to study coal miners, railroaders, truckers, farmers, fishermen, loggers, police and soldiers." As Hughes (1958:48–49) wrote:

Perhaps there is as much to be learned about the high-prestige occupations by applying to them the concepts which naturally come to mind for study of people in the most lowly kinds of work as there is to be learned by applying to other occupations the conceptions developed in connection with the highly-valued professions. Furthermore, I have come to the conclusion that it is a fruitful thing to start study of any social phenomenon at the point of least prestige. For, since prestige is so much a matter of symbols, and even of pretensions—however well merited—there goes with prestige a tendency to preserve a front which hides the inside of things; a front of names, of indirection, of secrecy (much of it necessary secrecy). On the other hand, in things of less prestige, the core may be more easy of access.

SUBGROUPS WITHIN OCCUPATIONS

The boundaries of an occupational group are not determined by geography. Nor can they be derived from either the Census Bureau's classification of occupations or its job titles. Indeed, job title and Census Bureau classifications can be particularly misleading (Abbott 1988). For instance, the Census Bureau's occupational category "professional, technical, and kindred" covers authors, draftsmen, striptease artists, and accountants; it is doubtful that these workers would recognize themselves as being part of the same occupational category (Van Maanen and Barley 1984). Similarly, the job title "manager" covers a wide range of workers who probably are not conscious of belonging to the same occupational group. Many high-status occupations are composed of subcultures of academics, managers, and practitioners (Freidson 1986).

Conventional labels, such as lawyer and librarian, are likewise somewhat misleading because insiders may recognize subcultures that are mutually exclusive and distinct in their minds. Thus, lawyers and librarians are often divided into subgroups, and attorneys who attended law school at night and graduates of prestigious law schools often occupy separate task worlds. The former, for instance, often practice in small-claims court, whereas the latter more often practice in large law firms that specialize in corporate law and government practice. Librarians become diversified by their clientele: school children, academics, industry, government, and the public (Abbott 1988:123). Commercial fishermen recognize several distinct groups within their occupation's boundaries, including "traditional fishermen" and "nontraditional

fishermen," "educated fishermen," "part-timers," and "outlaw fishermen" (Miller and Van Maanen, 1982; Van Maanen and Barley 1984).
These groups neither work together nor associate with one another outside of work, and the pursuit of a fishing career is different in each case.

The boundaries of journalists are even broader. It is a common practice for them to move in and out of public relations as well as into and
out of book writing and "investigative reporting." Thus, occupations
are not usually made up of one homogeneous community but increasingly may be characterized by distinct subcultures and internal status
systems that must adjust to one another. Systems analysis in computer
programming appears to be rapidly taking over a superior position vis-
à-vis programmers. Even the designation "professions" may well be a
"loose amalgamation of segments, pursuing different objectives in different manners, and more or less delicately held together under a common name" (Bucher and Strauss 1961:326).

Finally, it is relevant to note again the dynamic environments in
which cultures in general are embedded—the interlocking networks of
change that inevitably affect both the ideologies of the cultures and
related cultural forms. In particular, occupational cultures are part of
a larger culture that forces them into ongoing negotiations with managerial hierarchies out of which may emerge changes, including, perhaps, the total decline or reconstruction of the occupation.

CHANGES IN OCCUPATIONS OVER TIME

DEATHS AND DECLINES

Because occupations are dynamic, changing entities, they are subject
to decline, revival, and death. For instance, in the thirty years before
the mid-1950s, the watch repairer "ceased to be a craftsman and . . .
[became] virtually an assembler and adjuster—a person with primary
knowledge of spare-parts supply channels, plus experience and a degree of kinesthetic coordination" (Stodtbeck and Sussman 1956:604).
This simplification and subsequent demise of the occupation was due
largely to the increased availability of manufactured spare parts. Consequently, the machine skills possessed by most watch repairers became obsolete. It was much easier to secure a manufactured spare part,
or a substitute part, than to take the time to make the part from steel
stock.

According to Abbott (1988:91), software compilers replaced computer coders to the extent that the latter "simply withered with time." Likewise, domestic servants have all but disappeared; "only a century ago domestic service was among the most common occupational roles in all western countries" (Coser 1973:31). A recent study of Chicana women engaged in domestic service suggests that earlier mistress-servant relations "are being transformed into customer-vendor relations, reducing the personalism and asymmetry of employer-employee relationships" (Romero 1988:319).

Executions have become all but extinct because of the widespread abolition of capital punishment in Europe and America (Hornum 1968). Consequently, the employment of executioners has been reduced to part-time status. Apparently their demise is due to the significant decrease in the number of sanctioned killings, not to a shortage of persons willing to enter the field. Ironically, changes in public opinion about the hangman became more favorable during the twentieth century in the United States, while, at the same time, the reduction in the number of death penalties made it practically impossible to earn a living fulfilling society's mandate to commit legalized murder (Robin 1964). Similarly, profound technological changes between 1950 and 1978 in the mining of coal resulted in a drastic reduction in the number of miners: "Far fewer miners were necessary to produce the same amount of coal with these processes. Thus there are now far fewer miners" (Couto 1987:180). Specifically, in 1945, the total number of miners employed was 383,100; in 1983, there were only 173,543. There is a distinct likelihood that their numbers will be further reduced in the 1990s.

Abbott (1988:29) includes in his discussion of dead or declining occupations the fascinating story of the psychological medium. Persons in this role "flourished in the latter nineteenth century as the professional embodiment of spiritualism." After the turn of the century, however, they disappeared into the "organized Church of the Afterlife, complete with congregations and ministers." Nevertheless, from the mid-1850s well into the twentieth century, the psychological medium devised and evolved skills that promoted "communication between her audience and the inhabitants of the spiritual world." The mediums' Mutual Aid Society instructed all who wanted to use mediumistic skills, and the National Organization of Spiritualists attempted, unsuccessfully, to define the occupation's boundaries, paying close attention to charlatans. An official school was set up, and many well-known Americans patronized the practitioners. Disputes over their alleged ju-

risdiction brought the occupation into conflict with expansionist-
minded psychiatrists; "indeed a number of psychiatry's early battles
were fought with mediums and their descendants, the spiritualist
healer" (30).

During much of the same period, public lecturing became established
as a lucrative, distinct, and highly respected occupation. As Donald M.
Scott notes (1983:12), "Attendance at public lectures probably reached
close to half a million people each week during the lecture season."
Public lecturing flourished during the mid-nineteenth century and was
regarded as a major source of up-to-date knowledge about the sciences
and humanities. Its recognition as an established occupation faded during the 1870s, however, and largely vanished in its original form, giving
way to modern university faculties: "The emergence of the modern
university established careers that were organized around and gave
prestige and rewards to a life of scholarship, thus providing the broader
institutional context that underlay the emergence in the 1880s and
1890s of the modern academic professions" (27).

REVIVALS

In contrast, some occupations have gone through revivals following
obsolescence and decline. Pharmacists, for example, are reemerging
after experiencing occupational decline (Birenbaum 1982). In the 1940s,
technological advances in the mass production of drugs and persistent
efforts by doctors to curtail the pharmacists' ability to dispense drugs
without a prescription almost made pharmacists obsolete. In the 1960s,
"pharmacy was subject to much unfavorable public attention resulting
from a series of investigative committees into health care services. . . .
The net result was a serious questioning of the role of the pharmacist
in the modern health team" (Hornosty 1989:123).

Today, the long decline appears to be over because pharmacy educators and leaders have started to reprofessionalize the occupation with
a "visionary ideology" that they believe will permeate the formal and
informal socialization of pharmacists. This ideology "shifts the emphasis in pharmacy practice from compounding and dispensing of medications to patient counseling and drug consulting. . . . It involves a
commitment to a 'patient-oriented' rather than a 'product-oriented'
practice of pharmacy" (Hornosty 1989:123). Recent research has further
specified that the practice of pharmacy now includes information giving and advice giving about the use of prescription drugs (Sitkin and
Sutcliffe 1991).

Furthermore, competition from other occupations to perform the pharmacist's tasks seems to have subsided. Pharmacists appear to have carved out a niche for themselves among health professionals. Students in pharmacy schools may more and more be socialized into this belief system, a process that may well "reprofessionalize pharmacy" (Hornosty 1989:123; Holloway, Jewson, and Mason 1986:329). Additional evidence of a resurgence of pharmacy comes from a study of "the effects of computerized medical information systems on health care professionals in hospitals" (Aydin 1989:163). The study showed changes in the tasks of both pharmacy and nursing, "resulting in increased interdependence between the two departments." It now seems unlikely that anesthesiologists will move outside the operating room theater or that other physicians will effectively take on yet another area of responsibility.

At the same time, other research strongly suggests that doctors are preventing pharmacy from undergoing more than a limited revival. "Certain types of clinical pharmacy tasks are acceptable to physicians and certain ones are not. . . . Many physicians [though]—younger ones, those who have had experience with clinical pharmacy and those who practice much of the time in hospitals—are favorable to a limited expansion of the pharmacist's role . . . but it will not soon reach the ideal position espoused by pharmacy elites" (Ritchey and Raney 1981:90).

DESKILLING

Some occupations decline or disappear altogether because of the redesign of tasks, mechanization, and technological change. Harry Braverman (1974) suggests that through such changes management seeks to reduce the complexity of occupational skills by appropriating the knowledge needed to perform the set of tasks of an occupation, thereby simplifying performance and leaving members with less control over their work. According to some writers (e.g., Bright 1958), the result is a significant growth in the number of unskilled and semiskilled workers. Such routinization of complex skills via rationalization has steadily developed throughout the capitalist era, during which technological changes have been closely associated with deskilling (Simpson 1985).

Often referred to as scientific management (Taylor 1911; Braverman 1974) or as rationalized programs, numerical control, or computer-aided electronics, efforts to deskill an occupation have, in some cases, produced pronounced declines in its skill content. Indeed, machining and clerical work have been sharply downgraded in task complexity and status (Braverman 1974). And while occupations such as printing (Wallace and Kalleberg 1982), railroad driving (Stein 1978), social work (Patry 1978), and air traffic control (Shostak 1987) have not actually disappeared, their skill content has been sharply downgraded. Referring to printing, Arne L. Kalleberg et al. (1987:47) wrote that "indeed it is difficult to think of an industry where the transformations wrought by technological change have been so pronounced."

Barbara Garson (1988:10) argues that the use of computers in office work has practically eliminated employee discretion and that "office automation [is] rising almost floor by floor to engulf higher and higher strata of white collar workers." She reports, for example, that financial-service companies such as Merrill Lynch and Shearson Lehman have begun to translate the work of brokers into canned programs that use the "artificial intelligence" of computers to redesign the role of brokers, thereby reducing worker autonomy and limiting judgment.

Deskilling can occur swiftly and decisively. For example, the knowledge base and tasks of air traffic controllers consisted of knowing how to guide aircraft into crowded airports. In 1981, their craft union, the Professional Air Traffic Controllers Organization, threatened the Federal Aviation Authority (FAA) with a strike that could have disrupted most national air traffic patterns. On the eve of the strike, however, a new computer technology used hastily by the FAA established "flow control," and a "computer driven, 24 hour, controlled-from-headquarters schedule enabled the FAA to handle 83% of the system's former traffic load with less than 50% of its pre-strike work force" (Shostak 1987:168). The controllers were defeated, their union was decertified, and the occupation was dramatically deskilled. There is only sparse evidence to support the observation, but it seems likely that elements of their culture remain today.

Even though deskilling is a long-standing management strategy, managers have not been uniformly successful in their efforts to downgrade occupations. Results vary widely by occupation and industry. Indeed, Braverman's (1974) hypothesis that management is successfully deskilling workers everywhere finds support chiefly "in early case studies of dying crafts" (Form 1987:44). Older occupations, such as printing or machining, are more vulnerable to deskilling efforts than newer occupations. Moreover, efforts to deskill an occupation via new technology may actually increase or reskill an occupation. Ida Harper Simpson (1989:573) summarized this point: "But the losses of skill in

some instances have been more than made up by new skilled occupations and by technological and organizational changes that upgrade
skill on old occupations."

Kenneth I. Spenner (1979:973) for example, found no evidence that,
on average, skills were being downgraded in any of the occupational
sectors he studied; if anything, "work with data, people, and things,
had become slightly more complex." The position put forward by K.
Hall and I. Miller (1975) seems to reflect the overall dynamics: some
occupations have, indeed, experienced deskilling, and others have been
upgraded, but the net changes in the occupational structure have in all
likelihood been small. Van Maanen and Barley (1984:302) summarize
the overall pattern: "A population of occupations in a state of ebb and
flow may more accurately depict historical experience." Such a gen-
eralization fails to describe the fate of a given, specific occupation, however, and thus leaves the dynamics unexplored. In sum, "the patterns
of change over time are far more complex than a simple upgrading-
downgrading dimension would suggest" (Sullivan and Cornfield 1979:
184).

A final element in the nature of occupations is that they are cultures.
This feature, which is one of the main themes of this book, will be
explored in detail in the next four chapters.

SUMMARY

Occupations continue to be a prominent feature of how work is organized, even though managerial hierarchies have come to be the dominant force. In effect, occupations have become subcultures within
organizations. To varying degrees, members of occupations possess
and control the knowledge needed to perform specific, often complicated work tasks. Both this knowledge base and its control are in constant flux, however, as occupational decline, revival, or death remain
ever-present possibilities. Deskilling—a series of power moves by managers that fracture, reassign, and render obsolete many of the tasks an
occupational group has claimed for itself—is a potent force in this process of change.

2. OCCUPATIONAL CULTURES

Culture is a blank space, a highly respected, empty pigeon-hole. Economists call it "tastes" and leave it strictly alone. Most philosophers ignore it—to their own loss. Marxists treat it obliquely as ideology or superstructure. Psychologists avoid it by concentrating on child subjects. Historians bend it anyway they like. Most believe it matters, especially travel agents.

—Mary Douglas

UMANS CONSTRUCT CULTURES to make sense of the world around them. This is necessary because, unlike other animals, humans are "unfinished animals who complete themselves through culture" (Geertz 1970:61). Born with few, if any, instincts to guide their behavior, humans must invent collective meanings by which to adapt to their world, and these are modified and passed along from one generation to the next. Through culture, members of each generation try to manage the inherent uncertainty and anxieties that characterize the human condition and make some sense of the underlying chaos and disorder. Culture creates a distinct set of meanings and order and an ongoingness in human life (Leach 1976).

A culture contains two major ingredients: sets of taken-for-granted, emotionally charged beliefs, called ideologies; and mechanisms for expressing and affirming these beliefs, called cultural forms. Ideologies are the *substance* of a culture. Although abstract ideas, they tell members what is and in what actions they *ought* to engage. Cultural *forms*, in contrast, are observable entities that permeate actions with meanings. They accumulate, creating a repertoire of mechanisms by which members can share and express their ideologies with one another. Thus, through culture, members learn to express moral-evaluative ideas of "ought" and "should," defining what is right and wrong to feel, think, and do. These meanings are not neutral or rational. Rather, they are charged with intense feelings. When they are consistent with one another, emphasizing solidarity among members, they make for an established culture. Thus, a common ideology in occupational life is to embrace ethnocentrism, a "weness" that mobilizes members to be loyal insiders. Also common are occupation-based stories—a cultural form for transmitting the ideology. For instance, police officers Van Maanen studied (1973:413) told a story that illustrates how this "weness" extends to covering up one another's shortcomings and mistakes. According to the story, a patrolman was having a dalliance with a girlfriend who lived outside his assigned district. One day, while he was in the woman's apartment and his partner was in the patrol car, the partner received an emergency call on the radio. The partner tooted the horn to "get the horny bastard out of there," arousing the neighbors, who promptly called the police. When the officers showed up the partner recounted "an insane story about Sparky's girlfriend living there and how he always toots the horn when passing. . . . Nobody ever found out what happened, but it was close."

Other cultural forms include occupation-based myths, ceremonies, symbols, languages and gestures, physical artifacts, sagas and legends, rituals, taboos, and rites. Probably many of these cultural forms also operate within the police culture. The range of ideologies is more difficult to classify, since they range across a wide variety of possible sets of beliefs. Again, police culture probably has many ideologies in addition to the one illustrated above. This range of ideologies will be empirically examined for numerous occupations in the next chapter.

FEATURES OF CULTURES

CULTURES ARE COLLECTIVITIES:
CULTURES ARE GROUP PHENOMENA

Cultures cannot be produced by individuals alone. They originate as individuals interact with one another. Individuals may originate specific ways of managing the fundamental insecurities of life, but until they come to be collectively accepted, expressed, and put into practice they are not part of a culture. Persons who do not endorse and practice prevailing beliefs, values, and norms become marginal and may be punished or expelled. Belonging to a culture involves believing what others believe and doing as they do—at least part of the time (Trice and Beyer 1992).

CULTURES ARE INHERENTLY FUZZY AND AMBIGUOUS

Cultures come over time to include ambiguities, paradoxes, and contradictions. Consequently, every culture is relatively unique and, to

The section "Features of Cultures" is adapted from Trice and Beyer 1992.

some degree, in the process of change. Although each culture nurtures stability, harmony, and continuity, most modern cultures are also awash with change and ambivalence. Since these two forces—stability and ambivalence—often intermingle, cultures can be viewed as marked by change but directed toward member control.

Cultures are also inherently fuzzy, containing an array of forms, meanings, and sense-making messages, some more confusing than others (Pierce 1977; Moore 1975). One analysis viewed them as characterized by "enormous multiplicity" (Geertz 1983:161). Nevertheless, they can best be viewed as made up of central and peripheral elements. The central elements generate sufficient consensus to produce enough co-ordination and cooperation to avoid chaos and to allow members to "recognize their common identity through time and across lines of conflict" (Shils 1975:xii). Fuzziness resides in the periphery and slowly subsides, but by no means disappears, as the elements at the core come into focus. This feature makes it almost inevitable that a culture will contain numerous subcultures characterized by features that are divergent from those of the elements at the core.

Joanne Martin and Debra Meyerson (1988:107) have developed a useful paradigm for analyzing cultures. It emphasizes their inconsistencies and lack of consensus. Using the term *differentiation*, they suggest that inconsistencies occur when a culture's ideologies are not congruent with actual practice and when symbolic meanings are inconsistent with one another. Harmony, according to this view, can still be reached, but only cheek by jowl with conflict.

CULTURES EMERGE OVER TIME

Cultures are not generated overnight. They can be thought of as historically based. Before one can develop, people must spend time interacting with one another and facing common uncertainties. Under these circumstances, ideologies accumulate and become taken for granted, and cultural forms become routinized. The culture comes to have a life of its own.

A culture's fuzziness ensures that its transfer to another generation will be far from perfect. Nevertheless, close examination of a culture will "usually uncover residues of cultural ideas and practices that originated at earlier points in its history to deal with anxieties that may no longer exist. Even though these historical residues are buried under current preoccupations . . . they can still have powerful effects in guiding current behavior" (Trice and Beyer 1992).

CULTURES ARE DYNAMIC

Even though cultures produce the order necessary for life to have continuity, they are by no means static. On the contrary, they are dynamic. Their inherent, built-in fuzziness is the basis for their dynamic nature. Thus, they change continually. Numerous factors account for this feature of cultures. First, communications between humans are in no way perfect. Members of a culture learn different things at different rates about what a culture approves and expects. Second, individuals in most cultures—certainly American—have wide latitude for devising variations on central themes. Third, cultures tend to become taken for granted and unconscious, leaving many members ignorant and at "loose ends" about what their cultures prescribe. Further, symbols, the generic cultural form, are imprecise in their very makeup (Turner 1990).

CULTURES ARE INTRINSICALLY SYMBOLIC

Human actions serve both to do and to say things; that is, actions have both technical and expressive consequences (Leach 1968). This book focuses on the expressive side of human actions, what human behavior "says," even when the actors claim that the intended purpose of the actions may be purely technical. What actions "say" is what they represent, signify, and symbolize. For example, "shoes protect the feet, but in American society they also signify taste and income" (Gusfield and Michalowicz 1984:423). This book emphasizes the expressive or symbolic nature of cultures, in contrast with their technical and practical side.

Symbols so pervade cultural phenomena that they are thought to be the most basic cultural form (V. Turner 1969). As the basic unit of cultural expression, symbols often constitute a part of other cultural forms. A dramatic and rare rite of degradation in the U.S. Marine Corps demonstrates the power of symbols in a ceremony. When an officer was dismissed in disgrace, ranking officers were assembled and stood at attention to watch the ceremony. Drums played a muffled drumroll, and the commanding officer read the formal declaration of dismissal, stripped the symbols of rank from the officer's shoulders, and demanded the dress sword, which was then broken in half.

CULTURES ARE EMOTIONALLY CHARGED

Since cultures help their members cope with pervasive anxieties, they are shot through with strong emotions. In effect, a culture is a "gigantic effort to mask" the basic insecurities of life (Kluckhohn 1942:66). Members hold dear and cherish ideologies and the various social forms that become attached to them. Even though the intensity of emotions about ideologies will vary from member to member, and the emotions will probably fade with time, members' attachments to them are far from rational. Rather, members are infused with irrational feelings and elaborate rationales for them. Thus, when ideologies are questioned, their adherents show emotional reactions, often including anger and other intense feelings. Doctors, for example, have strong sentiments about "the ideology of affective neutrality" (Smith and Kleinman 1989:57). It is their way of avoiding emotional involvement with the diseases and deaths of their patients. Among craft workers in construction, strong feelings become attached to their beliefs about "responsible autonomy" (i.e., craft workers should arrange their work and resolve their own problems) (Steiger and Form 1991). And to suggest to a football coach that winning is unimportant will, in all probability, provoke a repetition of Coach Lombardi's famous remark that "winning is the only thing." Finally, emotional attachments to one's culture are encouraged by the repetitive nature of many cultural forms. The frequent performance of cultural forms increases and intensifies the awareness of the shared and collective sentiments.

CULTURES ENCOURAGE ETHNOCENTRISM

A collectivity may come to be very emotionally attached to a set of ideologies. As a consequence, its culture will be strengthened and the collectivity will come to distrust, fear, and dislike groups with other sets of beliefs. In effect, it will become centered on itself. A "weness," varying in intensity, will come to characterize the members, and cultural forms, such as an occupationally unique argot, will come to define the boundaries between insiders and outsiders, "we" and "them." Ethnocentrism, probably more than any other feature, characterizes cultures. Ideologies, especially, carry a sense of group superiority. People who embrace one set of beliefs come to distrust, fear, even hate those with different beliefs. The more emotionally charged these ideas are, the more likely adherents are to be intolerant of those with divergent ideas.

CULTURES ARE DYSFUNCTIONAL AS WELL AS FUNCTIONAL

Often overlooked is the tendency of cultures to generate dysfunctional consequences as well as functional ones. It must constantly be kept in mind that components of cultures can generate "inevitable dysfunctions" (Trice 1985:249) and that it is quite possible to overemphasize "the integrative and cohesion-producing side of culture" (Van Maanen and Kunda 1989:49). Research on organizations and occupations has focused almost exclusively on getting at and explaining what is functional about elements of cultures but has almost completely ignored the dysfunctional aspects (Pondy and Mitroff 1979). Both the ideologies and the forms of a culture typically have consequences that impede their effective ongoingness.

Strongly held ideologies add to the cohesion among members of an occupation, but, at the same time, they make for a rigidity and bitterness toward outside groups, often blocking needed cooperation. Similarly, cultural forms such as occupation-based stories may provide a means for expressing how to perform tasks effectively while at the same time delivering fictions that set up dysfunctional stereotypes of others in the organization.

CULTURES STRUCTURE SOCIAL RELATIONS

Cultures, guided by their ideologies, tend to produce mechanisms that arrange the relationship between their members; in other words, a structure of social relations. That is, cultures can rarely avoid the practical need for the management of administrative details and for the definition of ranks and divisions of labor among their members. This feature has been called the *grid* dimension of cultures and stands in contrast with the *group* dimension (Douglas 1982), made up of those elements set forth above that act to create and identify cultures. The *grid* dimension describes the amount of formal rules and hierarchical authority within the culture. The *group* dimension, in contrast, describes the amount of cohesiveness produced by the culture among members, thus emphasizing the pressures to conform to the culture's ideologies and forms.

Cultures vary in their strength in their grid and group dimensions (Douglas 1978; Mars 1982). Cultures that are strong on the grid dimension impose internal rules and rankings on members, provide explicit guidelines for their behaviors toward one another, and allow members little leeway to work out their internal relationships. In cultures that are weak on the grid dimension, there is a relative absence of these administratively imposed rules and rankings.

In cultures that are potent on the group dimension, members tend to interact with their own kind, emphasizing those forces that produce solidarity and conformity to expectations. Cultures weak on this dimension tend to have cultural features but less explicit ones. They tend to have blurred ideologies, and those that do form tend to be inconsistent with one another. Similarly, there are relatively few cultural forms, and they too are apt to be "fuzzy."

GROUP DIMENSION OF OCCUPATIONAL CULTURES

FORCES THAT FACILITATE GROUP IDENTITY

Because cultures are first and foremost collectivities with distinct ideologies, occupations fit the concept to the extent that forces are present that facilitate group identity among members. This is the group dimension of culture discussed above (Douglas 1978, 1982). The specific forces vary in strength from occupation to occupation. The major ones are (1) esoteric knowledge and expertise, (2) extreme or unusual demands, (3) consciousness of kind, (4) pervasiveness—the occupational culture permeates nonworking life, (5) ideologies that confer favorable self-images and social value to the tasks, (6) the extent to which members of the occupation are members' primary reference group, and (7) the abundance of consistent cultural forms. When all these *closely related* forces for cohesion are active, the occupational culture tends to be known as a community.

Esoteric knowledge and expertise. When members of occupations believe that they possess esoteric knowledge, skills, and abilities, the occupation is likely to arouse workers' involvement and to foster a feeling of specialness. Rigorous socialization experiences create such beliefs and feelings by underscoring that the knowledge, skills, and abilities are not easily learned by just anyone and that they require a special learning experience and a special person to grasp them. Shared beliefs, norms, and values, then, are more likely to arise among members when the socialization process is harsh, lengthy, and formal; when training takes place somewhere removed from members who are practicing the occupation; when there is uncertainty whether the newcomer will make the grade and be allowed to become a full-fledged member; and when the newcomer experiences a great deal of peer pressure to do things in the occupationally prescribed way (Van Maanen and Schein 1979).

Generally, those occupations that are rich in cultural forms have more rigorous socialization procedures than those that are culturally impoverished. For instance, lawyers, high-steel iron workers, and police officers experience very rigorous training because there is so much to learn about these occupational roles and the culture of which they are a part: the skills necessary to perform the work; the correct language; the right way to act toward one's peers, clients, and managers; and the appropriate emotional responses in specific situations. Consequently, the passage from raw recruit to full member of these occupations is arduous, and trainees will not see themselves as holding the particular occupational title until they have satisfied other members of the occupation and themselves that they have a right to this title (Salaman 1974). Trainees will generally ignore and resist premature labeling by uninitiated outsiders who, unaware of the subtleties in the passage, identify the trainees by the full occupational title when they have not yet earned the right to it. According to Howard S. Becker and J. Carper (1956:343), in well-defined occupations

> an important part of a person's work-based identity grows out of his relationship to his occupational title . . . [Occupational titles] imply a great deal about the characteristics of their bearers and these meanings are often systematized into elaborate ideologies which itemize the qualities, interests, and capabilities of those so identified.

Having earned the right to the title, members of an occupation think of themselves as possessing such qualities, interests, and capabilities.

Some social scientists suggest that it is becoming increasingly difficult for occupations to claim esoteric skills, knowledge, and abilities because technological innovations and bureaucratic controls have systematically appropriated them (Braverman 1974; Edwards 1979). For instance, cost-conscious managers, through the introduction of new technologies, have systematically dismantled occupational communities in the steel industry (Stone 1979; Marglin 1976) and printing (Wallace and Kalleberg 1982). New technologies, however, may also be the locus for developing new occupational communities if they provide workers with new skills (Van Maanen and Barley 1984; Form 1987; Salaman 1986). For instance, radiological (Barley 1988) and computer technologies (Pettigrew 1973; Schein 1985) have provided workers with new esoteric skills for which they may claim expertise and pride. New technologies may also strengthen older occupational communities by providing them with new esoteric skills. This has been true of butchers (Walsh 1989) and physicians (Freidson 1986).

Extreme or unusual demands. In occupations in which tasks are performed under conditions that produce a "thrill" or "emotional high," members can develop a sense of power and deep satisfaction. For example, Gary A. Fine (1987, 1988:125) found "peak experiences" among chefs and cooks in three Minneapolis restaurants during intermittent, short-term, and hectic periods in the kitchen, when the restaurant operated like "a well oiled machine" and "mundane experiences [were] transformed into something resembling joy." As one cook put it, "I'm pumped up till you wouldn't believe it. . . . I just want to go, go, go."

Detectives in a small southern city described a somewhat similar emotional high when "doing real detective" work with criminals and suspected criminals. They spent much of their time in monotonous tasks, such as writing reports, sitting in court, and performing other bureaucratic routines. In this context, "their encounters with criminals felt like a breath of fresh air" (Stenross and Kleinman 1989:439).

Joseph A. Blake (1974:208) suggests that the tasks of an occupation may be such that "a continual adjustment to the situation is necessary so that intensity of concentration varies intermittently over time . . . and a situational rhythm emerges in which the person becomes one among a number of elements coexisting and co-acting in the situation." Long-distance truck drivers experience such a rhythm. Their rig, the roadway, and the traffic all combine to generate a feeling of getting "high." A driver describes how it feels to command 40 tons of truck and load: "You're up there and you have a sense of cars swimming around you like minnows—you're continually monitoring your instruments and mirrors, checking the traffic and that trailer stretching out behind. It's far more intense than driving a four-wheeler (an automobile)" (Wolkomir 1985:93).

Blake (1974:212) found several self-images among truckers: "Knight of the Highway," the good samaritan who renders aid to people in trouble; the "brute monster," who terrorizes innocent travelers; the "sailor of the highway," a romantic adventurer embodying the ideals of independence and control of one's own destiny; and the "professional" or "king of the road," combining dominance of the rig on the road with the trucker's driving expertise and freight management.

Pool hustlers also derive great satisfaction from their work. According to Ned Polsky (1969:73), "When a hustler says of hustling that 'it beats working,' his emphasis is not on putting down the workaday world; his primary meaning is, rather, a positive one—that hustling is infinitely more pleasurable than any other job he would find."

Thus, task demands, especially emotional ones, increase occupational involvement (Salaman 1974). Many kinds of work and organizations make unusual affective or emotional demands on workers. These demands vary widely, from demands for unusual compassion to aggression, from friendliness to extreme remoteness, from genuine sincerity and caring to manipulation and exploitation of others. For instance, even though customers are often anxious, rude, and demanding, both flight attendants and bank tellers are expected consistently to project a demeanor of calmness, friendliness, and unfailing courtesy. Bill collectors, by contrast, must consistently project a demeanor of censure and instill fear in those who are tardy in their payments (Hochschild 1983): "Collectors are selected, socialized, and rewarded for following the general norm of conveying urgency (high arousal with a hint of irritation) to debtors" (Sutton 1991:245, 264). Members teach one another strategies for coping with the demands, and, in becoming adept at them, they begin to see themselves as unusual and distinctive people.

Peers as well as company officials often expect sales workers to display exaggerated positive affect concerning the products they sell. An extreme example is the wild enthusiasm that peers expect of those who sell Mary Kay cosmetics. Mary Kay expects her beauty consultants to fake such enthusiasm if they do not actually feel it. She expects them to take a "Vow of Enthusiasm" and to sing the company song, "I've Got That Mary Kay Enthusiasm" (Ash 1981). Less intense are the emotional expectations made on check-out clerks in convenience stores: friendly greetings, smiles, eye contact, and saying "thank you" to customers. When there are long lines of customers, however, clerks comply less with these expected norms because of the unpleasant feelings of pressure and haste (Sutton and Rafaeli 1988). Overall, "organizational life is structured to channel, mold, enhance, sustain, challenge and otherwise influence the feelings of organizational members—toward the organization itself, others in the organization, customers of the organization, and, crucially, themselves" (Van Maanen and Kunda 1989:43).

R. E. Clark and E. E. LaBeef (1982) studied the emotional demands made on physicians, nurses, police officers, and clergy when they deliver the news of a person's death to friends and relatives. They announce the death in a very somber way and then wait for reactions, which can range from crying, to silence, to anger. Depending on the reaction, they hug the relatives and friends, cry with them, or, if the response is anger, withdraw. Physicians, especially, seem to be socialized into ways to avoid getting too emotionally involved with patients (Bell 1984). Apparently they learn to appear concerned, but not to the extent that the patient's illness or death causes them genuine distress. Furthermore, throughout their careers, physicians must cope with chronic uncertainty and "fear of personal inadequacy and failure" (Gerrity et al. 1992:1043), emotions that are closely linked to clinical diagnosis and treatment.

Funeral directors must learn to cope with their feelings about death and the feelings of others (Barley 1983a, 1983b). They have devised several tactics to minimize the distressing emotional content in their work. When someone dies at home, they rearrange the room in which the death occurred to suggest that the body was not removed. Other "tricks of the trade" include posing the corpse in the casket at the funeral home to create the impression that the person is resting or sleeping. In addition, funeral homes are furnished so that they resemble private residences, places familiar to the funeral directors and to the mourners.

U.S. marshals must cope with the need to bear "bad news" to witnesses and prisoners (McClenahen and Lofland 1976). Tactics for managing the uncomfortable emotional demands emanating from this role include dribbling out the facts; normalizing the bad news during events such as the serving of a subpoena (e.g., "Oh, we serve thousands of these things; it's really nothing to worry about"); scaling down the importance of what is happening (e.g., "it's not as bad as you think"); omitting to mention truly bad experiences that may, and probably will, ensue (e.g., ignoring the possibility of sexual attack in prisons and emphasizing the positive features—"they feed you better in [these federal joints] than in other joints"; and engaging in gallows humor (e.g., "If these mug photographs turn out good, would you like to order some— I can give you a dozen 8 × 10 glossies for a mere twenty-five dollars").

Through such tactics, U.S. marshals come to recognize that they have the temperament to manage the unusual emotional demands associated with delivering bad news and come to think of themselves as special kinds of people.

In some cases, emotional demands may be unusually diverse. Anat Rafaeli and Robert I. Sutton (1987) describe the different emotions expressed by a team of surgical nurses. In the operating room they projected "an emotionally flat demeanor" (23) but were warm when talking with patients and their families afterwards. When they took breaks and met informally with other nurses, however, they encouraged each other to express feelings of rage, even disgust.

One dramatic and unusual emotional demand an occupation can make on members is to expect them to cope with immediate personal dangers. The great risks taken by high-steel workers (Cherry 1974), firefighters (McCarl 1980), soldiers in combat (Dyer 1985), longshoremen (Pilcher 1972), police officers in high-crime districts, and underground miners (Fitzpatrick 1980) are hard to imagine for people outside such occupations. Members of dangerous occupations often come to think of themselves as possessing exceptional character traits, particularly persistent courage.

According to John S. Fitzpatrick (1980:131), mining is characterized as a "subculture of danger." Miners view most mine dangers as having the potential to produce very serious injury or death. Some of these dangers are daily occurrences: falls, slips, machinery-related accidents, and rock falls. Less frequent but far from rare are misfired explosives, jammed ore chutes, and small cave-ins. The danger is complicated by the isolation in which many miners work: "Separated into small work groups and dispatched to the darkness of their work areas, the miners labor in places with a high degree of spatial isolation" (Fitzpatrick 1980: 153). Miners cope with these dangers with the help of their immediate work groups, and often the first lesson new miners learn is to protect other miners. For instance, although the Sandhogs, underground miners who construct tunnels, are well known for brawling among themselves, whatever hard feelings exist aboveground are put aside when they enter the tunnels (Sonnenstuhl and Trice 1987).

Herbert Applebaum (1984a) describes how members of danger-ridden occupations develop a variety of tactics for coping with the high risks of death and injury. They become attuned to signs of imminent disaster and act swiftly on these signs. Soldiers in combat learn to distinguish dangerous features from frightening ones, and a high-steel foreman "will observe how the men walk on to the steel in the morning, and if any of them seems shaky he will send them home" (Applebaum 1984a:100). Soldiers also try to avoid displaying fear because showing fear can cause distrust, wariness, and confusion in times of an emergency when "cool heads" are needed. For instance, Army General S. L. A. Marshall comments on the seeds of panic: "The retention of self-discipline . . . depends upon the maintaining of an appearance of discipline within the unit. . . . When other men flee, the social pressure is lifted and the average soldier will respond as if he had been given a release from duty" (cited in Dyer 1985:145). Similarly, social workers going into a crime-ridden ghetto where the danger of personal attack is considerable "concealed their fears from those who might exacerbate them" (Mayer and Rosenblatt 1975:234).

People in dangerous occupations also cultivate kidding, joshing, or mock aggression as ways of managing emotion. Machinists working with large lathes, surface grinders, drill presses, and other automatic machines "navigate successfully in a world of real physical danger" by coping via "machine shop humor" (Boland and Hoffman 1983:192). Meat cutters also encounter danger as they use tools and machines designed to rapidly cut animal meat and bone. Hannah Meara (1974) reported how butchers told stories and jokes about their injuries and scars. Members of many occupations exchange insults and threats within a friendly context, thereby expressing anger and fear in an acceptable, tacitly understood fashion. Longshoremen, whose work is often hazardous, are notorious for this form of danger management. In and after crisis situations, nurses may resort to gallows humor as a coping mechanism: "My God, we cut off the wrong leg."

Apprentices in dangerous occupations also absorb considerable amounts of verbal abuse and derision, in response to which they are closely watched to get a fix on how they will react under emergency conditions. If they respond angrily, it is a sign that they cannot be trusted. Firefighters, for instance, test recruits by giving them unannounced and prankish heavy dousings with cold water. Members closely watch to see which "can't handle it" (McCarl 1976).

Consciousness of kind. The emotional features of occupational cultures underscore their emotionally charged nature. These features also enhance a consciousness of kind, especially if it has emerged over a considerable period of time. The boundaries of an occupational culture are defined by members' consciousness of kind (Gusfield 1975; Van Maanen and Barley 1984); that is, members' definitions of who is an insider or outsider delineates the boundaries of occupational communities.

Occupations look different when viewed by insiders and outsiders. Insiders know their culture intimately because they live within it, behaving in accordance with its beliefs and enacting the cultural forms associated with those beliefs. From this perspective, they know who knows how to behave appropriately and who does not. Outsiders, because they do not live within the culture, do not know how to behave properly and are unable to discern accurately the subtleties in meaning conveyed by the cultural forms. Consequently, outsiders' criteria for determining membership in an occupational community are likely to vary substantially from the way insiders decide who is a member. "Members . . . see themselves in terms of their occupational role. . . . They see themselves as printers, policemen, army officers, or whatever, and as people with specific qualities, interests, and abilities" (Salaman 1974:21).

Pervasiveness. Pervasiveness refers to the number of activities inside or outside the occupation for which the occupation sets the norms. Some occupations establish membership norms and values that are relevant to a wide range of activities; others require nothing beyond the execution of specialized tasks during a set period of time. According to Morris Janowitz (1960:175), for instance, "The military profession is more than an occupation: it is a complete style of life. The officer is a member of a community whose claims over his daily existence extend well beyond his official duties." Studies of printers (Lipset, Trow, and Coleman 1956), longshoremen (Pilcher 1972), construction workers (Applebaum 1981), locomotive engineers (Gamst 1980), carnival workers (Bryant 1972), architects and railway workers (Salaman 1974), and jazz musicians (Becker 1951; Steffens 1972) detail the development of nonwork lives that have been deeply influenced by occupational ideologies and practices. In effect, members of these occupations build their lives around their work. Members of occupational communities extend their work relationships into their nonwork lives because they prefer to be friends with their colleagues. Becoming more than friends who work in the same occupation, colleagues share work-based beliefs about the world and can be trusted to understand how things really are. Members of such occupational communities spend leisure time together, tend to have other members of the occupation as "best friends," live near one another, link their families through marriage, and encourage their children to follow the same occupation.

Longshoremen, for instance, tend to associate with one another off the job and to intermarry with one another's families to such an extent that they feel another longshoreman is a sort of kinsman (Pilcher 1972). Similarly, the Sandhogs are known by their neighborhoods (e.g., Bronx Irish, Brooklyn Irish), intermarry, pass along their trade from father to son, and spend their off-hours enjoying one another's company and talking about sandhogging (Sonnenstuhl and Trice 1987; Breslin 1986). Railroaders build model trains and display them to one another during their off hours (Salaman 1974; Gamst 1980). And within the American printers' community:

> The formal community of printers' clubs is paralleled by an informal one. That is, large numbers of printers spend a considerable amount of their leisure time with other printers. In interviews, many printers reported that their best friends are printers, that they often meet in bars, go fishing together, or see each other in various places before and after work (Lipset, Trow, and Coleman 1956:70).

Several factors determine whether occupationally based activities extend into members' nonwork lives. People who are deeply involved in their work naturally tend to seek out and spend time with one another. Whether such melding occurs is also directly affected by the social status of the occupation and the extent to which occupational roles restrict opportunities for making friends outside the occupation. Studies of occupations with marginal status suggest that members are more likely to meld work and nonwork because their occupation offers them the highest status and most flattering image available. Cocktail waitresses, for example, tend to interact outside their homes largely "with others in occupational situs of bar business: other waitresses, bartenders, and musicians" (Hearn and Stoll 1975:111). They regard colleagues as the only people whose opinions and judgments really matter because only peers share their view of the nature of the occupation and the "real" status worthiness of its members; they have little recourse but to look to one another for positive support.

Although mining may require great skill, it has generally been accorded relatively low status; the Sandhogs convey this sentiment when they describe themselves as the "worms of society" without whom the infrastructure of New York City would collapse (Sonnenstuhl and Trice

1987). Unable to associate with members of higher-status occupations, they associate with one another because other Sandhogs provide the most positive self-image they can hope to attain. Similarly, printers, highly skilled craftsmen, have been forced to look to one another for support because they have been denied access to upper-middle-class status groups and have wished to avoid associating with "lower" groups (Lipset, Trow, and Coleman 1956; Salaman 1974).

The melding of work and nonwork is also facilitated when members are required to live with members of their work organizations (Salaman 1974). Members of such "total institutions" (Goffman 1961a) may be required to sleep, eat, and spend leisure time together. Examples include military personnel stationed on bases and encouraged to socialize with one another (Janowitz 1960); carnival workers who eat, sleep, and travel with one another (Bryant 1972); and counselors who hold full-time, live-in positions in college residence halls (Van Maanen and Barley 1984).

Finally, the melding of work and nonwork lives may be affected by such restrictions as the need to live in close proximity to one another, the times people work, and the amount of travel they must do. Police officers and some fishermen (Miller and Van Maanen 1979) need to work closely with one another and may live in such close proximity that their neighborhoods develop reputations for having people of these occupations. In contrast, jazz musicians spend so much time traveling long distances to fulfill short-term engagements that they have little time to make friends with people who are not musicians.

According to E. Blakelock (1960), the times people work have especially pronounced effects on their nonwork lives. For instance, the scheduling of work at night, symbolically and actually, separates people into two social groups: day and night people (Zerubavel 1981). A dramatic instance of the differences between these groups emerged in Jane C. Hood's (1988) study of janitors at a large state university. To tighten its budget, the university moved janitors from night to day work. While on the night shift the janitors had performed "clean work"; on the day shift they did "dirty work" because the transition brought them into an entirely different work setting that "turned a good job into demeaning dirty work. . . . Overall, custodians experienced diminished control over both their work and its setting, found it more difficult to take pride in their jobs, and were more affected by the stigma of doing dirty work after moving to the day shift" (Hood 1988:99). Taxi drivers have reported to J. M. Henslin (1973) that they feel more trust toward daytime passengers because they can more easily see and "size up" these passengers and there is therefore less likelihood of being robbed. Overall, they divide themselves into day drivers and night drivers.

People who work after dark find their lifestyles different from those in daytime society and think of themselves as "night people" (Melbin 1978, 1987). Jazz musicians, who share the constraints of both night work and transient engagements, define themselves as different from the "squares" who inhabit ordinary society (Becker 1966). Nightclub strippers are also part of "the night people's subculture"; they see the world outside their occupation as hostile and have little choice except to associate with one another (Becker 1951; Boles and Garbin 1977). Cocktail waitresses are geared to working primarily at night and "get the days and nights mixed up and are out of touch with the 'straight world' " (Hearn and Stoll 1975:111). The work-substitution system in printing, which allowed manual and nonmanual workers to substitute for one another, and frequent night work encouraged printers to interact with one another off the job (Lipset, Trow, and Coleman 1956). Similarly, the enslavement of railroaders to precise time schedules, federal regulations on work hours, and variable shift work precluded their development of friendships outside of work (Cottrell 1940; Salaman 1974).

Favorable self-image and social value in tasks. Members of occupational cultures derive valued social identities that they present to others as central to their image of themselves (Van Maanen and Barley 1984; Van Maanen 1977). Erving Goffman (1961b:87–88) states this point as follows: "A self virtually awaits the individual entering a position. . . . He will find a 'me' ready made for him." For example, the Sandhogs in the Tunnel and Construction Workers Union have a distinctive image of themselves as hard working, fun loving, hard drinking, and "two fisted." Tunnel workers take great pride in being Sandhogs, in living up to the image that they try to outdo each other at work and in their carousing. As one miner aptly put it:

> "The word [*Sandhog*] itself gives them a lot of pride. They enjoy being Sandhogs. . . . It's not the money; they get a lot of pride out of what they do. There's a lot of camaraderie among the workers.

... A lot of joking and kidding around. ... A lot of socializing off the job, people going to each other's wedding, parties, and social events" (Sonnenstuhl and Trice 1987:232).

Jazz musicians identify with their occupation and see themselves as possessing special qualities, interests, and abilities (Becker 1963; Mack and Merriam 1960; Cameron 1954). Believing in artistic autonomy, and seeing themselves as "cats" who possess a precious and mysterious "gift" that cannot be acquired through education and that sets them apart from the "squares," of the world, the jazz musicians in Becker's study saw themselves as "better than other kinds of people" (1963:86). As one "cat" put it: " 'You know man I hate people. I just can't stand to be around squares. They drag me down so much I can't stand them' " (Becker 1963:99). When work involves emotional commitment, individual members are likely to develop a *self-image* organized around their occupational roles.

Bartenders have constructed a favorable self-image by emphasizing their service to society. For instance, when compared with barbers and professors on occupational self-esteem indexes, bartenders ranked higher. As Edward J. Walsh and Marylee C. Taylor (1980) note: "The bartender is often an important person for a stable core of regular patrons who use his services to counter the tension of mainstream society, and the resulting subculture in bars and taverns may tend to buffer bartenders from mainstream stigmatization of their work." This favorable occupational self-image may also derive from the importance of the bartender in the social structure of the tavern. James P. Spradley and Brenda J. Mann (1975:71) describe bartending as central to the social roles played by bouncers, regulars, managers, "real" regulars, and walk-ins in cocktail bars. The first thing new waiters and waitresses learn is that "bartenders are very important people." The pervasiveness of one's occupational role also increases the likelihood that one will organize one's self-image around one's work identity (Salaman 1974).

Members of occupations also tend to construct ideologies that confer social value on their work. In a case study reported by Whyte (1956), a vice-president's remark that a skilled job was "just a watchman's job" so infuriated workers that they joined the Congress of Industrial Organizations (CIO) in large numbers. Garbage collectors emphasize the public-health benefits of their work and call themselves "sanitation engineers" (Lasson 1971). Nightwatchmen see themselves as surrogates for absent managers, standing ready to manage crises at late hours (Trice 1964). Janitors conceive of themselves as the "guardians of the building and its occupants" and emphasize their mechanical abilities (Gold 1964:9). Rangers in Yellowstone National Park see themselves as protectors of the wilderness and enhancers of the visitors' park experiences (Charles 1982). Ward attendants in psychiatric hospitals think of themselves as therapists since it is they, and not the psychiatrists, who interact frequently with the patients (Simpson and Simpson 1959). A grave digger commented:

> "Not anybody can be a grave digger. . . . You have to make a neat job. . . . A human body is going into this grave. That is why you need skill when you're gonna dig a grave. . . . It's like a trade. It's the same as a mechanic or a doctor. . . . A grave digger is a very important person" (Terkel 1972:658).

An occupation that can claim to have social value also promotes involvement in the work and the occupational role. When peoples' health, safety, or welfare is highly dependent on how members of an occupation perform, members of the occupation can easily construe their work as having great social value. Air traffic controllers, nurses, doctors, firefighters, and locomotive engineers, for example, feel important because other people's safety and well-being depend on how they perform their jobs. They extol the virtues of service as an occupational creed and, because they have responsibility for life-and-death decisions concerning others, they may be accorded a certain awe and prestige.

Primary reference group. To maintain a social identity, support and confirmation from others are required (Mead 1934; Goffman 1959). Members of occupational cultures derive much support and confirmation from taking one another as their primary reference group. Because they share common values, members look to one another as the only ones who are really capable of judging their work performance, defining their problems, or understanding. Consequently, as members of occupations become integrated into their cultures, they increasingly take one another as the main points of reference. Thus, mental maps or "schemas" (Louis and Sutton 1991; Bartunek and Moch 1987) become central in individual perception, connecting person and culture. These mental maps direct behavior at the individual level, guiding the acquisition and processing of information and the individual's response to it. Thus, beginning nursing students expect to have the value of their nursing performance confirmed by patients, but advanced nursing students look to their superiors and doctors for guidance in defining expectations and for assurances about their performance. Likewise, computer data processors look to other data processors rather than to members of management, senior management, or user groups for information on how they are doing (Hebden 1975). Jazz musicians consider the judgments of other jazz musicians as valid and worthy of shaping their lives (Mack and Merriam 1960; Becker 1966). And "federal district judges see themselves as part of a great national fraternity, a brotherhood of individuals who daily encounter the same demands, difficulties and traumas. . . . : 'we understand each other; we all have the same problems and we help and sympathize with each other' " (Carp and Wheeler 1972:389).

Abundance of cultural forms. Since cultures are intrinsically symbolic, cohesive occupational cultures—communities—are rich in cultural forms that reinforce meaning and motivate members of the culture to have beliefs that are in accordance with the occupation's ideology (Douglas 1975). Doctors, for instance, have a very rich culture with a unique language, many occupational heroes and stories, complex rites of passage meant to transform premeds into skilled physicians, and a potent occupational association that translates its beliefs to the lay community and fights for the interests of its members. These cultural forms surround physicians' everyday lives, continually signaling them how to act properly. The meaning conveyed by a particular cultural form is readily understood by members as signifying something in particular. For instance, they know what a phrase, or gesture, means and do not need someone to interpret it for them.

Less cohesive cultures, in contrast, have few cultural forms, and those they do have are subject to varying interpretations. Employee assistance workers, for instance, have few shared cultural forms that are unique to them. They have no unique language, no occupational heroes, few myths and stories, and only a rudimentary rite of passage, so that practically anyone who wishes can call himself or herself an employee assistance worker. Consequently, individuals feel relatively free to enact the role of employee assistance worker as they see fit. Only a dim outline of an occupational community can be discerned.

DEVELOPMENT OF ETHNOCENTRISM

When members of an occupation take their self-image from their occupational role, share a reference group composed of members of the occupation, extend their work roles into nonwork life, and develop a keen consciousness of kind, a potent occupational ethnocentrism emerges. Members will see themselves in terms of their occupational norms and beliefs. Accordingly, members of many fishing communities in the United States put themselves into one of two basic categories: "fishermen" and "outsiders" (Miller and Van Maanen 1979, 1982).

In the case of longshoremen, drinking behavior symbolizes the ethnocentrism. Members drink in tightly structured groups inside taverns. "Outsidemen," who work irregularly on the docks, drink unobtrusively in cars or nearby in random clusters out in the open (Mars 1987).

In less established occupations, members will have other identities that are more important, or as important, as their occupational role, take other groups as their primary points of reference, and keep their work and nonwork lives separate. As cohesion increases, however, members become more ethnocentric, believing that their group is superior to others and that outsiders should be viewed and treated with suspicion. Edgar H. Schein (1985:37) cogently describes the ethnocentrism of the data processing "fraternity":

> [It] has its own norms, its own traditions, its own vision of its importance, and its own perspective on how the technology ought to be used, none of which may match the language, perspectives, and norms of potential users of the system. . . . [It is] often intolerant of ambiguity, impersonal, concrete and output oriented, compulsive and precise, and therefore, likely to misunderstand and clash with the general manager, who perceives his world as ambiguous, imperfect, and unprecise.

Occupational ethnocentrism sets the stage for conflict with management and other occupational groups that may have their own ideas about how work is to be organized. Indeed, the literature on organizations and occupations is replete with examples of workers' refusal to cooperate with management expectations (e.g., Roy 1954; Roethlisberger and Dickson 1946). Similarly, ethnocentrism can make it difficult for groups of workers to understand and cooperate with one another. In universities, librarians constitute a world all their own, forming a subculture that views itself as unique and apart, even though it must operate in close conjunction with students and faculty (Wallace 1989; Reeves 1980).

Technical workers in Silicon Valley organizations hold such contrasting views of one another that cooperation is difficult. They identify one another by their occupational subcultures:

> "Hardware," "Software," "Engineering," "Marketing," "PAC Division" or "Scientist" orientations were often mentioned. . . . Employees holding such contrasting viewpoints may try to interact and coordinate their actions to produce computer products but may find that their conflicting cultures complicate these attempts or even make direct coordination unproductive (Gregory 1983:372).

Although every occupational culture is relatively unique, members of most occupations behave according to what Eliot Freidson (1973) has termed "the occupational principle." This code of conduct holds that the members of the occupation, not managers, should control the main aspects of the work. It stands in sharp contrast with the managerial principle—a code of conduct that holds that managers should hold these prerogatives. Even workers who are unable to exercise control over the major features of their work will attempt to control its minor aspects (Greenberger and Strasser 1986). For instance, brewery workers who are overpowered and outflanked by management "go to great lengths to assert their personal autonomy" (Molstad 1988:359).

An ethnographic study of deputy court clerks (Purdum 1985:358) concluded, "The type of informal exercise of power, often in subversion of formally defined organizational goals, displayed by the clerks is common in bureaucracies in which people at the lowest levels have no direct say in decisions that affect their jobs."

Caught up in the ideology of the occupational principle are beliefs in the primacy of occupational expertise and of group solidarity. Each occupation, to varying degrees, constructs a set of beliefs that binds its members together and helps them make sense of their world. Prostitutes, for instance, believe that they serve important social functions by helping to ensure the permanence of marriage and by providing comfort, insight, and sexual satisfaction (Bryan 1966), and accountants believe that they are designers of order who reduce ignorance and generate consensus in organizations by means of rational knowledge and fact (Montagna 1973).

GRID DIMENSION OF OCCUPATIONAL CULTURES

Occupational cultures also contain structural features—the grid dimension—although they are less potent and certainly less interesting than the features of the group dimension. While the group dimension consists of the emotionally charged beliefs that organize and maintain ideologies about how to create meaning and control in work life, the grid dimension consists of the tangible structures through which members of an occupation attempt to order their relations with one another. Most analysts conclude that these two dimensions are distinct though interrelated: neither is a mirror reflection of the other; each must be considered in its own right (Keesing 1974; Kroeber and Parsons 1970).

Thus, the grid dimension sets up a pattern whereby members are supposed to interact with one another (Douglas 1982). It underscores hierarchical authority, formal rules, impersonal relations, differential rewards, and divisions of labor (Mars 1982) *within the occupation.* Three prominent parts of this dimension are rankings, members' autonomy over their work and their control over other workers, and the imposed and formal rules that execute these arrangements (Sonnenstuhl and Trice 1991). In occupations with a strong grid dimension, individual members' behavior relative to other members' behavior is tightly constrained by formal rules; in occupations with a weak grid dimension, constrained by few, if any, rules, so that members have a great deal of freedom to behave as they choose vis-à-vis one another. Occupations with strong grids emphasize one's place and role in the occupation's structure; weak ones emphasize that one's place and role are poorly defined. Grid dimensions reside primarily in formal occupational associations or in labor unions, although informal expressions of the dimension may emerge spontaneously.

Typically, occupations form fewer and less intense grids than do work organizations, where managerial hierarchies and formal rules are common. Also, when practiced inside an organization, occupations may come to absorb management's administrative structure, making it a part of the occupation's culture. Thus, occupations that practiced in large bureaucracies tend to develop a strong grid dimension. Many well-established craft occupations also have a substantial degree of grid dimension. Apprentices, journeymen, and masters, in one form or another, are apt to be common in such occupations. Further, and independent of the work organization, members of some craft occupations, such as construction work, perform numerous functions that might otherwise be done by management—planning, directing, and controlling work processes (Freidson 1986)—and therefore have stronger grid dimensions.

Using a combination of the group and grid dimensions, it is possible to construct four ideal types of occupations that become subcultures in work organizations (McKinney 1966; Scott 1981, 1987). Each type focuses attention "on one or a few features of organizations that are asserted to be of primary importance" (Scott 1981:28).

Based on Mary Douglas's analysis of the major dynamics of an organization's culture (1982), I have selected two features to be of primary importance in constructing these ideals. They are the degree of cohesiveness or "sticking together" (group dimension) and the degree to which there are norms governing the relationships between members of the occupational (grid dimension).

Each of these four types of occupations typically adapt in some fashion to the administrative hierarchies within the management subculture. In the process there is the distinct possibility of a clash between the occupational and managerial subcultures. There is also the distinct possibility that the occupation's ideology will be so compatible with that of management that members of the occupation will readily accept and become assimilated into the managerial culture. Thus, in effect, an occupation's grid dimension can become so blended into management's administrative structure that the two become indistinguishable from each other. Since managerial hierarchies strive to achieve well-defined structures, this blending usually means there is a strong grid dimension for the occupation even though the grid is not native to the occupation itself. Chapter 7 explores in detail how the following types of occupations will probably adapt during the dynamic processes involved in reducing—at least temporarily—culture clash. For the moment, I will merely list and briefly describe them.

STRONG GROUP/STRONG GRID OCCUPATIONS

These occupations approach being communities (i.e., their cultures have in abundance many of the features of cultures described earlier in this chapter). In addition, they have prominent structural features. These features are independent, however, of the organization's administrative structure. Thus, they have a ranking system relative to the other occupations with which they interact in the organization and a

ranking system within their own group. They adapt to managerial subcultures by *accommodating* their culture's definitions and practices to
those of management so that neither prevails. Corporate physicians are
an example.

WEAK GROUP/STRONG GRID OCCUPATIONS

Occupations in this category have ideologies that closely resemble
those in the managerial hierarchy or management has been successful
in dismantling and redistributing the occupation's tasks and body of
knowledge. Thus, the occupation becomes *assimilated* and over time
takes on management's ideologies and strong grid structure. Members of the occupation have weak consciousness of kind and low cohesiveness. Examples are engineers, accountants, and personnel
administrators.

STRONG GROUP/WEAK GRID OCCUPATIONS

These can be found in organizations where all or almost all of the
organization's members are in one well-developed occupation. As a
result, members generate their own grid structure to administer the
organization and are also responsible for planning and controlling
work processes (Freidson 1986). Consequently, such occupations have
relatively weak grid structures but *dominating* group features. Occupations in secondary schools, police departments, and social welfare
agencies are examples.

WEAK GROUP/WEAK GRID OCCUPATIONS

These occupations have tended to reject both occupational expertise
as well as administrative hierarchy, substituting instead the authority
of democratic consensus. They abandon both grid and group features,
attempting to create new work organizations in which they can express
the ideology that everyone has an equal role in deciding how work will
be organized and relationships structured. Examples are producer cooperatives, alternative schools, and feminist health collectives.

SUMMARY

In general, cultures have distinct characteristics. They are inherently
fuzzy and ambiguous because they spring from ideologies and symbols. These, in turn, are inherently colored by paradox and contradic-
tion. Despite these features, cultures are essential since they provide

much of the guidance human beings need to survive, adapt, and achieve collectively. Their base in ideologies and symbols makes them dynamic and ever subject to change. They are also historically based and have emotionally charged sense-making capacities.

Some of the features of occupations encourage the formation of cultures. These include esoteric knowledge and expertise and unusual or extreme emotional demands, such as night work and danger, which lead to a consciousness of kind. This, in turn, tends to generate a situation in which the occupation may pervade members' nonworking lives. Both a favorable self-image and beliefs that confer social value on the work flow from all these favorable conditions. Ethnocentrism is the overall consequence—a belief that their "our" views on work and life are superior to those of others and that outsiders must be viewed with suspicion.

In addition to their group features, occupational cultures also have grid dimensions. These consist of the rules, ranks, and procedures by which members of occupations order their relations with one another. When group and grid dimensions are combined, it is possible to construct ideal types of occupations that reflect the various adaptive modes that arise between occupational and managerial subcultures.

3. IDEOLOGIES IN OCCUPATIONAL LIFE

*Men plug the dikes of their most needed beliefs with what-
ever mud they can find.*

—Clifford Geertz

T HIS CHAPTER EXAMINES the concept of ideology as it applies to
occupations. In chapter 4 we will review the concrete and specific
cultural forms that convey ideologies to the members of occupations—argot, myths, stories, rituals, ceremonies, symbols, and physical artifacts. Cultural forms and ideologies are closely related.

Recall that an occupation's culture consists of the ideologies that are
relatively unique to it and the cultural forms that transform these abstract beliefs into a "natural system" (Swidler 1986) that expresses these
ideologies in concrete form to the occupation's members. Ideologies
are "understandings that represent credible relationships between objects, properties and ideas" (Sproull 1981:204 and are imbued with
powerful emotions and moral obligations. Their "oughtness" is akin
to religious fervor because they possess a moral significance such that
members often view them as crucial for the maintenance of proper
behavior and the guidance of social action, including the proper distribution of resources. The bundle of beliefs comprising an occupation's
ideology explains and justifies its ongoing arrangements in a way that
the human relationships and distribution of resources generated by
these arrangements seem natural and morally acceptable.

As Robert Wuthnow has noted (1987:156), "Ideology creates, as it
were, models of moral order that can be visualized and experimented
with symbolically, enacted in ritual, or in idealized, communities."
Moreover, these models "can crystallize within virtually any long-
lasting human group, including national cultures, social classes, occupations, professional groups, formal organizations and organizational
subunits" (Beyer, Dunbar, and Meyer 1988:483).

When a constellation of beliefs develops into an ongoing cluster (Williams 1970), it sets up a continuum between ideology, tradition, and "common sense" (Swidler 1986:273). At its first inception, the ideology is articulated as a self-conscious belief and ritual system. With repeated expression and further articulation, however, the ideology becomes taken for granted as a inevitable part of life. Over time, and with continuing expression, the original beliefs come to be viewed as guides for behavior and for assigning moral meanings to concrete action. For individual members, the constellation of beliefs are their "oughts," their values. They may be either semiconscious or largely unconscious, but in either case they have become common sense. As such, these stable clusters of beliefs legitimize concrete actions, make others heretical, and create meanings for events yet to come, thereby linking past and future (Meyer 1982:47). In short, a generalized, abstract system of meanings develops, becoming the "of course" or the "it is only natural" of continuing interactions. As Eric Carlton (1977:28) concludes, ideologies "dispel conceptual uncertainty by supplying a blueprint."

The basic nature of ideologies and the cultural forms that express them, however, do not guarantee a clear-cut and unambiguous expression of explicit meanings. As Ritzer and Walczak (1986:391) comment, ideologies may "be vague and very general . . . may also be highly integrated or be made up of values that are disconnected and, perhaps, inconsistent." Hospital social workers, for example, have "irreconcilable contradictions within their ideology" (Meyerson 1988:7). On the one hand, the social workers place great faith and authority in science and the status it brings to the doctors in hospital settings. On the other hand, they believe they are patients' advocates and should empower patients to question and defy the medical model of doctors. Although this is a rather extreme example, it nonetheless illustrates the intrinsic fuzziness of cultures and their ideologies.

According to Brenda E. F. Beck and Larry F. Moore (1985:335), ideologies "never provide a completely consistent set of ranked values or action guideposts; there are always ambiguities, even contradictions." Further, most cultures contain a multiplicity of ideologies, often in competition. In modern cultures there are few reasons to assume ideologies are necessarily harmonious. Some deliver crisper messages than others and conflict less with other ideologies in the culture, while others are fuzzier and deliver less precise messages (Pierce 1977). As cultural forms act to deliver meanings, contradictions are likely to emerge, so that ambiguities permeate practically all expressions of culture: liberty conflicts with order, stability with inevitable change, precision with flexibility (Geertz 1964:54). Despite these inherent flaws, ideologies are, in some fashion, expressed and made manifest by cultural forms. In essence, ideologies are the substance of a culture, and, as such, they are inevitably a part of human experience.

EXAMPLES OF OCCUPATIONAL IDEOLOGIES

Ideologies, as we have seen, are emotionalized, action-oriented beliefs held by members of an occupation about their work. Accountants, for example, may at times question their "dominant assumptions" (Boland 1982:126), but they have mounted and sustained a vigorous attack against outside critics of these assumptions. Moreover, they have carefully cultivated a professional elite—certified public accountants—that rigorously controls membership and carefully distinguishes between outsiders and insiders. Above all, accountants legitimate their actions by their ideology of orderliness and rational control—an appeal to a cherished "higher value."

Among accountants, a dominant ideology is the deep-seated conviction that order and rationality can be made a vital part of the behavior of work organizations, especially their financial control and planning. Consensus and the governance of workplaces, they believe, are possible by means of rational knowledge and factual information. Conflict, strain, and power struggles exist, but these are secondary to the "bottom line," where financial profit or loss are cold-bloodedly assessed.

Dan Gowler and Karen Legge (1983:210) view accounting "as a form of moral and technical reckoning, where the careful husbandry of scarce resources is not only treated as a sign of management competence, but also a moral superiority." Moreover, accountants believe that the independent certified public accountant has the competence and objectivity to "properly deal with problems of materiality and remain both competent and objective while doing so" (Montagna 1973:142).

In short, accountants believe they are the designers of order: they reduce ignorance, preserve order, and represent the rational maintenance of the status quo. As Louis Pondy (1983:174) puts it, accounting "creates a rational *context* within which natural processes of organizations are worked out." Accountants believe they can get at the "truth" in organizational life. Indeed, a widely accepted proverb among accountants testifies to this assumption: "The accountant's job is to protect the company against the manager."

A recent study revealed the basic content of craft ideology among construction workers:

> We found that work behavior on all construction sites is governed by a rich craft ideology that pervades day-to-day events such as the pacing of work, job techniques, and the choice of tools. This ideology links the work autonomy of the individual craftsman with efficient and high quality work standards. Supervising workers too closely threatens their status as craftsmen, and their work becomes less efficient and of lower quality. . . . Workers, foremen, supervisors, subcontractors and general contractors all emphasized that workers should organize their work and solve many of their own problems (Steiger and Form 1991:261-62).

Thomas L. Steiger and William H. Form suggest that the term "responsible autonomy" could be aptly applied to this ideology.

Social workers embrace an "ideology of care: treat the whole person including his/her psychological, social, and economic conditions; empower the client by giving him/her as much control as possible. The nitty-gritty of their work entails rolling up one's sleeves and talking with all sorts of people in their own language. Many of the trappings of professionalism oppose the core values of social work" (Meyerson 1988:5–6).

Midwives are nurses who justify their occupational role as one "in which birth is viewed as a normal, family-centered event" (Langton 1991), not a pathological state.

Arlie R. Hochschild (1983:147) suggests that the increasing commercialization of human feelings among airline flight attendants, bill collectors, waiters, salespeople, and others "require[s] the worker to produce an emotional state in another person—gratitude or fear, for example," all as a belief in the expediency of selling emotions for monetary income (also see Nielsen 1982).

Nightclub strip dancers studied by Jacqueline Boles and A. P. Garbin (1977) believed they provided opportunities for sexual fantasy that fulfilled therapeutic and protective functions for society in general. Some pimps and prostitutes claim that their work has social and psychological functions, including deterring rapes and related crimes and saving

troubled marriages (Bryan 1966). Indeed, Jim Wall (1986:26) cites a
high-class brothel manager who claims

> "we have a mission here. We contribute to society. I show society
> that this profession can have positive aspects. One example: I just
> fully equipped this place so that it's accessible to the handicapped.
> Handicapped people don't get a fair shake in society when it comes
> to the freedom to have sexual relationships."

These beliefs give prostitution a positive image, allowing members of
the occupation to respond to the social consensus against them (Jackman, O'Toole, and Geis 1963).

Ideologies are closely associated with and often molded by the tasks
members of the occupation perform. Among doctors, for example, "the
ideology of affective neutrality is strong" (Smith and Kleinman 1989:
57). Emotional neutrality becomes socialized into their reactions to patients so that intimate contact with the human body has an aura of
detachment and objectivity. Advertising agents emphasize their crea-
tivity and challenge, dentists believe in their independence and autonomy, and university librarians tend to think of themselves as protectors
and keepers of books and the equality of access to them by students
and faculty. Each of these ideological stances reflects the tasks of its
respective occupation (Gerstl 1961).

Male actors who face chronic unemployment believe in egalitarianism—no actor may claim sole responsibility for what he has done because the triumphant performance belongs to all of them (McHugh
1969). Similarly, shrimp fishermen value voluntary cooperation as a
means of reducing work risks and believe in egalitarianism, albeit while
recognizing the captain's final authority (Acheson 1981). The ideal skip-
per-crew relationship is one in which the skipper hardly says a word
or rarely gives an order. Apartment janitors, by contrast, work in an
environment and perform tasks that promote an "I'm-my-own-boss"
ideology (Gold 1964). Lacking co-workers or supervisors, they feel an
unusually high level of personal responsibility for their buildings and
are especially angered when tenants go over their heads and complain
to owners or real estate agents. Similarly, longshoremen see themselves
as macho workers who are able to cope with problems on their own
(Pilcher 1972). They view white-collar workers as "pencil pushers" and
"office pinkies," and they are ever ready to resolve disputes with their
fists.

DOMINANT IDEOLOGIES

Although every occupation has its own unique set of ideologies, many have beliefs that may be referred to as "overarching." Professionalism and unionism are two examples of overarching ideologies. Both are expressions of the occupational principle, the belief that workers rather than administrators should control the way work is organized. Many occupations have adopted these overarching ideologies to maintain control over their work. This section examines professionalism and unionism as overarching ideologies by locating their source in the disruption of the social order of the eighteenth century and examining their functions for workers.

The occupational principle predates the Industrial Revolution and the rise of complex, bureaucratic organizations. The guilds of the Roman Empire and the Middle Ages strictly controlled whether one could work at a particular craft (Kranzberg and Gies 1975). By the thirteenth century in Europe, there were hundreds of guilds whose masters were a combination of merchants and craftsmen who sold the products of their shops at their front doors. The carpenter, for example, originally both a house builder and a furniture maker, divided into carpenter and joiner. A third craft, wood carver, split off to do the most delicate woodworking, and a fourth was developed by those who painted the finished wood products.

Like their Roman predecessors, medieval guilds provided welfare assistance to their members, but their chief function was to protect the craft as a whole by strictly regulating production. They imposed strict quality-control standards on guild members. When brewing ale, for instance, brewers could use no ingredients except grain, hops, and water; chandlers had to use four pounds of tallow for each quarter-pound of wick. Guild officers inspected workshops, checked scales, and confiscated substandard goods. In the interest of fair competition, work on Sundays and on a saint's day was forbidden; to preserve meticulous craftsmanship, night work was banned. Guilds restricted recruitment and put recruits through long and arduous training.

Generally, guilds were divided into masters and apprentices, but some added a middle grade, journeyman. Although masters could employ as many sons, brothers, and nephews as they chose, most guilds could have only one or two nonfamily apprentices. The apprentices started out with the most menial tasks and throughout their apprenticeship were given increasing responsibilities. After several years of hard work, apprentices could become masters by fulfilling the following obligations: paying a license fee to the political sovereign, accumulating enough capital to go into business, taking an oath to uphold the guild's laws, and producing a masterpiece.

In the United States, the guild system of apprenticeship flourished until the close of the eighteenth century. Originally formed to meet the needs of a purely local trade, the guilds were less and less at home in a production apparatus geared to the needs of regional, national, and international markets. The role and function of merchant came to predominate over that of the craftsman, a subtle but far-reaching change in the organization of work. Instead of the craftsmen exercising the sales function, as in the old days, the new merchant-salesmen began dictating the organization of production. Forced to find cost-cutting advantages, the merchant-salesmen sacrificed the apprentice system by hiring unapprenticed labor, generally women and children, whom they paid very little; farming out work to prison inmates; and cutting the wages of those apprentices and journeymen remaining in their employ. In addition, they increased the hours in the workday, subdivided work into easily completed operations requiring few skills, and hired aggressive supervisors to enforce newly tightened work standards. Unskilled workers reacted by looking for new employment opportunities on the frontier; skilled craftsmen, however, unable to count on moving into the master class and unable to put together the capital to open their own enterprises, found they had few choices: either accept wage cuts, nonapprenticed labor, and harsh working conditions or join in collective action against their employers.

UNIONISM

Unionism in America thus, emerged with the growth of industrial capitalism and the breakup of craft apprenticeships (Rorbaugh 1986; Filippelli 1984; Dulles and Dubofsky 1984). As an overarching ideology, unionism emphasizes beliefs in group solidarity and collective bargaining as a way to ensure workers economic security, welfare, and dignity. Accordingly, employers are believed to be responsible for paying workers a living wage, providing them with secure jobs, and ensuring them decent working conditions. In addition, employers may not withhold these responsibilities without consulting their workers. In return, workers are responsible for providing employers with a fair day's work and are entitled to strike and withhold their labor if employers renege on their responsibilities. Underlying these principles is the deeply held belief that if workers are to prevail, they must act collectively. These were unionism's initial "bread-and-butter" issues, and they remain so today.

In the United States, unionization took two forms: craft unionism and industrial unionism. Craft unions, like the guilds of earlier times, were organized by members of a particular skilled trade or craft (i.e., carpenters, steam fitters), and until the 1930s, craft unionism was the dominant form of unionization. Industrial unionism, by contrast, organized skilled and unskilled workers according to industry (e.g., steel, oil, rubber).

Initially, the great mass of unskilled factory operations concentrated in the mass-production industries lacked the economic ability and opportunity to form stable unions. Passage of the Wagner Act in 1935, however, changed that situation by giving workers the right to join unions and bargain collectively.

In general, craft unionism gives workers more control over the practice of their work than industrial unionism does because the crafts set the standards for who will be recruited into their apprentice programs and decide when the apprentices qualify to become journeymen and masters. A craft union's control over the content of its work is not absolute, however, for, if there are no legal constraints on who may perform a particular kind of work, employers may recruit whomever they choose. Industrial unions, because they represent a diversity of workers who are generally trained for their jobs by their industrial employers, lack formal control over the content of their work. Both craft and industrial unions, however, bargain with employers over the terms and conditions of members' employment and often have been willing to concede control over the content of their work for improvement in wages, benefits, and working conditions.

Since the formation of the first trade unions at the end of the eighteenth century, swings in the growth of American unionism have often been extreme. Usually, the number of adherents has increased during periods of economic downturn and government favor and has decreased when those conditions were reversed (Sloane and Witney 1985; Ritzer and Walczak 1986). For instance, by 1836, total union membership had grown to 6.5 percent of the labor force; however, with the business depression of the following year, the union movement collapsed. After that, the movement regrew very slowly, although it received a major boost as a result of President Abraham Lincoln's support for unionism and the labor scarcity created by the Civil War. By 1865, it stood at 2 percent of labor. In 1878, the number of unionists plummeted to 50,000, but it increased to 447,000 in 1897 and to 2,073,000 in 1904. After World War I, the number increased to 5.1 million in 1920, but it declined to 3.8 million in 1923. Spurred on by the Wagner Act, the number grew to 23 percent of the labor force in 1946, peaking at 25 percent in 1970. It declined again, to 18.8 percent, in 1984.

The recent decline in union membership has led some observers to predict the demise of unionism; however, a historical overview highlights its remarkable staying power. For many workers, there simply has been no alternative to collective bargaining for maintaining and improving working conditions. The current environment has not been beneficial to unionism because the blue-collar sector of the economy, which has been contracting, has been largely organized and the white-collar sector, which is expanding, has been generally resistant to unionization. Seeing themselves as "professionals" and "managers," most white-collar workers reject unionism as inconsistent with such self-images and as a hindrance to being promoted into the highest echelons of corporate life.

PROFESSIONALISM

Professionalism as an ideology also came into existence with the rise of the market system of capitalism (Larson 1977; Wilensky 1964a). According to this ideology, professionals possess special knowledge that permits them to act in the interest of the public rather than in their own self-interest. Consequently, they argue that society should permit them to define what tasks make up their work and who should be allowed to perform them. As professionals, they claim to possess the following special traits (Carr-Saunders and Wilson 1941; Parsons 1939):

- a systematic body of knowledge learned within the university and known only to members of the occupation;
- a norm of autonomy, which requires that they be free of external control because outside interference will reduce the quality of their service;
- a norm of altruism, which requires members of the occupation to put the interests of the community before self-interest be-

cause they are more concerned with symbolic than with economic rewards;

- a norm of authority over clients, which requires that members of the occupation have virtually uncontested authority over clients because a questioning clientele, incapable of judging its own needs or the ability of a given professional to satisfy those needs, will reduce the quality of service and;
- a distinctive occupational culture manifest in its associations, training schools, and those organizations in which professionals work, that reinforces the norms of professional service.

During the Middle Ages, the term *profession* was used to refer to religion, law, and medicine—those occupations associated with the medieval church and universities. With the rise of industrial capitalism, however, the term became associated with efforts by middle-class workers to create a market for their services.

Under the old order, the traditional professions were stratified into two social worlds: the learned and the common. The learned were distinguished by their training in the university and ministered only to the elites. Common practitioners learned their trades as apprentices in guildlike relationships with master craftsmen and competed with one another for commercial advantage.

With the reordering of society during the growth of capitalism, learned practitioners lost their special relationship to the dominant classes and had to compete with commoners and anyone else who claimed to be a professional. To bring about order, the learned and the commoners joined forces to make the case for the superiority of their services over those of others. They did this by standardizing their services, which made their "commodities" both distinct from those of others and recognizable to the public.

Standardization was achieved by controlling the production of the "new professionals." The "old professionals" claimed sole control of superior expertise and sought a monopoly from the state to teach that expertise to recruits. Members of the old professions of medicine, law, and religion continued to teach recruits within the university and established occupational associations to fight for their self-interests. Occupations such as social work, school teaching, and librarianship that were seeking professional status established guildlike associations that administered the new symbols of professionalism to their members—

formal training in a common curriculum, a diploma, a qualifying examination, and a certificate. Later, professional schools in universities took on these functions.

The grand prize in obtaining control over one's work is state licensure, and it has been pursued by both the crafts and those occupations striving to be called professional. Licensure means that the state grants licenses to practice to workers in an occupation; all others are barred from performing such work. The state generally establishes licensing standards in accordance with what the occupation's professional or trade association claims are the minimal requirements for someone to practice, and such standards often emerge only after prolonged battles on the floors of state legislatures. But the outcomes of licensure seem to be significant: it restricts entry quite effectively and enhances the monetary returns of those licensed to practice (Pfeffer 1974).

A wide variety of occupational groups have sought state licensure so that the last two decades of the nineteenth century were characterized by a licensing movement. During this period plumbers, doctors, barbers, horseshoers, pharmacists, embalmers, and members of sundry other groups sought and were granted licensing protection. They sought state protection because they feared competition from the large corporations that were coming to dominate the economic landscape. Predominantly self-employed, most of these professionals and tradesmen worked out of small shops that had been established with little capital, and they generally sold their goods and services to individuals rather than to corporations. Their trades and occupations were easy to enter and consequently beset by competition; licensure laws restricted entry and gave members a monopoly. These occupations were successful in obtaining licensing because there were no organized buyers or employers who stood to lose by the monopoly and because they stipulated that anyone in business at the time could qualify for licensure under the statutes.

Although licensure is the grand prize in the occupational battle to control work, because it ensures that the occupation will be able to set the standards for what constitutes appropriate practice, it does not necessarily give workers, especially those in organizations, complete control over the content and terms of their employment. For instance, a variety of forces contributed to the erosion of control in the professions referred to by some observers as "deprofessionalization" (see Haug 1975; Haug and Sussman 1969; 1971; Toren 1975; Rothman 1984). Marxist theorists, such as Derber (1982) call it the "proletarianization of the professions."

Among the political, social, and economic forces that have contributed to deprofessionalization are the rising educational level of the population, which has meant that laypersons have become knowledgeable about matters once believed to be in the exclusive domain of the professional (Rothman 1984). Routinization and computerization of expert knowledge make it possible for laypersons to perform these tasks (Rothman 1984; Toren 1975; Denzin 1968; Haug 1977). Another such force is the increased specialization within the professions which produces schisms that make it difficult for occupational associations to mount cohesive campaigns with state legislatures and regulatory agencies (Rothman 1984). Client awareness of self-interest and abuse among professionals has led to closer scrutiny by individuals, consumer groups, and state legislatures, of the traditional prerogatives of professionals (Haug and Sussman 1969; Betz and O'Connell 1983). Further, allied occupations have successfully encroached on the once-exclusive jurisdiction of some professionals. Realtors and title insurers, for instance, now perform work previously done by lawyers (Rothman 1984; Rosenstein et al. 1980; Waldman 1980). Finally, outsiders such as government regulatory agencies and the organizations for whom professionals work are increasing their control over professional work (Starr 1982; Rothman 1984; Betz and O'Connell 1983).

With their moral order shaken, professionals are searching for ways to refurbish the ideology of professionalism. In a few instances, they have sought relief in unionism, whose conflict orientation they previously perceived as being inconsistent with professionalism (Haug and Sussman 1971). According to Charles Derber (1982), professionals, faced with performing a narrowing range of tasks, subjected to external controls by nonprofessionals, and battered by large-scale market conditions, are being forced to move toward collective bargaining and/or the formation of more militant occupational associations. For example, four thousand legal-aid attorneys are members of a national union (Waldman 1986), and staff lawyers for the California Bar Association have gone on strike over wages (Galante 1986).

It remains unclear to what degree professionals will move toward unionism or what impact such a movement will have on the ideology of professionalism. As professional workers struggle to reorder the chaos caused by deprofessionalization, however, new beliefs about their place in the division of labor will be put forth, tested, abandoned if found lacking, and embraced if found convincing.

In sum, to assume that professionalism is a unified ideology ignores the state of flux and conflict within its parameters. As we have seen, different groups wrestle over control of the tasks of a particular occupation. Often these conflicts are ideological ones, even though they may compete under the umbrella of professionalism. Like so many other dimensions of occupational life, professionalism is subject to dynamic flux and change, to inevitable shifts and faults.

EVOLUTION OF OCCUPATIONAL IDEOLOGIES

Ideally, ideologies set forth the appropriate moral obligations that people in the occupation should hold toward one another and toward those with whom they must interact, as well as the correct distribution of resources to maintain those obligations. It follows that disturbances in this moral order are likely to create opportunities for the production of new ideologies. Wuthnow and Marsha Witten (1988:65) formulate the process as "changes in the social environment that add to levels of uncertainty, and therefore provide opportunities in which new ideologies are likely to be produced."

Three phases make up the evolution of ideologies (Wuthnow 1987). These can be thought of as responses to the opportunities provided by the disturbances in the existing moral order of a collectivity such as an occupation. According to Wuthnow (1987:151), these phases are (1) the social production of ideological innovations following the interruption of existing ideologies; (2) selection from among the number of ideologies that respond to the opportunity; and (3) the institutionalization phase, in which the successful ideologies develop features that make them less vulnerable to competition from other ideologies.

The first phase emerges during rifts in the existing moral order (i.e., during those periods when social expectations and obligations become uncertain and chaotic). Since chaos inherently generates numerous ideologies to fill the void, in the second stage, a "selective process weeds out some of the competing ideologies because they perform less effectively in governing social resources" (Wuthnow and Witten 1988:65). In the third phase, institutionalization, those ideologies with the most plausible pattern for using resources take on additional features that make them less vulnerable to competition and less subject to radical changes in the environment. The second and third phases tend to appear once an ideology is under way. The explicit tasks that evolve in the occupation, and the body of knowledge on which these tasks rest, may prove to be incompatible with parts of the emerging ideology and thus get weeded out. As these tasks continue to evolve, they further mold, reinforce, and fit with the emerging bundle of beliefs. As a consequence, ideologies tend to be closely associated with, and grow directly out of, the tasks an occupation performs as it evolves over time (Breer and Locke 1965).

JOURNALISM AND NURSING

Although not perfect examples, journalism and nursing illustrate well the three phases in the evolution of ideologies. Before steam-powered presses, editors such as Horace Greeley collected, wrote, edited, and printed the news themselves. Journalists evolved an occupational image of themselves as being independent, resourceful, and determined to get accurate and detailed news stories.

As Richard Kluger explained (1986:272):

> According to tradition, the journalist would willingly sacrifice money, comfort, sleep, love, food and hope of eternal salvation to the spirit of his craft; his compensation was to be on the inside of things, to know the dynamics of his society, to confer celebrity or promote social justice and to feel he was as good as any man through his access to the printed word.

The advent of steam-powered presses, accompanied by the evolution of the railroads and telegraphs, profoundly disturbed this ideology and set the stage for ideological innovations. Newspapers became cheaper to produce, were able to gather news more rapidly, and had expanding circulations. Enterprising editors began going after the news and sending reporters for it, rather than waiting for it to come to them (Lee 1937; Kluger 1986). Although some measure of objectivity remained, newspapers soon became closely allied with political parties and commercial interests, giving rise to an ideology of sensationalism. According to this ideology, the way to increase circulation was by adopting an extravagant and extreme style:

> People would scold and fret, but they would read, and with much zest, devour those articles which were most declamatory and personal and least instructive and valuable. . . . People must have [sensationalism] just as the Chinese take opium, the ignorant take

whiskey, and the higher class person takes a philosophical discussion (quoted in Lee 1937:650).

William Randolph Hearst, a leading practitioner of "yellow journalism," trained his reporters to be managers of sensation and jugglers of catch words. An offshoot of this ideology was the emergence of the journalist turned public relations representative. These journalists came to believe their tasks should be the manipulation of press accounts and stories so that their employers would be portrayed in the most favorable light possible.

In summary, then, two innovative ideologies challenged the original ideology of objectivity and truth in reporting. One was that it was necessary to sensationalize the reporting of news. The other was that it was necessary to manipulate the news for monetary gain and for the benefit of a few who had paid to have the news manipulated.

There was a long-term compatibility between objectivity and the actual tasks of journalists that tipped the occupation toward the selection and revival of objectivity as the prevailing ideology. After all, at bottom, the distortion of news was not a basic feature of gathering and reporting it. To distort it was an unrealistic, discomforting, and onerous task. Simply to report it as accurately as possible was consistent with the task itself. In addition, a new morality was emerging within the ranks of editors and reporters that was guiding the institutionalization phase of the development of the ideology.

Fed up with the press's antics, several groups undertook attempts to reform it. Schools of journalism were developed at Washington and Lee University in 1869, at New York University in the 1870s, at the University of Missouri in 1903, and at Columbia University in 1912. Although many of the graduates of these colleges were recruited by the larger metropolitan dailies, most reporters were still trained on the job. Accordingly, in an attempt at news reform, in 1918 Joseph Pulitzer established his "prize for the most distinguished and meritorious public service rendered by an American newspaper during the year." In 1913, the *New York World* established a Board of Accuracy and Fair Play, supervised by its legal department, to correct carelessness and stamp out fakes and fakers. In 1922, the American Society of Newspaper Editors adopted seven ethical canons: responsibility; freedom of the press; independence; sincerity; truthfulness, accuracy, impartiality; fair play; and decency. And in 1924, the American Bar Association sought to curb the "unwholesome" tendency toward "crusading," which it described as "a rich man's game" leading ultimately to lost advertising, circulation, and prestige.

The coup de grace in news reform, however, was delivered by journalists. Always reluctant to unionize because they saw themselves as professionals and reporting as a way into management, they disdained joining the labor movement, believing that they would find financial relief through individual initiative. Consequently, the many attempts between 1886 and 1935 to create a craft union were doomed to failure. As the Depression deepened, however, news reporters found they were the most readily dispensable part of any news operation. Their numbers and salaries were drastically cut, while those of unionized printers were left largely intact. Discontent over bread-and-butter issues, mobilized by Heywood Broun's 1933 column "A Union for Reporters," led to the establishment of the American Newspaper Guild, and at their 1934 meeting, the delegates adopted a "freedom of conscience" resolution and a code of ethics.

According to the freedom of conscience resolution, freedom of the press is a right of readers and a responsibility of the producers of news; owners of the news media had abused this right and degraded the high calling of news writing; and the American Newspaper Guild would strive tirelessly for the integrity of news columns and the opportunity for reporters to discharge their social responsibility. The code of ethics loudly proclaimed that the reporter's first duty was to give the public accurate and unbiased reporting, legitimate news concerning the privileged should not be suppressed, and the news should be edited exclusively in the editorial room instead of in the business office.

Today, the code of ethics of the American Newspaper Guild is an article of faith among journalists who strive to be objective, and objectivity in reporting remains a much examined issue both inside, and outside of journalism (eg., Boyer 1988; Tuchman 1972, 1978; Gans 1982). According to Gaye Tuchman, objectivity is a strategic ritual (1972) and news reporting is an artful accomplishment attuned to specific understandings of social reality that are constituted in specific work processes and practices and legitimate the status quo. Similarly, Steven E. Clayman (1988) argues that journalists maintain neutrality in television news interviews by embedding statements within questions, attributing statements to third parties, and mitigating the force of their own statements so that they appear less violative and more acceptable than they might otherwise be. Interviewees generally cooperate to preserve the interviewers' neutrality, but occasionally they undermine it and unmask the interviewers' biases. In this sense, the construction of objectivity is a social accomplishment.

Herbert J. Gans (1982) argues that journalists try hard to be objective but that neither they nor anyone else can in the end proceed without values. Television commentator James Lett (1987) reports, for example, that even though the medical evidence was irrefutable, his supervisor admonished him to remain "objective" in a news program about the impact of cigarette smoking. Values in the news, however, are rarely explicit and must be found between the lines—in what actors and activities are reported or ignored and in how they are described. Generally, the news supports those enduring values described as "motherhood and apple pie": ethnocentrism, altruistic democracy, responsible capitalism, small-town pastoralism, individualism, moderation, social order, and national leadership.

These values are revealed, for instance, in stories that describe welfare programs as subject to "waste" and military expenditures as "cost overruns" or that describe the president as "arriving" somewhere while a black militant is said to have "turned up." Magazine and television stories about the good life in America center on the small town and its presumed sense of community and absence of "urban ills." "Self-made" men and women are featured, as are people who overcome bureaucracy and poverty. Domestic news reporters judge other societies by American practices and institutions. Americans are urged to compete with one another but, in the process, to refrain from making unreasonable profits on grossly exploiting workers or customers.

The evolution of ideologies among nurses followed, in general, the major phases put forward by Wuthnow (1987), with distinctive idiosyncrasies. The opportunity to introduce ideological innovations came about in part because of the activities of journalists during the Crimean War, who, for the first time, widely reported in British newspapers the horrors of war and the despicable medical facilities the military provided for the sick and wounded. Their reports would probably have not been enough, however, to cause a widely felt disturbance of the moral obligations of the military physicians and unskilled and undisciplined workers in public hospitals of the period. Nursing, at that time, was merely an extension of housework, accompanied by rather primitive hygiene and care. It was conducted by "women of questionable character, of inordinate thirst for alcoholic beverages, and other unmentionable vices" (Whittaker and Olesen 1964:125). The results were often horrible, but that was war. The prevailing ideology seemed to be one of fatalism, despite a sense of crisis created by the newspapers (Strachey 1918).

Without this context, however, Florence Nightingale would probably have never blossomed into the charismatic leader who transformed nursing. Born into an aristocratic family, she had been attracted to voluntary hospital work as a young girl and had worked in hospitals before the Crimean War. Contrary to the legend of her as a dedicated, gentle, and saintly woman whose chief purpose was to serve the sick, she was, in fact, aggressive and somewhat masculine. She was "one who could be interpreted as power-loving, coolly manipulative and hypochondriacal . . . not as self-abnegating as the woman of legend, but rather a woman of authority, a woman who mercilessly drove others and within whom lurked fierce and passionate fires" (Whittaker and Olesen 1964:125; Strachey 1918).

Learning of the scarcity of medical help for wounded British soldiers, she volunteered to set up military hospitals in which to demonstrate the value of trained, compassionate nursing care for the wounded. Although medical and military authorities resisted, she succeeded in recruiting and training women volunteers for the Crimean theater of war, and she did indeed organize medical supplies, develop rules of hygiene, establish clean kitchens and laundries, and provide regular hot meals in many military hospitals and recovery barracks. Her spectacular accomplishments in the field led her to attract many supporters, including Queen Victoria, who encouraged her to continue her work in reforming health care both in the military and at home. Convinced that she was following God's will, Nightingale forsook marriage to devote her life to caring for the sick and injured.

Her efforts had just begun with the Crimean War. Her legend tends to end with the story of her standing outside a battlefield late at night, holding a lamp amid the wounded. In fact, modern nursing emerged in the mid-nineteenth century primarily as a result of Florence Nightingale's efforts to elevate health care from domestic tasks performed by women in the household to skilled work carried out with a sense of service, charity, and obedience to male authority. Drawing on the traditions of religious education and military discipline, Nightingale trained middle-class women to provide skilled nursing care for the sick and general assistance to physicians and caretakers of the weak.

Nightingale single-handedly, and against great odds, created the caring ideology of nursing and its enduring public image of the "angel in white." She defined a specific area of work tasks, carved them out of both military and civilian bureaucracies, and created schools to transmit knowledge about how to do them, as well as an occupational association to control who does them. She had seized upon disturbances and change in the social environment as an opportunity to generate a new set of beliefs about the care of the sick and wounded (Strachey 1918).

Competing ideologies also emerged, however, even as Florence Nightingale pursued her long career. Thus, she vigorously asserted that "every woman is a nurse" yet warned that womanly virtues alone were not enough to make a good nurse. Expert skills in caring were also required. In these declarations, she captured the dual beliefs that have come to characterize nursing and have, at times, split it into warring factions.

The first U.S. nursing school was established in 1873, and by the turn of the century, nursing, like other occupations of that era, was well on its way toward institutionalization and the acquisition of the trappings of professionalization. At the same time, nursing was being split into two factions: the traditionalists, who emphasized the helping aspects of nursing, and the professionals.

The traditionalists looked upon the acquisition of expertise and professional status with suspicion, arguing that nursing was not merely a profession but a vocation and that it was not solely for gainful employment but a ministry (Melosh 1982). Looking to the selfless woman and the nurturing mother as their role models, rather than the expert, they believed that by seeking professional prerogatives, nurses would lose sight of the intense personal commitment and humanitarian sentiments required of them and reduce nursing to "mere skill."

The professionals, by contrast, saw the tasks and skills of nurses as empowering them to professional status by pushing them beyond the confines of domesticity and its idealized image toward the possibility that nursing could be judged by the standards and values of the world of paid work. Nursing leaders, rejecting the limiting conventions of gender, used the ideology of professionalism to defend nursing as paid work, thereby distinguishing it from the diffuse category of women's domestic duty, and to preserve this new occupation for an elite group of women—those trained in schools of nursing.

In sum, as the tasks in nursing evolved and the body of relevant knowledge accumulated, competing ideologies emerged. Based on the complex tasks that came to characterize the occupation, a strong theme of professionalism began to intermingle and compete with the original theme of compassion and care. Although the original theme has not been eliminated, it appears to have been deemphasized among nurses as the occupation has entered the institutionalization phase in the development of its ideologies. Finally, underlying these conflicts are the current dynamics of change in sex roles and gender ideologies among women in general.

Social transformations in medical care (e.g., germ theory, shifting care from the home to the hospital) created a labor market for trained nurses and enhanced their efforts to professionalize; consequently, today nursing is a well-established and relatively prestigious occupation within the health industry. Although debate rages about whether nursing is a semi- or a fully developed profession (Katz 1969; Melosh 1982), its current code of ethics highlights the nurse's professional skills and responsibilities. At the same time, nursing remains predominantly a female occupation and popular stereotypes perceive the nurse as a caring angel of mercy clothed in white.

In 1860, Nightingale set up the Nightingale Training School for Nurses to teach novices the attitudes and skills required of nurses. In 1893, the Fervand School of Nursing in Detroit formulated these attitudes and skills into the Nightingale pledge; today, this pledge and its emphasis are clearly reflected in nursing's code of ethics (Rothman 1987). Within the United States, schools of nursing have proliferated, and today nursing is taught within three-year hospital diploma schools, two-year community colleges, four-year baccalaureate degree programs, and graduate schools of medicine. Today, there are approximately 1.7 million nurses in the United States, the great majority of whom are women. Most nurses still revere Nightingale for her dedication to her vision and strive to emulate her behavior.

Despite the internal strains in nursing, care giving and humanitarian sentiments have remained important to its ideology. Support for this view comes from modern codes of ethics for nurses, which, although they have often been modified with the humanitarian/professional codes in mind, are still very similar to the Nightingale pledge of dedi-

cation to service. Elvi Whittaker and Virginia Olesen (1964:130) summarized Nightingale's career as follows: "In short, the image of
Florence Nightingale is so elastic that it is able to reflect a large range
of values and concerns, both in society and the occupational subculture."

FUNCTIONS AND DYSFUNCTIONS OF IDEOLOGY

Both strain and interest theories are useful in explaining the functions
and dysfunctions of ideologies. Strain theory suggests that ideologies
grow out of "the chronic malintegration of society" (Geertz 1964:54).
According to this theory, regardless of how human relationships are
organized, anxiety is inevitably produced within a given culture because no social arrangement is or can be completely successful in coping with the functional problems the culture inevitably faces.
Consequently, individual members experience unsolvable contradictions and ambivalences. Ideologies simplify, even resolve, these anxieties, making occupations ongoing and adaptable at the level of the
individual. As Harry M. Johnson has said (1968:77), ideologies "help
many people to cooperate toward the same goals."

Ideologies function to reduce tensions within an occupation in two
other ways: by projecting these tensions onto scapegoats and outsiders
and by legitimating the occupation's actions by attaching a "higher
value" to them. Ideologies also create or enhance a sense of solidarity
and ethnocentrism despite internal strains and ambiguities.

Early in their history, journalists viewed newspapers with political
allegiances and sensationalist reporting as having chosen this approach
as a way to compete and boost circulation. Although an ideology of
objectivity had tentatively crystallized among journalists, it was the
acceleration of the sense of independence and dedication to the desire
to create an accurate and full news story that enabled them to develop
a sense of occupation.

In contrast, according to the interest theory, ideologies are "a mask
and a weapon" (Geertz 1973:201) used by groups to advance their economic and political interests in the midst of ever-present struggles for
advantage. For Clifford Geertz (1973:201), however, the strain theory
and the interest theory need not be incompatible: "The two theories
are not necessarily contradictory, but the strain theory, being less sim-
plistic, is more penetrating, less concrete, more comprehensive." In essence, ideologies can reduce inconsistencies within a group while at

the same time promoting the interests of that group in the larger context within which it operates. Thus, scientists advance their own occupational interests by describing themselves to politicians and the general public as sources of impartial information about public policy. Journalists advance their own prestige and social values by claiming they are objective. Finally, social workers press their own interests to gain prestige and job security by readily adapting to the authority of physicians in hospital settings.

Waiters, salespeople, and flight attendants embrace an ideology that emphasizes service to customers and passengers, promoting their interests. Egalitarian sentiments among fishermen promote higher monetary shares for each at the end of the voyage, and prostitutes obviously promote their own competitive interests vis-à-vis exotic dancers and waitresses through their claims that they provide therapy and protect the society. Accountants profit by the power and prestige they accrue in organizations through their emphasis in order. Clearly, ideologies do serve the economic and power interests of persons in specific occupations.

These two theories are not competing to explain the functions of ideologies; nor are they mutually exclusive. Nevertheless, strain explanations are broader, more realistic, and subtle and reveal more about the basic nature of ideology. Consequently, strain explanations typically receive more attention, although they should not be regarded as eliminating the interest functions of ideologies. In summary, ideologies function in occupational life to reduce internal strains and anxieties, project emotional tensions on outsiders or scapegoats, legitimate behaviors that reduce tensions as having a "higher value," promote occupational solidarity, and advance the economic and power interests of those in the occupation.

Ideologies also provide occupational groups with a sense of place within a moral order. An occupation's ideology clearly delineates members' functions in a division of labor and their relation to other occupations, clients, and the government. Thus, ideologies are functional in that they provide members with clear guidelines for performing their tasks and relating to other groups.

The various functions of ideologies are often offset by distinct dysfunctions. Although nurses and accountants learn from their ideologies their appropriate moral obligations and a comforting sense of their place in the order of things, ambivalences and conflicts nevertheless emerge. Thus, the ideology of caring conflicts with nurses' desires to better themselves, insofar as caring people are not supposed to be assertive and demanding. Similarly, the rationality of accountants conflicts with the nonrational realities of social life—most things cannot be reduced to accounting practices. Consequently, while accountants may feel that they are morally correct, they are often perceived by outsiders as being out of touch with the "real" world and, therefore, having little to contribute.

Projecting tensions onto symbolic enemies can increase the number of targets for bitterness, making it difficult to elicit the necessary cooperation from others to get on with one's work. This was the case with the managers Melville Dalton studied (1958), who projected their hostility onto accountants and, consequently, devised ways to weaken and bypass them.

Similarly, legitimating tension by invoking some higher value may create such a wide gap between reality and ideology that people give up. This is currently the case in nursing, where it is no longer sufficient to motivate individuals by appealing to the higher values of service, dedication, and charity (Aiken 1983).

Ideological commonality produces solidarity, but it also creates opportunities for schisms within the occupation. Pathologists (Bucher 1962; Bucher and Strauss 1961) and pediatricians (Pawluch 1983), for instance, although they identify with their occupations, have seen schisms develop in their fields as opportunities for new areas of practice have emerged. Further, the clash of ideologies over how to manage a particular tension may publicize the problem, but it may also escalate the rhetoric so that all efforts to manage the difficulty are precluded. According to Alan D. Meyer (1982:60), ideologies "can . . . cause groups to become excessively deviant, rigid and stagnant. . . . [They] . . . may be perceived by nonmembers as iconoclasts, heretics and fanatics. Members . . . can suffer mass hallucinations about the outside world."

Ideologies may also oversimplify complex reality. People naturally simplify situations, and existing ideologies act to structure that oversimplification in the form of stereotypes, which are gross overgeneralizations of a few accurate and inaccurate characteristics. Consequently, stereotypes are misleading. In this regard, ideologies are quite dysfunctional. They are, however, inevitable. Actually there is considerable opinion that any collectivity, including an occupation, needs to develop insights, both internally and externally, into its complexity (Weick 1979). Ideologies are largely dysfunctional in this respect.

Finally, theories and studies of occupational cultures need to incorporate the concept that cultures can have dysfunctional consequences as explicitly as they do the idea that they have functions. Theories about organizational cultures have focused unrealistically and exclusively on order, even though disorder is also an obvious outcome. Louis Pondy and Ian I. Mitroff make this point repeatedly (1979:14, 15, 16), declaring that the "myth of the stable state" (Schon 1971) blinds students to the need to understand dysfunctions if one is to achieve a comprehensive analysis of organizational life. Perhaps the study of occupations can profit from the oversight in the study of organizations and consistently incorporate dysfunction into its efforts.

LEADERS AS PURVEYORS OF IDEOLOGIES

Leadership is defined by the reaction of the leader's followers because leaders, by definition, are able to get people to do things.

Leaders of occupations perform a variety of roles. Founders of occupational cultures, drawing on their visions of what the occupation ought to be, literally create its ideology and construct its unique cultural forms. Other leaders preserve the culture by embodying in their actions and words what it means to be a member of the occupation; they are especially adroit at performing and dramatizing its myths, symbols, and ceremonies. According to Schein (1985:317), "The unique and essential function of leadership is the manipulation of culture"; leaders are skilled at constructing, performing, and embellishing the myths, stories, songs, symbols, and other forms that convey a culture's meanings. In particular, leaders dramatize what it means to be a member of the culture and make being a member exciting (Pfeffer 1981).

Still other leaders are consensus leaders, who bridge the schisms that develop in any occupation by the adroit use of rites of conflict reduction, renewal, and integration. (Chapter 4 discusses these rites.) Finally, leaders may be change agents, people who are able to enunciate changes in the occupation's basic beliefs and to convince members to accept the proposed shifts in ideology and practice.

Founders of new occupations are frequently charismatic leaders (Weber 1947). Florence Nightingale was clearly in that category. They possess extraordinary personal qualities, emerge during times of social crisis, provide radical solutions to the crisis, and attract followers who attribute extraordinary powers to them and their successes. Finally, their radical solutions—complete with ideology and cultural forms—become institutionalized (Trice and Beyer 1986).

Other leaders preserve the occupational culture by becoming symbols of what it means to be a group member. As heroes, they embody the occupation's ideology, and by their actions they dramatize its meaning. According to Terrence E. Deal and Alan A. Kennedy (1982: 37), the first American astronauts possessed the "right stuff" and have become genuine folk heroes:

> Like John Wayne or Burt Reynolds . . . they create role models for others to follow. The hero is the great motivator, the magician, the person everyone will count on when things get tough. They have unshakable character and style. They do things everyone else wants to do but is afraid to try. Heroes are symbolic figures whose deeds are out of the ordinary, but not too far out. They show— often dramatically—that the ideal of success lies within human capacity.

Edward R. Murrow embodies journalism's ideology of objectivity; indeed, his crusading career is held up to newcomers and old-timers alike as an example of the journalist's responsibility and freedom to disclose the "true facts" as a service to the public. During World War II, he described the horrors of London's bombing from its rooftops. Likewise, during the reign of Senator Joseph McCarthy, his devastating broadcasts against the demagoguery of McCarthyism earned him worldwide applause. Finally, his controversial CBS documentaries set the standard for the likes of Bill Moyers, Mike Wallace, and Charles Collingwood. Throughout his career Murrow spoke out against management attempts to influence news reporting, steadfastly insisting that deciding what to report was the journalist's responsibility and not subject to negotiation with management and its censors. Rather than submit to CBS censorship, he resigned, denouncing management for its immoral behavior (Sperber 1986).

Upon his death, Murrow was hailed as "broadcasting's true voice" (Sperber 1986:703) and eulogized around the world for his contribution to the maintenance of freedom and integrity in journalism. Today, he is described as embodying the "heroic tradition" and the "fighter spirit" of journalism (Turnstall 1971:72) and as the "sainted Murrow" (Boyer 1988:8). Journalists are said to pursue the "high and holy calling of Murrow," and those who worked with and followed him at CBS are affectionately called "Murrow's Boys" (Boyer 1988). At CBS, the struggle to maintain autonomy from censorship continues, and Dan Rather publicly invokes Murrow—warning all journalists of a fall from Murrow to mediocrity if they are not ever vigilant in upholding his sainted tradition (Boyer 1988:9). Murrow, through his actions, dramatized for his generation and future ones what it really means to be a reporter and imbued it with a sense of excitement.

Vince Lombardi exemplifies the leader who is capable of changing an occupation's cultural beliefs and practices. He embodied the ideology of intense competition, a status achieved by his bringing about the miraculous turnaround of his disheartened and defeated football team, the Green Bay Packers. Although famous coaches such as Frank Leahy and Earl Blaik had previously spoken about the importance of winning in football, Lombardi became the dramatical personification of the central importance of winning, as exemplified by motto: "Winning is not the most important thing; it's the only thing." He devoutly insisted that competition was virtuous, and football players dramatically embraced that virtue. He justified his intense insistence on going all-out to win with his observation that business, politics, and law are, first and foremost, competitive struggles. Winning for him "was a uniquely modern form of immortality" (O'Brien 1987:197).

As a leader who facilitated drastic changes, Lombardi was spectacular. In 1958, the Packers' season was a total disaster: they won one game, tied one, and lost ten. The disgust of fans, the resignation of coaches, the angry letters, the sarcastic reviews of sportswriters, and the almost unbelievable contrast with the team's earlier years, when they had won six league championships—three in a row (1929, 1930, 1931)—made for a crisis atmosphere. In the eleven years since those proud days, there had been twenty-seven wins, ninety-three losses, and two ties. Hopelessness pervaded the team's efforts. Moreover, during the late 1950s, the Packers' coach had been a "nice guy" who was lenient and permitted gross infractions of curfew rules and public drinking.

In contrast, Lombardi's first year as the Packers' coach and general manager brought dramatic changes. Insisting on his clear-cut authority, he imposed rigorous training and curfew rules, enforced dress codes, and demanded unremitting drills and practice as ways to increase the players' physical conditioning and preparation. These changes resulted in five victories, five defeats, and a resounding vote of approval from businessmen, labor leaders, and the mayor of Green Bay, as well as roaring crowds.

The turnaround the next year was even more spectacular. In 1961, the Packers won the western conference with a 11–3 record and played the New York Giants for the National Football League (NFL) championship. In this game the team members—many of whom had been with the demoralized team two or three years earlier—played almost flawlessly against an opponent of equal experience and accomplishments, winning 37–0. The team's amazing victory resulted in President John F. Kennedy, who attended an award ceremony for Lombardi at the *Sports Illustrated* silver anniversary banquet, offering him the job of head football coach at West Point. Lombardi reluctantly declined and went on to win the western conference title for the third consecutive year. In 1962, his team again played the New York Giants for the NFL championship and won.

All occupations contain factions and schisms. Consensus leaders integrate them by emphasizing the commonalities, balancing each faction's power vis-à-vis the others, and striving for some sense of harmony. For instance, colleges are characterized by faculty members from a wide range of disciplines, and deans must function as consensus leaders in order to weld them into a company of equals. Similarly, the president of the American Medical Association, which represents physicians' diverse interests, must work toward reconciling their differences and achieving united action.

Unfortunately, many occupations are unable to develop consensus leaders who are genuinely able to bridge differences. Social work, for instance, has been relatively unsuccessful at achieving consensus about its basic tasks and who should perform them. Indeed, Meyerson (1988: 4), after closely studying hospital social workers, wrote that "members, as well as outsiders, hold extremely diffuse ideas about what social work is and is not, and about who is and is not a social worker." And Stephen Fineman (1985:21), in an ethnographic study of social workers, reported "a deep sense of confusion and distrust about the nature and purpose of their work."

This ambiguity delayed adoption of state licensure. Daniel B. Hogan (1979) concluded that the most active opposition to licensure came from within factions of social workers and not from psychologists or psychiatrists. The divisive issue apparently was the appropriate requirements for licensure. One faction argued that a bachelor's degree or less should be the minimum requirement for licensure. Others argued for more extensive academic requirements. This split has made for a relatively weak occupational association. This is ironic because the American Association of Social Workers set up a committee on licensing at the national level as early as 1945, but it has never been able to create consensus because of opposition from local chapters and other national social work bodies. As Hogan notes (1979:47), "This lack of unity made licensing laws almost impossible until the 1960's." Even then there was only a modicum of consensus among social workers about how to define their work because there were apparently few, if any, integrative leaders producing reasonable and collective harmony.

ROLE OF OCCUPATIONS IN SHAPING PERSONAL VALUES

Occupations shape and mold members' individual beliefs so that they often come to internalize the group's ideology. According to Hughes (1958:23), "A man's work, to the extent that it provides him a subculture and an identity, becomes an aspect of his personality." Scott Turow (1977) reported the case of a law student who had difficulties with his wife. He could no longer engage in mundane discussions with her, as he would with other people, since she was "too emotional." He insisted that emotions had no part in thinking like a lawyer.

Cartoonists, using these insights, illustrate occupations in highly stylized forms. Although some may find such vignettes offensive, Wilbert E. Moore (1969:881) defends them

> In social situations outside the workplace, popular occupational stereotypes may have some merit: the fussy accountant, argumentative lawyer, didactic teacher, crude and materialistic businessman, inarticulate mechanic or engineer, television-addicted factory worker, and the tense and brittle advertising man. It would be surprising if work did not leave its mark.

Research generally supports the notion that occupational conditions influence personality rather significantly. M. L. Kohn and C. Schooler (1978:48), drawing on ten years of data, concluded that their findings "come down solidly in support of those who see occupational conditions as affecting personality and in opposition to those who see the relationship between occupational conditions and personality as resulting solely from selective recruitment and job molding."

They further concluded that habituation to work of low complexity limits intellectual flexibility and the capacity for self-direction, while more demanding and challenging occupations have the opposite effect (Kohn and Schooler 1983). One of their consistent findings was that specific features of a given occupation correlated closely with occupational self-direction, a series of feelings characterized by perceiving oneself as competent, effective, and in control of the forces around one. The occupational characteristics associated with these personality features were the presence of substantive complexity and freedom from closeness of supervision and from highly repetitive and routinized processes that restrict possibilities for exercising initiative, thought, and judgment.

In this regard, these features closely resemble the characteristics of a well-formed occupational culture, which has a distinct body of knowledge and considerable control over how it is used, evaluated, and by whom, including use of independent judgment relative to the possession and performance of specific tasks. Apparently, occupational cultures tend rather uniformly to generate an ideology of independence from managerial control in the uses of the knowledge members have mastered to perform the specific, rather complex tasks of the occupation. Moreover, the presence of these three features of an occupational role—complexity, freedom from supervision, and freedom from routine—is also "significantly related to all facets of psychological functioning, a condition that suggests that occupational culture is receptive on an individual level to belief systems other than occupational self-direction" (Kohn and Schooler 1978:48).

In a sample of twelve hundred female and male workers, Yitzhak Samuel and Noah Lewin-Epstein (1979) found (1) that those whose work functions were mainly integrative (e.g., education, welfare) held collective values; (2) those workers who performed adaptive functions (e.g., manufacturing, maintenance) held individualistic values; (3) those workers who performed primarily economic functions (e.g., building, transportation) held materialistic values; and (4) those workers who performed cultural functions (e.g., science, art) and those who performed integrative functions (e.g. education) held collective and humanistic values. These findings imply a consistent correspondence between abstract value systems and the central tasks performed in a work role such as a specific occupation.

Research also shows that values appear to change across the life course so that they become more consistent with those required in one's work. College students, anticipating their future employment, change their work values so that they are compatible with their future occupational aspirations. Consequently, "even as a student, . . . the individual is learning to think of himself as a doctor or lawyer or teacher, and is rehearsing, either in his mind or overtly, the behavior appropriate to that status" (Rosenberg 1957:125). J. R. Hinrichs (1972) found that eight years after attaining their Ph.D.s, chemists who entered academic and industrial employment differed significantly from each other in their values. In particular, academic chemists were often more inclined to want to perform independent research and rejected organizational controls on their work more than did their industrial colleagues, who had come to accept collaborative research and controls as a "normal" part of their employment.

Occupations also have pronounced effects on political beliefs. In comparing professional workers, nonprofessionals, and business executives, Steven Brint (1984, 1985) found that professionals were conservative on most economic issues and on their commitment to core American values; like business executives, they were comparatively liberal on civil rights and civil liberties issues; and like nonprofessionals, they were comparatively liberal on welfare, state, and military issues. Unlike nonprofessionals and business executives, however, they were liberal on issues of personal morality and military force. In addition, he found that members of specialties that had close associations with businesses and business practices—those that encourage aggressive, command-oriented activities—were more conservative than those without business contacts and practices. Consequently, corporate, tax, and patent attorneys were more conservative than labor, criminal, and civil rights lawyers (Heinz and Laumann 1982). And line managers were more conservative than personnel in consultative staff jobs.

OCCUPATIONS AS IDEOLOGICAL MODELS FOR ORGANIZATIONS

If occupations shape members' personal values, it is also possible that occupational cultures provide metaphors for work organizations themselves. Managers frequently promote a particular image of an occupation as a guide for behavior in an entire organization. When they do this they are speaking metaphorically, using the occupational culture as a tool for clarifying the ideological stance members of the or-

ganization are expected to take. Thus, accountants and accounting
metaphors often become "a form of moral and technical reckoning"
in large corporations (Gowler and Legge 1983:210; Burchell et al.
1980). Meeting profit commitments is expressed as "hitting" or
"missing your numbers" and becomes a prevalent, potent, and quan-
tifiable index of success for many ranks of managers (Jackall 1988:62).
According to Pondy (1983:174), the quantification of accounting creates a rational context within which other processes of the organization are acted out.

When incorporated into the typical bureaucracy, accounting simpli-
fies answers to complex problems by reducing them to countable monetary terms. As a result, organization personnel are frequently required
to use cost-benefit analysis to interpret the past, forecast the future, and
determine corporate strategies (Chambers 1980). The language of accounting permeates whole organizations as managers and employees
speak of the "bottom line," "standards," "writing off" people, someone
as "a liability," and the need to focus on output. The accounting image,
then, conveys the proper attitude for managers to emulate; but in
adopting the language of accounting, managers do not become accountants, and, in some instances, they may even come to dislike them
(Dalton 1959).

The cowboy as a metaphor for organizational behavior draws on the
ideology of rugged individualism found among ranchers and rodeo
cowboys. Kanter (1989:70) coined the phrase "cowboy management,"
meaning that some companies hold strong beliefs about unbridled individualism and competition. In such organizations, the cowboy is a
metaphor for the frontier entrepreneur and is often invoked as a model
for behavior:

> What a cowboy manager likes best is being alone out there in the
> wilderness with a few trusty pals, no restraints (like government
> regulations, family obligations, or corporate reporting), and a few
> foreign savages to fight. Cooperation, in turn, is seen as "soft," as
> something for "sissies." . . . "Tough" management styles are reg-
> ularly glamorized in the press, as in *Fortune* magazine's listing of
> the "ten toughest bosses in America."

Moreover, as Kanter (1989) also observes, competition can be likened
to a rodeo, especially when a company is "restructuring." Under these
conditions internal groups are put into direct competition, and their

fate depends on their performance in this "rodeo." Thus, a company with an already successful product line adds a competing line internally and lets the two compete for higher ratings with the distinct possibility that one will be dropped entirely.

Another prominent organizational metaphor comes from the professional athlete. Indeed, classic ethnographic studies suggest that in many cultures games metaphorically illustrate how life ought to be lived (Simmel 1971; Eitzen 1981). Among the Tangu people of New Guinea, for instance, teams play to a draw rather than a victory, expressing a basic value in the Tangu culture: "the concept of moral equivalence, which is reflected in the precise sharing of foodstuffs among the people" (Leonard 1973:45; Eitzen 1981).

In Bali, cockfighting is a metaphor for life's conflicts: "As much of America surfaces in a ballpark, on a golf link, at a race track, or around a poker table, much of Bali surfaces in a cock ring. For it is only apparently cocks that are fighting there. Actually it is men" (Geertz 1973: 417). Geertz comments that the Balinese cockfight is an indicator of what being Balinese "is really like," as useful in understanding the culture as more studied features, such as law, art, and patterns of child rearing. And while competitive dart throwing in Polynesia took on "considerable importance in general economic and religious life" (Firth 1930:95), among the Timbira of Brazil ritualistic competition between teams of log racers was brisk and vigorous but winning or losing was unimportant (Luschen 1967:130).

Prominent sociologists, such as Goffman, have also embraced the game analogy (1961b). His microscopic examination of social relations often assumes the game metaphor. Likewise, George Simmel (1971) set forth a series of propositions that the dynamics of society are closely associated with its forms of games and play.

In America, winning, or success, is of even more importance than trying mightily to win. Here poker, as Geertz has pointed out, is a revealing ritual in that the winner takes all; sharing the spoils is unheard of. As Robert Jackall says (1988:3), "Hard work, it is frequently asserted, builds character, [but] business people, and our society as a whole, have little patience with those who, even though they work hard, make a habit of finishing out of the money."

In American corporate life, football and baseball serve to carry the message of winning at all costs: "The American brand of football is *un*exportable. . . . No one else can imagine what the natives see in it. . . . When we consider football, we are focusing on one of the few things we share with no one outside of our borders, but do share with everyone within it" (Arens 1976:6).

According to Susan P. Montague and Robert Morais (1976:39):

> The football team looks very much like a small scale model of the American corporation: compartmentalized, highly sophisticated in the coordinated application of a differentiated, specialized technology, turning out a winning product in a competitive market. . . . As a small scale enactment of the commercial structure and process, [it] renders visible and directly comprehensible a system that is far too large and complex to be directly comprehended by an individual.

The specific metaphorical meaning of football players for work organizations is expressed through what Jackall (1988:49) terms "football phrases." During his field work with large corporations he compiled the following list of these phrases:

Football phrases	*Metaphorical meaning for managers*
Players	Anyone who has a stake in and is therefore involved in a decision
Carrying the ball	Responsible for an assignment
Taking the ball and running with it	Showing initiative and drive
Fumbling the ball	Messing up in an assignment
Passing the ball	Getting rid of a responsibility
Punt	Employ a defensive strategy while waiting for things to sort out
Sidelined	Taken out of the game; benched
Running the clock down	Wear out an opponent by stalling
Huddle	Quick meeting
Reverse or reversing fields	Changing one's story or public rationale for an action
Going over the top	Achieving one's commitments
Running interference or blocking	Using personal influence to knock down opposition to a client's plans
Broken field run	Virtuoso, individual performance
Getting blindsided	Being unexpectedly undercut by another in public
Quarterback	Boss

Both football and baseball players illuminate the obsession with winning by emphasizing team play. Firefighters, for instance, are like baseball players in that their success requires that individuals subordinate themselves to the larger unit. At the same time, individual achievement is much applauded when the team wins (McCarl 1984). These attitudes are conveyed to employees in sports jargon that permeates companies. Thus, corporate strategy becomes the "game plan"; companies present their "most valuable player award" (Rosen 1985); executives complain about the quality of "blocking" and "tackling" and vow to recruit "star players" (Nussbaum and Beam 1986); and top athletes deliver inspirational messages "at sales meetings, award dinners, conventions, store front openings, or whenever else the color and excitement of sports can help you shine" (Keidel 1984:5).

Even academics studying leadership and organizational effectiveness have used the sports metaphor. Many (Eitzen and Yetman 1972; Pfeffer and Davis-Blake 1986; Allen, Panian, and Lotz 1979) assume that team sports approximate organizational life and that therefore their findings on sports are generalizable.

Although there are similarities in the metaphors from professional baseball and football for thinking and acting in a work organization, there are also differences. Compared with football, baseball is "highly individualistic—elaborate teamwork is not required except for double plays and defensive sacrifice bunts. Each player struggles to succeed on his own" (Eitzen 1981:62). Failure is largely an individual's responsibility. Baseball calls for "only occasional or situational teamwork" (Keidel 1985:5).

Football, by contrast, is team controlled and brutally competitive. Individual players subordinate their personalities to the team's collective strategy and to the commands of its head coach and his staff. Losing any game is a bitter disappointment, since, by comparison with the baseball season, the football season is very short. Each game is thus marked by extreme intensity and competitive aggression.

The antipopulist theme of football also sets it apart from baseball. Football players come from colleges and universities and must be physically big men. In contrast, baseball players have never been identified with higher education, and it can be played by men of all sizes. Moreover, baseball players, regardless of the position they play, have a roughly equal chance of becoming stars. Adding to this egalitarianism, all baseball players must play both offense and defense. Stardom in football is largely accorded to players in certain positions—backs, passers and receivers, and runners, who also generally get higher salaries (Eitzen 1981).

Because of these sharp differences, the management of each sport is significantly different. In baseball, it is "the management of individuals—of independence" (Keidel 1985:23). In football, it is "comprehensive planning, coordination, and execution. . . . Success in football turns on organizational planning" (39) and the specialized division of labor that grows from it. Both planning and execution are under hierarchical direction, which, as in a classic bureaucracy, is coordinated in a "top-down" fashion.

Regardless of the approach one takes to the use of athletics as a metaphor for organizational life, the analogy seems to be an appropriate one. Robert W. Keidel (1985) uses not only football and baseball but also basketball as metaphors. He goes so far as to speak of "basketball organizations" (55), "baseball organizations" (26), and "football-like companies (9). His detailed comparisons may make one question the credibility of these metaphors, but they nevertheless affect and influence many persons in organizational life. Furthermore, they have been recognized as potent influences on the larger culture in which work organizations are embedded.

SUMMARY

Ideologies are the substance of a culture. They are clusters of beliefs, often inconsistent with one another, that explain and justify ongoing behavior for members of a collectivity: when applied frequently, they become taken for granted, that is, "common sense." Despite their ambiguities and contradictions, they become guides for the assignment of moral meanings to concrete actions. They become emotionalized and thus constitute the "oughts" and the "ought nots" of work behavior.

Although occupations typically have their own unique ideologies, many occupations in America have one of two overarching ideologies. One of these ideologies is professionalism; the other is unionism. Both embrace the occupational principle, but each has a highly divergent way for putting it into practice.

Unionism strongly encourages collective action, including strikes, against employers as the way to ensure that the occupational principle prevails. Those who embrace professionalism believe that members of an occupation should master a unique body of knowledge and apply it in the name of public service and responsibility. As a result, members of these occupations insist on norms of authority over clients and autonomy of actions, thereby carrying out the occupational principle. With these credentials in hand, members of an occupation should, according to the ideology of professionalism, press for licensure from the state, which is a way of barring all those without licenses from performing the tasks the occupation claims for itself.

Journalism and nursing provide concrete and imperfect instances of the evolution of both overarching and unique occupational ideologies. In both occupations the three phases of ideological development can be identified, within the historically different contexts in which each emerged.

Although they are essential features of cultures, including those of occupations, ideologies can also be dysfunctional. Often this negative side is overlooked and the functional aspects unduly emphasized. Two theories about their functions and dysfunctions—the strain and interest explanations—are in many ways compatible with each other, although the strain theory is more comprehensive.

Cultural leaders can be purveyors of ideologies within occupations. This was especially true of such leaders as Florence Nightingale, Edward R. Murrow, and Vince Lombardi. Finally, occupational ideologies can influence both the personal values of members, on the one hand, and act as metaphors for parts or all of large corporations, on the other.

4. CULTURAL FORMS
IN OCCUPATIONS

And what have kings, that privates have not too,
Save ceremony, save general ceremony?
And what are thou, thou idol Ceremony?
　　—William Shakespeare, *King Henry the Fifth*

AS I DISCUSSED IN chapter 3, occupational cultures are composed of ideologies and the cultural forms that express them. Rites and ceremonies, for example, express ideologies by dramatizing ideological meaning, thus acting as "sense making practices" (Gephart 1978:553); elsewhere they have been described as "secular rituals" (Warner and Low 1947:41). This chapter reviews an array of cultural forms, including occupationally unique symbols, myths, sagas, and legends; languages and gestures, physical artifacts, and settings; and rituals, taboos, rites, and ceremonies.

The meanings attached to some cultural forms are quite consistent with one another, while others may be ambiguous and "fuzzy." Nevertheless, all cultural forms symbolically convey ideological meanings that are learned by members of the occupation (Douglas 1975). Cultural forms are "the symbolic action through which ideology is brought to life" (Kunda 1991:91).

Myths, for instance, are imaginative, taken-for-granted explanations for techniques and behaviors that are not supported by demonstratable facts. Often expressed in narratives, myths recount concrete but unconfirmed events through the use of images that direct members of occupations as to how they should organize their everyday lives. A saga is a well-formed narrative myth that describes the alleged unique accomplishments of a group and its leader—who is often charismatic—using heroic terms. Occupational stories are based on true events but are a combination of truth and much fiction. Rather than telling about momentous events, as sagas do, stories are about the everyday lives of relatively normal people; they are often told for humor and sociability.

Although these forms involve language in their narrations, language is itself a cultural form in which members use vocal sounds and written signs to convey meaning.

Gestures, artifacts, and physical settings also express meaning. In contrast, rituals are standardized, detailed sets of behaviors that both manage anxieties and express meanings but seldom produce intended technical consequences of practical importance. Rites and ceremonies are elaborate and dramatic planned activities in which several cultural forms are consolidated into one public event.

MYTHS AND FICTIONS

Guiding myths and fictions are characteristic of occupational cultures. As expressions of an occupation's ideology, myths provide unconfirmed images about how to conduct one's work life. These images are, to a considerable degree, shared and unquestioned by members of the occupation. Myths differ from ideologies in that they are tangible accounts and images rather than abstract ideas about behavior. Frequently, they deal with the origin of the culture; that is, they are ancestral and underwrite the essence of the culture in narrative terms. Although unconfirmed, myths permit the occupation to organize its members and get on collectively with its work; consequently, they are often referred to as organizing or rationalized (Meyer and Rowan 1977; Boland 1982).

Even though they cannot be empirically demonstrated, myths are widely accepted within an occupation. Academic researchers, for example, especially those who do behavioral science research about the workplace, embrace a myth of utilization in which their research findings are actually applied by managers and businesspeople (Beyer and Trice 1982). In addition, academics in general share a myth that teaching and research are compatible endeavors in their ongoing daily work lives. Often, myths are widely accepted outside the occupation as well; this is particularly true when an occupation has won a mandate or license that gives its members the exclusive right to their work.

Rationalized myths elaborate rules and procedures, adding to the accumulation of what an occupation or organization considers "proper, adequate, rational and necessary" to incorporate into its structure in order "to avoid illegitimacy" (Meyer and Rowan 1977:345; Trice, Belasco, and Alutto 1969). Rather than being pejorative, myths are reference points around which humans organize their lives. In a world of hazard, uncertainty, and endemic change, they provide validation and confirmation, enabling people to act even though there is scant opportunity to investigate, calculate, and decide rationally what is "best" under the circumstances. Indeed, for Joseph Campbell (1949:3), "throughout the inhabited world, in all times and under every circumstance, the myths of man have flourished; and they have been the living inspiration of whatever else may have appeared out of the activities of the human body and mind."

Myths permeate occupations as diverse as accounting, personnel management, computer programming, carpentry, bricklaying, and rodeo work. Before World War II, old-line carpenters and bricklayers expressed their ideology of craft control in the myth of the boy apprentice (Myers 1952:302). This myth was of a boy "growing up in the trade," dedicated to a course of action "involving patience, abstinence, and the arduous acquisition of high skill." From such imagery grew a sequence of apprenticeship training characterized by the development of stamina, foresight, rigor, and dedication to a vocation. Flowing from this myth came sharp restrictions on the number of apprentices who could enter training.

The extent of fiction in the myth of the boy apprentice was partly revealed in a 1941 study of building tradesmen in the Great Lakes area (Myers 1952). Forty percent of the sample had entered their trade at twenty-five years of age or older, and 42 percent indicated that they had no formal, regulated apprentice training; rather, they had come in as "back door mechanics." Unlike the myth of principles in accounting, for example, the myth of the boy apprentice has been susceptible to change and is less potent today than it was in the years before 1940.

Among bricklayers, there are myths and stories involving tremendous output and individual performance. Delbert C. Miller and William H. Form (1980:397) describe one they collected in the form of a folk tale told by a young bricklayer:

> "You know I'm not much good in the afternoons. None of us are, I guess. We're not as tough as the old folks. I can remember as a kid when old John Kiddy was building a house next door to us. One Saturday morning him and his old lady decided to lay the north wall of the house. The old lady mixed the mud and John laid the bricks. You should of seen the old man work; he was seventy years old then. He was a demon; not a useless move, just laying row after row without a minute's rest. The old lady kept right up

with him. By two o'clock they had her done. After cleaning up they went to a square dance. Yes sir, John Kiddy worked with my father's gang until he was eighty-five. Guess we ain't like the old folks. Just too soft."

In another occupational myth, health workers visiting England used "atrocity stories" to establish that they were distinctive from and just as good, if not better, than social workers (Dingwall 1977). The following describes another prominent occupational myth:

of the "real" lawyer as the fellow who hangs out a shingle and settles down to handle the business and civic affairs of small-town America. No matter that town and that lawyer hardly exist any-more, and perhaps never did exist as they are portrayed in the bucolic fantasies of Norman Rockwell and Walt Disney. The image remains. It is in this small-town, small-office work that professional values can best be realized. . . . The reality, of course, is somewhat different. The law addresses itself less to general problems of justice or conflict resolution than it does to the problems of acquiring, maintaining, and transferring property (Spangler and Lehman 1982:94).

Unconfirmed, taken-for-granted myths support the ideology of professionalism. Indeed, the professional enterprise is possible only if members of an occupation and their clients believe that such people possess the special traits of professionals. To a great extent, however, the assertions made by "professionals" are mythical because most occupations simply do not approach the idealized standards of professionalism. Members of occupations that perform personnel testing and employment interviewing, for instance, embrace myths of science, on which they rest claims of predictability and professionalism (Trice, Belasco, and Alutto 1969; Arvey and Campion 1982), and for social workers, "the myth of professionalism cannot withstand a rigorous examination of the actual working conditions of most social workers" (Cohen and Wagner 1982:141).

Only a few occupations, such as medicine, engineering, and the physical sciences, begin to approximate the professional ideal. In the majority of cases, however, the knowledge base is either too general and vague or too narrow and specific for the occupation to achieve the exclusive jurisdiction and autonomy of a profession (Wilensky 1964a). In some instances the tested knowledge base may be thin or nonexistent, and the prospects for increasing it significantly may be low as well. In others, considerable progress in generating a body of generalizable knowledge may have taken place but much controversy and additional research remain to be done before generalizable confidence in the body of knowledge is justified. A good example is the mythical use of testing and selection procedures by personnel workers in the 1960s to justify their professionalism. According to Harrison M. Trice, James Belasco, and Joseph A. Alutto (1969), the personnel occupations claim to have a tested body of knowledge. Upon closer scrutiny, however, the apparent scientific rigor and legitimacy of their selection procedures is exaggerated. Despite these shortcomings, personnel workers attribute to themselves the features of professional behavior.

A belief in the mythical traits of professionalism presses an occupation to organize itself in accordance with the idealized structure of the professions so that it can convince its clients and the state that it actually possesses those valued traits. This is necessary if the occupation is to win a mandate giving it control over the specialized tasks and duties under the occupation's jurisdiction. Consequently, the occupation establishes a professional association to spread the word that it is indeed "professional" and can be trusted to pursue the public good. In addition, it establishes relationships with universities and colleges to symbolize that it possesses a rational, codified, and tested body of knowledge, and it creates certification exams to demonstrate that members have mastered its body of knowledge. Finally, it writes a code of ethics to convey its lack of self-interest and overwhelming commitment to its clients and the public good. These rationalized myths enable the occupation to get on with managing the perplexing and complicated environment that increasingly characterizes its work. At the same time, these myths allay clients' and the state's fears of exploitation.

Observing that the "so-called traits" of a profession provide a strategy for "occupational communities currently attempting to convince relevant audiences that its members should be accorded professional status," Van Maanen and Barley (1984:319) suggest that "new traits are being added to the old list." They note, for example, that burnout is becoming a mark of occupational status among human service occupations such as nursing, social work, counseling, and clinical psychology (320). Persons in these occupations visualize themselves as being dedicated and hard working to the point of being so exhausted that they are no longer able to perform. They argue that the notion of job stress is a perfect vehicle for conveying the symbolic virtues of an occupation not yet recognized as professional.

Studies show that nearly ten times the number of articles dealing with job stress appear in police and nursing periodicals than in comparable periodicals of law and medicine. Yet empirical evidence to support the claims of greater stress in the occupations of policing and nursing than in law and medicine is sparse (Terry 1981; see also Barley and Knight 1988). Nonetheless, "stress stands as an indicator of a larger family of occupational claims (e.g., service goals, responsibility for other people's problems, personal sacrifice, bureaucratic interference or indifference) residing under the sacred canopy of 'being called to a set of higher ideals' " (Van Maanen and Barley 1984:321).

The ideology of rational objectivity in accounting is expressed in its myth of generally accepted principles. According to Richard J. Boland (1982:118), accountants won the sole right to perform audits because of a belief in the expertise of accounting:

> The profession implied that this expertise encompassed a body of generally accepted standards, principles, and practices, and that audit judgments would be based on good reason. These were deceptive myths, for the profession had yet to create a codified body of knowledge or to define appropriate practice. . . . These myths gave rise to a technology of standard setting by three quasi-legislative boards. Apparently, the profession hopes that by mimicking legal procedures a body of accounting principles will emerge that is analogous to common law. . . . The characterization of accounting as technology gives opportunity for the myth of principles. The myth of principles, in turn, affords a basis for belief in a technology of standard settings.

Myths of accounting have been remarkably resistant to objective analysis. R. J. Chambers (1980:176) notes that "if a rule or practice can be said to conform with generally accepted principles, *ipso facto* it commands allegiance . . . and those who raise doubts about the existence of any such thing as a corpus of generally accepted principles are treated—politely, by ignoring them—as heretics." Leslie Wayne (1989: 12) summarized the general principles of auditing as consisting of "only 10 general standards expressed in less than 350 words: among them that the auditor must be proficient, independent and use profes-

sional care, that accurate records be kept and sufficient evidence collected to form an opinion."

In practice however, accountants are often influenced by the interests
of the large corporations that employ them (Chatov 1975). Wayne
(1982:F15) concludes that with the computerization of corporate accounts "the individual accountant is freed to become more involved in
the management of the client's finances, in designing internal financial
systems and in consulting on troubling financial problems." Critics
have referred to such professional latitude as "creative accounting,"
and Abraham J. Briloff (1972) describes their highly proclaimed independence as "unaccountable accounting." Indeed, Boland's (1982:122)
view is as follows:

> Today, accounting firms subject themselves to conflicts of interests
> by providing management-advisory and tax-advisory services for
> the same clients they audit. They propose methods for structuring
> and recording transactions that minimize taxes, and later they cer-
> tify that the recorded data provide sound bases for economic and
> investment decisions. They design and install computer systems to
> provide internal control, and later they judge these systems' ade-
> quacies for internal control during an audit.

One observer offered the suggestion that in hindsight

> it would be judged madness to invent a system where the one to
> be audited hired the auditor, bargained with the auditor as to the
> size of the fee, was permitted to purchase other management serv-
> ices from the auditor, and where the auditor in turn had the social
> responsibility for setting the rules and for enforcing them and ap-
> plying sanctions against themselves (Klott 1985:D22).

During the recent crisis in the savings and loan banking industry,
accountants failed "to detect the shenanigans that triggered one of the
biggest financial calamities this country has ever seen" (Wayne 1989:
1). Moreover, according to Wayne (1989:12), the "savings crisis is so
widespread that accounting firms of every shape and size are potential
defendants. . . . Again and again, accountants were called on to make
hundreds of judgement calls in an industry that was engaging in some
of the riskiest financial ventures around." Nevertheless, accounting
firms competed vigorously for these accounts and realized handsome
profits.

In one notorious case—Sunbelt Savings of Dallas, Texas—the management team responsible had already resigned by the time the auditors detected the gross misuse of depositors' money for real estate speculation. In essence, there are often "myriad political factors which have intruded in the setting (and subsequent criticism) of standards, factors the impact of which is not registered in the accounting model which has traditionally provided the dominant frame of reference for discussing accounting practices and the reasons for adopting them" (Burchell, Clubb, and Hopwood 1985:408).

Despite these disclosures, spokespeople for the accounting profession insisted that the dramatic failures of auditors in the savings and loan business was unrepresentative of the work of accountants and that they should not be blamed for what went on since they tried to avoid the cover-ups with accounting methods and techniques. Such a response might easily have been predicted from evidence that accumulated in the early 1980s. A summary of the growth and influence of the accounting profession during that period suggests that accountants were well entrenched in America's businesses.

> The accounting business is bursting not only in the Park Avenue towers where the leading firms are based, but also in the offices of certified public accountants throughout the land. Greater demands ... for more precise information of all types, particularly more accurate financial information, have made the accountant a much sought after individual (Wayne 1982:1).

Dalton's (1959) ethnographic description of internal audits in a chemical plant illustrates the mythical nature of cost accounting and how easily it can be turned to political purposes. When the central office did audits, they were supposed to be on a surprise basis. Warnings of their imminence, however, were secretly given to those on the list, which

> provoked a flurry among the executives to hide certain parts and equipment. . . . Materials *not* to be counted were moved to: (1) little known and inaccessible spots; (2) basements and pits that were dirty and therefore unlikely to be examined; (3) departments that had already been inspected and that could be approached circuitously while the counters were enroute between official storage areas, and (4) places where materials and supplies might be used as a camouflage for parts. . . . As the practice developed, cooperation among the [department] chiefs to use each other's storage ar-

eas and available pits became well organized and smoothly
functioning (Dalton 1959:48–49).

Similarly, Robert J. Swieringa and Karl E. Weick (1981) describe a company that had tight controls over maintenance tasks but no controls
over construction projects. As a result, foremen encouraged workers to
boost the time reported on the construction project and to underesti-
mate the time on maintenance tasks in order to make the foremen look
good.

   Abuses of accounting systems notwithstanding, accountants, like
priests and magicians in an earlier age, play an important guardian
role in modern society (Cleverley 1973; Gambling 1977). Like priests,
they possess an arcane knowledge that rests on a simple base, restrict
membership to those who complete elaborate and lengthy initiation
rites, seldom defrock initiates, and generally act to protect the moral
order. By symbolically mediating between stockholders and managers,
who depend on their reassuring presence and blessings, accountants
assure the citizenry via their myths that their models of reality are
"truth."

   An influential and long-standing occupational myth is that of the
lone American cowboy who fights against great odds for justice and
freedom. During the fifteen years between 1870 and 1885 the cowboy's image "in the public mind was that of hired men on horseback who led monotonous lives of unenviable drudgery and had no
romantic connotations," and the cowboy at this point was "far from
being considered a hero" (Lawrence 1982:46). The mythical image
of the cowboy as hero was promoted by theatrical spectacles and
by novelists, especially of the dime-store variety, who capitalized on
Buffalo Bill's Wild West shows of the 1890s. These shows featured
salaried performers who demonstrated horsemanship skills and enacted such bits of drama as a Pony Express ride, a buffalo hunt,
and Custer's last stand. Within the span of a few years at the turn
of the twentieth century,

   the dull routines involved in the occupation of cattle herding had
   been transformed almost overnight into a bold and free, colorful
   and individualistic, way of life that would become the dream and
   envy of virtually every time-bound and machine-oriented worker
   who felt imprisoned by the newly industrialized American society
   (Lawrence 1982:46).

Coincidentally, Owen Wister's *The Virginian*, a novel that cast the cowboy in a heroic mold, appeared to enormous popular acclaim in 1902.

The characteristics of the mythical cowboy hero are an amalgam of exaggerated, romanticized, and fictionalized traits, personifying "rugged individualism." The cowboy earns his livelihood outside the constraints of conventional society; relies chiefly on himself; enjoys nomadic freedom; and is stoic, uncomplaining, humorous and droll, disdainful of routine, and completely free of the past. He strives to adapt and succeed in his demanding work, regardless of the costs. Women and family life are largely irrelevant; horses are a priority. Although he is distinctly a member of a team—there is camaraderie around the campfire, and he is loyal to his "outfit"—he nevertheless is a loner, learns the hard way, and calls no man his master (although he reveres the trail boss and will go "through hell" for him). The "cowboy code" is one of hospitality, cheerfulness, enormous personal courage, and pride in one's work.

Unconcerned with lifetime employment or security, a cowboy follows his star and finds a job wherever that leads. His self-worth comes from doing his job well. Like Shane, the cowboy hero rides off into the sunset having successfully defended the basic value of American culture. Similarly, Will Kane, the hero of *High Noon*, having singlehandedly defended the community from a gang of killers, throws his sheriff's badge into the dust of Main Street and rides off with his bride into the desert.

The rodeo was the first organized cultural form in which the hero myth was refined, followed quickly by the movies. Recently, cowboy "art" has become popular. Demand is soaring, and a painting by an outstanding artist sells, on average, for $30,000 to $50,000. The motif of this art is "middle class values of striving and prospering, optimism and rugged individualism" (Gilder 1982:35).

The uniqueness of the cowboy as an American symbol is evident when one contrasts American and Canadian culture. Canada had relatively little "Wild West" culture even in those provinces that were adjacent to the American West. Rather, the Royal Canadian Mounted Police was a widespread symbol of crown and provincial authority. In sharp contrast to the cowboy, they stood for law, civilized conduct, and respect for authority.

From the cowboy myth emerged the occupation of rodeo cowboy.

Like the boxer (Weinberg and Arond 1952), the rodeo cowboy is indifferent to pain and continues a performance despite it, and this pain becomes the basis of an ideology of stoicism and individual autonomy. The cowboy has become "that most mythic individual hero. . . . His significance lies in his unique individual virtue and special skill. . . . It is as if the myth says you can be a truly good person, worthy of admiration and love, only if you resist fully joining the group" (Bellah et al. 1985:145). This myth forms the underpinnings of the red-meat industry and is seriously hurting its competitiveness.

What ranchers fear most is loss of their autonomy (Lawrence 1982). Unfortunately, as the eating patterns and lifestyles of millions of Americans are changing significantly, the ranch and cattle industry is hampered in making market adjustments and adaptations because it clings to its cowboy myths. Rather than emphasizing the importance of collective, disciplined action to meet the competition, its occupational myths convey a deep-seated belief in autonomy and individualism that is fracturing the industry.

Fictions serve the same functions as myths. Unlike myths, however, they are more deliberate artifices constructed by occupations to enhance their status and power and enable everyone to get on with business (Smith 1962; Dubin 1951). Personnel managers, for instance, carefully cultivate the image that they are neutrals in organizational decision making even though they give line managers advice and, although they do not broadcast it, often are independent decision makers (Ritzer and Trice 1969a; Trice and Ritzer 1972; Watson 1978). Similarly, when computers were introduced into a large British firm, programmers insisted on an image of themselves—soon to become widespread—that they were unique, performed esoteric tasks for which they were especially qualified, and had to be free of time constraints to operate effectively (Pettigrew 1973). Skilled maintenance workers in France have kept secret details about repair problems and strategies (Crozier 1964), and industrial relations specialists have protected their unique influence by deliberately keeping union-management agreements either totally secret or as vague as possible (Goldner 1961).

STORIES AND SONGS

Occupational stories and songs dramatize group beliefs and practices by depicting everyday events in emotionally charged terms. Although understood to be the truth about the occupation, these descriptions of events include a liberal mix of historical fact and fiction. Songs, or stories set to music, produce an "interplay between pride-in-skill and social statement" (Green 1978:97). Songs interweave myth, ideology, historical fact, and occupational ethnocentrism.

Both stories and songs are mechanisms whereby members of an occupation develop a sense of kinship with the past, along with a sense of sharing current experiences, that produce inferences, or instructions, about how members should feel and behave while performing the occupation's tasks and responsibilities. As one firefighter explained, "'You learn a lot by listening to the stories that the guys tell you in the firehouse; the more you hear about things, the more that stuff flashes in your mind when you have similar experiences on the fire ground'" (McCarl 1980: 81–82). Accountants, consistent with their basic ideology of rational, quantitative, and accurate calculations, tell the story of David B. Chase, an accountant who pursued a tiny Internal Revenue Service overcharge (75 cents) through years of appeal and finally won (Montagna 1974).

Many occupational stories and songs describe dangerous working conditions and emphasize workers' sense of superiority over other workers because of their courage and expertise in managing risks. Coal mining, for example, is replete with songs depicting its dangers, and they are sung for instruction and amusement in the mines, miners' homes, and barrooms (Reuss 1983; Dorson 1973). "The Mines of Avondale," for instance, describes a fire that started in a Pennsylvania mine shaft in midmorning on a September day in 1869 and swept rapidly throughout the chambers of the mine, blocking all exits. One hundred eleven miners and boy helpers perished.

"Only a Miner," called by folklorists the "American miner's national anthem" (Green 1972:64), tells a similar tale. Sung from California to Virginia in coal, gold, silver, copper, and lead mining areas, it describes the constant threat to life and limb faced by miners and the casual way others treat the miners' injuries and deaths: "The hard-working miners, their dangers are great, many while mining have met their sad fate" (66). These first two lines sound the note of extreme danger and relentless exploitation by outsiders. On the basis of the history of this song and other evidence, Archie Green (1972:76) concludes that "no industry in the United States produced more disaster songs than coal mining" and that "Only a Miner" describes how miners cope with the harsh reality of accidental death.

In sharp contrast, the auctioneer has devised an "auction chant" that is "the theme song of the performance" (Smith 1989:117). Instead of dramatizing danger, its

> major function is rather to orchestrate the auction rhythm. The chant controls the temporal order of an auction, the movement of the bids. . . . Auctions are ripe with uncertainty and ambiguity. The chant introduces form where it is sorely lacking. It is a basic structure around which other meanings, namely price and allocation, can be built. . . . It manages to take what is a very erratic, disjointed process and meld it into an ongoing, comparatively harmonious process. Like any music, it provides a unifying rhythm or theme (Smith 1989:117).

Some occupational stories include grim admonitions to take safety precautions. Welders, for instance, tell stories about electrocutions caused by spilled coffee or partial blindness due to cracks in the glass of their helmets (McCarl 1974). Iron workers instruct journeymen and apprentices in the danger of wind by telling the following story:

> I remember I was on this job putting this bridge over the seaway and this stupid son of-a-bitch is up there and he had his hat on backwards, so this wind comes and lifts the peak up and the hat starts flying off his head. So this guy comes and reaches up with both hands and grabs his hat and goes overboard with it. . . . [He] should have known better and let the god damn hat drop. So there he is falling down through the air about 100 feet still holding on to the god damn helmet. . . . I don't know how stupid guys can be (Haas 1977:163).

Similarly, Mormon missionaries tell the following tale, which illustrates the dangers they face at the hands of hostile people and conveys a message of divine protection. Two elders were "tracking" and were invited into a woman's home where she voluntarily fed them. She also requested that they return on a specific date and time because she was looking for the "true church" and wanted to be baptized. When the missionaries returned on the appointed day, she immediately asked to be baptized without further talk. When asked what accounted for her instant conversion, she told them that on their first visit she had fed them poisonous food and yet they were unharmed, proving that they were true servants of the Lord (Wilson 1981).

Other stories illustrate how members of an occupation ought to feel about and act toward management. Jack Santino (1978) points out that the hero in many occupational narratives is a trickster who outwits authority figures. He recounts how a railroad engineer got even with his office managers, who had developed specific cleanup requirements for his engine. The engineer perceived these requirements to be an intrusion into his area of expertise and ordered that steam pressure be gotten up. He then backed his engine near the office and sent water spilling all over the office floor. In doing so, he was enunciating the guideline that management should be forced to clean up its own act (Santino 1978).

In the same vein, workers in shipyard occupations told an enduring and time-tested story that was subsequently adapted and retold by automobile workers, railroad mechanics, and soldiers (Green 1965:57). It told how a tough, hard-boiled foreman chewed out a worker who appeared to be loafing on the job. The man was sitting down near the launching ways on a keg of nails, a violation of the most basic rule at work: never sit down. His elbows moved around in a peculiar fashion as the boss descended upon him and kicked the keg from underneath him. Upon recovery, goes the story, the worker knocked the boss down, exclaiming, "Listen, you S.O.B., I don't work for Bethlehem, I'm a cable splicer for Pacific Tel. and Tel." Apparently the appeal of this story did not subside with retelling; quite the opposite; it grew in its appeal among diverse occupational groups.

Other stories, however, convey the message that when push comes to shove, the boss is undoubtedly the boss. For instance, on one railroad it was quite common to get fired. At the least infraction, the foreman would send workers to see the general foreman, who never got to work before 9:00 A.M. One trainman, who came in at 7:00, discovered that the general foreman's office was air-conditioned and had comfortable chairs. Consequently, he would engage in some minor infraction just after reporting to work in order to enjoy a respite of an hour or more in that office. After a number of such episodes, the general foreman told the trainman, "Look, if you don't stop getting fired, and wasting all this time in my office, I am really going to fire you." The trainman later said, "That put an end to that, but I did have a good time while I was doing it" (Byington 1978:210).

Still other occupational stories set forth guidelines about how to interact with customers and clients. An old airline story illustrates that the customer is always right. The stewardess asks if the passenger and

his wife would like something to drink. He says, "I'd like a martini."
But when the stewardess asks the wife, she does not say anything. Then
the husband says, "I'm sorry, she's not used to talking to the help"
(Terkel 1972:78).

Another story, told often among jazz musicians, also illustrates that
customers are supposed to get what they expect. A player had a rep-
utation for behaving outrageously toward audiences, but during an
engagement at New York's Village Gate he was unusually quiet and
well behaved. The co-owner, so went the story, called the musician's
agent and demanded some action: "Mingus has been here for a week
and so far no trouble, no telling the customers off. Talk to him and tell
him to get moving, will you? It's bad for business."

Another legendary airline story reflects flight attendants' anger over
abusive passengers who expect them to smile all the time. When asked
by a businessman why she was not smiling, a flight attendant put his
tray on the food cart, looked the passenger in the eye, and said, "I'll
tell you what. You smile first, then I'll smile." When the businessman
smiled at her, she replied, "Good, now freeze, and hold that for fifteen
hours," and walked away (Hochschild 1983:27).

Other stories underscore the relationships that are expected among
the members of an occupation—particularly the expectation that they
will support and protect one another. Robert S. McCarl, for instance,
recounts a tale that highlights the taken-for-granted faith firefighters
have that other firefighters will come to their aid in an emergency:

> "I came close to buying the farm on this one. We pulled up and
> the nails were burning in this place; I mean it was well off. We
> went in the front door. . . . Well, I got in this room and got turned
> around and I couldn't find my way out and man it was getting
> some kinda hot in there. So I thought, well this is it. I thought of
> my family and my kids, and I really wondered what the hell I was
> doing there. But I figured I had to try at least once more so I took
> five good sucks of pure oxygen out of the McCaa and somehow
> made it to the top of the stairs where the other animals from the
> squad were coming up to get me" (McCarl 1980:90).

Storytelling, then, is an integral part of occupational life, dramatizing
for newcomers and old-timers alike what constitutes proper and desirable behavior. Stories highlight many aspects of such life, such as members' courage (Gillespie 1984:3), appropriate hair length (Lawrence

1982:94), and the proper way to display one's feelings (McCarl 1980: 89). They produce in members a consciousness of kind that links the past, present, and future.

Stories may also relate events involving the occupation's leaders and heroes. Michael O'Brien (1987:193) recounts a story told by a player about Vince Lombardi, the legendary football coach. Describing a rainy morning just before a crucial game, the storyteller said:

> "We had a longer meeting than usual, figuring we'd never get out to the field to practice, and Lombardi was pretty unhappy, walking around, wringing his hands, looking disgusted with the weather. Finally he cut out pacing and looked up at the heavens and shouted, 'Stop raining! Stop raining!' And there was a huge clap of thunder and flash of lightning, and the rain stopped. . . . I'm a hard-shelled Methodist, but I've been eating fish every Friday since then" (Lombardi was a very devout Catholic who went to Mass practically every day and obeyed church rules about eating meat on Friday).

In the same category is the legend of the batting power of Babe Ruth. The story is that he jested to the opposing team—the Chicago Cubs— that he would hit the next pitch into the center field stands. Actually, he was holding up one and then two fingers as the first and second strikes were called. But he did hit the next pitch into the spot toward which he seemed to be pointing. A story immediately sprang up about his bold and brash gesture, but it consisted mostly of legend.

SYMBOLS

Symbols pervade all aspects of behavior; social life for example, is couched in an endless array of manners, speech, dress, and behaviors while eating and drinking that stand for and signify a relationship among people (Goffman 1967). Prominent examples of occupational symbols are uniforms, titles, and argot. They signal individuals' roles and how others should react. Hairdressers, for instance, in an effort to set themselves apart from barbers, have consistently insisted on the "hairdresser" title as a means of claiming higher status and fees than barbers.

A uniform is an ensemble of clothes that communicates instantly to most viewers the tasks, ideologies, and mandates possessed by the person wearing them. The whiteness of nurses' uniforms stands for their work, performed under very clean and hygienic conditions, whereas the black of the police officer's uniform denotes official authority. Joseph Sassoon expands on this point:

> It is no coincidence that the uniforms of the police and guards of many countries, the robes of judges, and university professors, the habits of priests and nuns, are black. . . . The spirituality of the color white is evidenced in priestly vestments of the highest religious authorities in both Christianity and Judaism. The Pope always wears white, but the garments worn by rabbis on particular solemn occasions are also white (1990:171, 172).

When in uniform, the wearers focus on their occupational selves and duties. Airline flight attendants, for instance, interpret the donning of their uniforms as a signal to activate the "managed heart"; their smiles become "professional smiles," and the uniform transforms them from the real world to the flight world (Hochschild 1983:4).

Occupations depend on members' uniforms to create an identity, especially in their organizations. Consequently, soldiers, athletes, priests, clowns, rodeo cowboys, and members of many other occupations feel they represent their occupations when they are in uniform. Smoke jumpers attach particular significance to their garb: blue jeans, jump boots, fire shirts, jumpsuits, ditty bags, cargo packs, and signal streamers (McCarl 1976); and chaplains may wear their clerical collars even when in military uniform (Zahn 1969). Construction workers distinguish one another by their coveralls (Applebaum 1981): painters and plasterers wear white, carpenters wear blue and white striped coveralls; and plumbers and electricians don dark ones.

On construction sites, apparel also closely approximates the stages of the job and suggests expected behavior (Riemer 1979). Consequently, during excavation and framing, construction workers wear dirty clothes and engage in foul acts such as urinating on the ground and throwing around trash. During the finishing stage, however, they are likely to be neatly dressed and very careful about the appearance of the work site.

A final example of how uniforms can create identity is the garb worn by many domestic servants. They have historically worn a clean cap and apron during the workday—livery—typically as symbols of cleanliness and their lower status than the employer (Katzman 1981:237).

Members of occupations without explicit uniforms often dress in ways that approximate a uniform. Funeral directors, for instance, wear near-black, very conservative clothes (Barley 1983b); businessmen wear conservative suits and ties with color-coordinated shoes and belts (Molloy 1975); enterprising young managers in the 1970s wore attire that made them look the same—button-down collars and Hickey Freemen suits (Jackall 1988). British architects identify one another by their gray suits, colored shirts, bow ties, suede shoes, and brightly colored socks (Salaman 1974). Still others, such as British barristers and college professors, have uniforms that are worn on special occasions.

In some instances, however, a uniform alone does not sufficiently communicate the wearer's occupation and other signals must be used. Women forest rangers in uniform, for instance, are not accorded the same authority by the public as male rangers; however, when the women are on horseback, the public gives them equal respect (Charles 1982).

In some instances, titles or initials are used to denote the nature of an occupation. Clergymen are typically addressed as "Reverend" or "Father"; university teachers are called "Professor," and lawyers are frequently addressed as "Attorney Jones," for example. Medical doctors insist on being called "Doctor" and follow their name with the letters M.D., whereas veterinarians define the boundaries of their occupation with the initials D.V.S. (doctor of veterinary science). Literally hundreds of such initials have appeared in the last two decades, all symbolizing, some more effectively than others, the occupational focus of the user.

LANGUAGE AND ARGOT

Occupational language and argot are even more common than either uniforms or titles, constituting a unique form of language—"a special, almost secret language, that is often unique to a single occupation or work setting" (Graves 1989:56). Among train dispatchers, for example, the degree to which their special "railroad language" structures and controls their behavior is practically complete (Gamst 1990).

Pondy (1978) suggests that well-developed occupations constitute "jargon groups" whose specialized languages set them apart from other occupational groups. Applebaum (1984b:12) illustrates the variety of argots:

> The printers' "dead horse," is the recomposing of type already printed (Jacobs, 1962); the loggers' "whistle punk" gives signals

when a tree is coming down, and "widow makers" are branches
which might unexpectedly break off and hit a logger (Bergren,
1966; Holbrook, 1962). Safecrackers perform a "jam shot" or
"gut shot" designed to open a "can" (safe) which "drinks" the
"grease" (nitroglycerin) set off by a "knocker" (detonator), but
the "can" can also be "peeled," "unbuttoned" or "punched"
(Letkemann, 1973). In the oil fields, a "rabbit" is an obstruction
in a pipe or a device to remove it; a "whale" or "wildcat" is a
producing well; and a "bird dog" is a geologist (Boone, 1949).
In logging a "king snipe" is the boss of a track-laying crew and
a "cat skinner" is a tractor driver (Holbrook, 1962). In railroading, "frog" stands for a cross-over plate or a rerailing implement; a "donkey" is a section man; a "hog" is a locomotive run
by a hoghead or hog jockey; a "rabbit" is a derail iron; and a
"monkey house" a caboose (Cottrell, 1940).

The work vocabularies of manual occupations are often earthy and
are generally drawn from a few major sources. The names of animals
provide a galaxy of special argot: all sorts of dogs stop or hold objects,
while bulls denote strength. Body parts, such as the knuckles, elbows,
nipples, belly, head, and toes, are used in the names given to various
tools. Other argot uses sexual imagery: objects that fit into one another
are called male and female, including clutches, pipefittings and shafts,
and bushings (Meissner 1976:265).

Longshoremen use profanity extensively to manage their work relationships and to cope with their fears of accidents (Pilcher 1972). For
instance, they create new and colorful blasphemous expressions as a
form of psychological release from work tensions and employ sexual
and excretory expletives as forms of affection toward one another.

Highly skilled pipeline construction workers have an argot that com-
bines rural language with common slang. A "bronc" on the line is a
worker who does not yet "know the ropes"; his counterpart is an undo-
mesticated horse. Pipeline workers refer to sewer work as "turd lin-
ing"—a term that "both graphically describes and expresses contempt
for a kind of work that pipeliners sometimes have to do (Graves 1985:31).

Occupational specialists in the navy typically come to have nicknames. Thus, radio operators are known as "sparks," signalmen are
"skivvy wavers," and communications technicians are "spooks."

The argot of white-collar occupations is far less earthy than that of
manual workers. Nevertheless, brokers involved in mergers and ac-

quisitions make liberal use of cowboy imagery, speaking of white hats, black hats, shootouts, tombstone hill, and the code of the West.

White-collar workers have also borrowed imagery from their products and their work. Thus, managers in Western Electric referred to those who knew a great deal about what was going on as "being wired in." And saleswomen in posh department stores during the first four decades of this century devised a shop-floor vocabulary used during their many idle moments interacting with one another:

> A "crepe-hanger" was a saleswoman who ruined a sale by talking a customer out of something she had resolved to buy; a "stoker" was an eager-beaver saleswoman; the "main squeeze" was the supervisor; "spiffs" or "kokum" were premiums; a "looker" or a "rubber neck" was a customer who didn't intend to buy; a call of "oh Henrietta" signaled that a customer was a "her," a hard to please person (Benson 1986:245).

Cattle brokers in the Omaha stockyards communicate their esoteric knowledge of cattle economics to one another through such specialized jargon as "ready for the tank" (poor quality), "wastey" (too-fat hindquarters), and "single-gaited" (a specialist in the market) (Leary 1978). Computer programmers have a specialized argot that sets them apart from other occupations (Pettigrew 1973; Schein 1985), even though some people, especially those who use personal computers, have picked up many key computer terms and incorporated them into their everyday jargon. Finally, Wall Street stock traders in securities have a language that is so abbreviated and incomplete that it is unlikely to be understood by the most attentive layman without sustained study.

All of this colorful language and jargon serves to maintain the specific boundaries of the occupation:

> Jargon functions to outline the boundaries of an occupation because 1) Any person who is unable to understand the language used in that particular occupation cannot possibly be a member in good standing in that occupation, and 2) the language serves as a short hand, allowing expression of complex thoughts in single words or short phrases.... In a sense, a person who did not understand would be ... a stranger—and his lack of knowledge would clearly mark him as such (Runcie 1974:421).

Gestures frequently accompany spoken language and are sometimes used as a substitute when circumstances do not permit verbal communication (Bocock 1974). A surgical operating team, for example, often becomes so close-knit that verbalizing is unnecessary: "A language of gesture has developed whose meanings are crystal clear to persons following the operation" (Wilson 1982). Iron workers typically take for granted an elaborate set of hand signals for bringing steel beams into position (Haas 1972). Sawmill workers, police who control traffic, and sailors are examples of workers who use gestures so frequently that they have developed their own languages.

Often gestures are used to convey solidarity and group control. For example, a pat on the head (in the case of children), on the buttocks (in the case of football players), or, more generally, on the back expresses approval and conveys emotional support. Hitting another person on the upper arm expresses antagonism and has been used to regulate co-workers' output (Roethlisberger and Dickson 1946:421-23). A rodeo cowboy's hat often comes off during his ride, and he is apt to walk slowly over, pick it up jauntily and casually, projecting the image of the lone cowboy, put it on his head and walk from the ring.

Longshoremen engage in mock physical assaults—playful pats on the shoulder and rough scuffling—as prework warm-ups and to reaffirm group solidarity and identification (Pilcher 1972). Only close friends engage in this behavior; those who truly dislike one another never insult one another or josh in such an extreme way. William DiFazio (1985:87) has captured the full extent of these playful gestures:

> Joking behavior consists of paper throwing, hair messing, head rapping, insults, joke telling, and so on. To an observer outside of the work group, the behavior would be interpreted as hostile and overtly aggressive. Instead I saw it as behavior that "serves as an important boundary and symbol of group solidarity for the longshoring group and probably contributes to some unknown degree to the maintenance of this solidarity" (Pilcher 1972:112).

The settings in which members of occupations work also convey meaning. For instance, the chiropractor's adjustment table with its movable sections appears formidable to a new patient (Cowie and Roebuck 1975:56).

RITUALS AND TABOOS

Rituals are standardized, detailed techniques that workers use to manage anxiety and promote ethnocentrism, although they seldom produce consequences of practical importance. Young lawyers, for instance, are apt to look up all the past cases related to a current case and to go over all the arguments even when they know that the court's decision will be based on other considerations (Hughes 1958). School teachers, pharmacists, and nurses keep highly detailed records as ritualistic protection against making mistakes. News reporters use "strategic rituals" as a presumed guard against deadline pressures, libel suits, and the wrath of superiors and to ensure "objectivity" (Tuchman 1972:669). Thus, they view the judicious use of quotation marks around other people's opinions and the presentation of conflicting views as symbolic ways of removing themselves from stories.

Nurse's aides in operating rooms are much influenced by the demanding exactness of surgical work and as a result fold towels ritualistically and with mechanical perfection (Wilson 1982). Baseball pitchers ritualistically engage in "tugging the cap between pitches, touching the resin bag after each bad pitch, or smoothing the dirt on the mound before each batter" (Gmelch 1971:39). Professional wrestlers ritualistically perform the motions that are expected of them, using grunts and gestures that they exploit to the limit of their meaning: "A man who is down is exaggeratedly so, and completely fills the eyes of the spectators with the intolerable spectacle of his powerlessness" (Barthes 1972:16). Burglars often engage in a truly bizarre ritual: leaving piles of excrement in a prominent place at the scene of their crimes (Friedmaan 1968). Many thieves deposit this "calling card" in such prominent places as the center of a room, a bathtub, or a porcelain table.

A fascinating example of ritualistic behavior occurred among motorized British artillerymen during the early period of World War II. A moment before the artillerymen fired their guns, two members of the gun crew ceased all activity and saluted. They stayed in this position for the six to eight seconds doing which the gun was discharged. Puzzled by this behavior, a time-motion analyst inquired of an old colonel of artillery what the saluting was all about. After much ruminating, he replied, "I have it; they are holding the horses" (Morison 1982:84).

Taboos are behaviors and topics that are viewed as prohibited within the occupation. They are usually unspoken and unwritten and constitute an empirical example of a "taken-for-granted" expression of the culture. Baseball players, for example, scrupulously avoid dropping bats on top of one another in resting positions, fraternizing with players of opposing teams, and making umpires look foolish in public (Charnofsky 1974:267). Longshoremen have a strong taboo against the use of profanity if women are present or even in earshot (Pilcher 1972:104). High-steel iron workers prohibit talk about their obviously appropriate fears (Haas 1977:167), and a potent taboo is covertly learned among medical students: "[They] learn to manage the inappropriate feelings that they have in situations of clinical contact with the human body, but two years of participant observation revealed that the subject of 'emotion management' is taboo" (Smith and Kleinman 1989:56).

Among funeral directors, certain forms of public behavior, for instance, drunkenness, boisterousness, or even the luxury of not attending religious services regularly, are taboo not only for the funeral director but for his family (Van Maanen and Barley 1984). Similarly, the cowboy tradition prohibits complaining (Lawrence 1982:96), and loggers will not break up a log jam on a Sunday because it will lead to death (Santino 1978).

Cocktail waitresses learn taboos regarding their relationships with bartenders: don't yell at them when you need them to mix drinks; don't correct them when they make mistakes with change; don't demand if they forget to hand you beer glasses; and don't scowl when they mess up the tray (Spradley and Mann 1975). According to H. L. Hearn and Patricia Stoll (1975:108), it is also taboo for waitresses to become personally and emotionally involved with bartenders: "Each waitress expressed a recognition of the hazards of becoming too friendly or personally involved with [bartenders]. . . . It is taboo to become personally involved."

In the case of prostitutes taboo concerning intimacy are even more explicit and are directed at their "tricks" (customers). Lip kissing is especially taboo as part of their sexual services because it connotes an emotional involvement, which they wish to avoid (Prus and Irini 1980: 17). Finally, nightclub strippers must never "bad-mouth" another stripper to a customer (Boles and Garbin 1977:235).

RITES AND CEREMONIES

Rites and ceremonies are elaborate, dramatic, and planned public activities that consolidate several cultural forms into one event, thereby delivering a set of meanings (Trice and Beyer 1984). When performing these activities, cultural leaders and group members use symbols such as language, gestures, rituals, and artifacts to heighten the expression of shared meanings appropriate to the occasion, and often these activities are reinforced by myths, sagas, legends, or other stories. Rites and ceremonies differ in magnitude: a rite amalgamates a number of discrete cultural forms into an integrated, unified public performance; a ceremony connects several rites into a single occasion or event (Chapple and Coon 1942; Gluckman 1962).

Among academic occupations the conferral of tenure is a ceremony composed of several rites. Typically, the ceremony entails meetings and votes by the tenured faculty in one's academic department, review by an ad hoc committee of one's peers outside the department, and subsequent evaluations by university committees. Finally, the president and board of trustees decide to promote or deny promotion, usually the former. If the individual is promoted, other celebrations follow. This series of events either enhances or deflates the prestige of the individual being reviewed for promotion, and it renews the commitment of all the people involved in the process to their occupation; that is, it helps resocialize them to the ideologies of individual performance and competitive excellence (Trice and Beyer 1984).

Rites and ceremonies are classified according to their social consequences, including the ideologies they deliver. All rites and ceremonies can be classified along two dimensions (Trice and Beyer 1984): their technical versus expressive consequences (i.e., what do they do or say?) (Leach 1968) and their manifest versus latent consequences (i.e., their intended and unintended functions) (Merton 1936). Combining the two dimensions yields four possible social consequences, as illustrated in table 4.1.

Typically, rites and ceremonies are classified according to their manifest expressive consequences rather than their manifest technical, latent technical, or latent expressive consequences. Thus, the tenure-conferral ceremony described above is categorized according to its manifest expressive consequences as the enhancement of the social identity of the successful candidate among his or her peers, as well as the renewal of collective commitment by those peers to the occupation.

Rites of passage facilitate the transition of persons into occupational roles and statuses that are new to them. In a seminal analysis, Arnold Van Gennep ([1909] 1960) observed that within tribal societies certain behaviors typically accompanied common and unavoidable events such as pregnancy and childbirth, the onset of sexual maturity, betrothal, and marriage. Because such events create marked changes in

Table 4.1. Four Possible Social Consequences of the Tenure-Conferral Ceremony

Technical consequences

Manifest	A thorough evaluation of candidates' performances over fairly extended periods so as to promote only the qualified to permanent membership in the system.
Latent	Faculty learn about one another's work; the relative priorities placed on various areas of performance are decided, communicated, and enforced.

Expressive consequences

Manifest	The enhancement of the social identity of the successful candidate among an immediate audience.
Latent	The enhancement of the prestige of the professional role; untenured faculty are motivated to perform according to the priorities made evident; and a collective renewal of commitment.

Source: Adapted from Trice and Beyer 1984:656.

roles and status for the individual involved, he called the accompanying sets of behaviors "rites of passage."

Rites of passage are composed of three distinctive, consecutive subsets of behaviors: rites of separation from the old status, rites of transition to the new status, and rites of incorporation into the new status. The manifest intended consequences of all these rites are to aid individual members of a social system in reestablishing the equilibrium in their social relationships that was disturbed by their move from one social role to another.

Although frequently truncated in modern life, rites of passage do occur. Occupations have them both for newcomers and, although less frequently, for older workers as they progress in their careers. Van

Maanen (1973), for instance, found rites of incorporation among police officers as they went from the police academy into active police work. Because rites of passage are such a prominent part of the socialization process in an occupation, they will be discussed in detail in chapter 5.

Rites of enhancement act to enhance the personal status and social identities of members of an occupation. The tenure-conferral ceremony in academic occupations is one example. It provides public recognition, of individual faculty members for their accomplishments and motivates others to make similar efforts. In addition, the series of meetings and decisions by various faculty groups made up largely of the professors' peers reinforces their collective authority to evaluate and judge one another and to make all decisions relative to academic matters. Even high-status tenured faculty members outside the university are normally called upon to judge their colleagues during this process. All of the effort expended to reach a decision carries the message that being tenured is an important role and status and thus serves to increase the prestige and power of the focal professors and their occupations.

Rites of degradation dissolve an individual's occupational identity and the power associated with it, ritually destroying the individual's claim to an occupational role and status. They deliver messages about boundaries; that is, that violations of prevailing belief systems will not be tolerated and will be met with by expulsion from the field. Among some clergy, defrocking involves the physical and public removal of the priest's robes and ornaments. The expulsion of soldiers also takes place in a public ceremony, characterized by the destruction or removal of parts of the uniform—the buttons, denoting legitimacy; the bars, showing rank; and, on some occasions, the sword, denoting honor (Young 1965; Joseph and Alex 1972).

As the polar opposite of rites of passage, rites of degradation act to dissolve an occupational identity and strip away some, or all, of its accompanying power. Although somewhat rare, they nevertheless demonstrate that role transitions in careers can involve the loss of a role as well as the acquisition of a new one. A dramatic, but infrequent, instance of such a rite occurred in 1983 when the U.S. House of Representatives voted to censure Congressmen Daniel Evans of Illinois and Gerry Studds of Massachusetts for having had sex with teenage pages. The rite that accomplished this process consisted of a formal confrontation between the two congressmen and the members of the House, at which a judgment about the nature of their deviant act was announced, followed by their assignment of a special role, namely "censured" legislators. These proceedings were performed in a ritualized setting (Roberts 1983; Erikson 1962) in which the two men stood before their colleagues in the well of the House while the Speaker, Thomas P. O'Neill, read the censure resolution. They were automatically stripped of any committee chairmanships for the remainder of the congressional session, and the proceedings were broadcast on national television and radio, as well as widely reported in news magazines and newspapers.

On balance, however, compared with organizations, occupations appear to have developed few public degradation ceremonies. This probably reflects the norm that only other members of an occupation are qualified to judge the work of other members and they must not criticize their work publicly (Freidson 1976) unless driven to do so by irresistible forces.

Rites of renewal rejuvenate and reinforce existing ideologies and arrangements within the occupation, refurbishing the status quo and making it palatable. Auctioning the tools of deceased members is a rite of renewal among members of many manual craft occupations (Green 1965). When an old-timer dies, his expensive, often ornate tools are meticulously auctioned off one by one to fellow union members, emphasizing the ongoingness of the trade.

Rodeos renew commitment to ranch life. Calf roping reenacts the precursor of cattle roundups, while steer wrestling, bull riding, bareback bronco riding, and wild horse racing recall the dominance of ranchers over animals and nature. At the same time, the festival atmosphere surrounding the rodeo celebrates shared understandings: nostalgia for rugged frontier life, stoicism, extreme individualism, and a macho view of animals, women, and bodily functions (Lawrence 1982).

Many rites of renewal entail role reversals. In British hotels, for instance, once or twice a year during staff parties managers and waiters reverse roles (Mars and Nicod 1984:100). Waiters act above their stations, possibly imagining for a few hours that the whole world lies at their feet; and managers "wait on their tables and perform other menial services for them." As is classic in such situations these reversals last only a short time. When the old roles are resumed, however, not only has latent conflict been blunted but the essence and authority of the normal roles have been renewed by the contrast.

Surgeons' "grand rounds" and "mortality and morbidity conferences" are potent rites of renewal in that they dramatize the attending physicians' clinical and scientific mastery (Bosk 1979, 1980). Mortality and morbidity conferences, which examine the failures of attending physicians, renew the surgeons' authority by permitting them to "put on a hair shirt" and state publicly that they made a mistake in handling the case and to point out why some other course of action might have been better. Charles L. Bosk notes that grand rounds "celebrate the extraordinary success of surgeons" and that in morbidity and mortality conferences following operations, surgeons "are able to use unexpected failure to serve the same ends" (1979:122, 127). "Putting on the hair shirt" dramatizes the "humanity, humility, and the scope of the physician's wisdom" (Bosk 1980:75); junior staff are not allowed to "wear the hair shirt," however, because their competence is still an issue. Another observer of these conferences concluded that they are "a ritual designed to reaffirm the profession's worth after doubt was cast upon it" (Light 1980:216).

Rites of conflict reduction reduce conflict and aggression among hostile, or potentially hostile, factions. Occupational cultures contain at least four kinds of rites that reduce such conflict. First, committees, such as task forces and project teams, reduce conflict by forcing hostile parties to find common ground. Helen B. Schwartzman (1981:80), for instance, found in her study that committee meetings between social workers and mental health professionals served "as a homeostatic [internal stability] in the system to validate the current social structure and to regulate and maintain order." Second, status reversals, such as those just described and practiced by British waiters and managers (Mars and Nichod 1984), serve as safety valves in that they give people an opportunity to vent their anger and resentment (V. Turner 1969). Third, ritual rebellions allow individuals to act out their anger without destroying the group. Some academic departments, psychology, for instance, have annual dinners at which graduate students perform elaborate skits in which individual faculty members are portrayed as callously disregarding student feelings and espousing impossibly high academic standards. Fourth, and finally, joking relationships bond together individuals who might otherwise have a problem cooperating with one another because of the structure in which they interact or their roles; What might otherwise be regarded as an insult becomes a play or joke. For instance, "joking [between bartenders and waitresses] takes on a reciprocal quality in which the exchange of words, much like the

exchange of gifts, creates and solidifies the social ties between [them]"
(Spradley and Mann 1975:90). Similarly, the joking relationships that
develop between novice machinists and old-timers reduce the conflict
between members of different generations and underscores the newcomer's proper place (Boland and Hoffman 1983).

Rites of integration encourage and revive the common feelings that
bind members of an occupation together and express commitment to
a social system. Meetings of occupational associations reinforce members' mutual sense of identity with other members of the occupation.
Pavalko (1971:106) summarizes the manner in which such meetings act
as rites of integration:

> Persons who may in their normal work activities be in competition
> with one another, or physically and spatially separated (physicians,
> academics from different universities, bricklayers working on dif-
> ferent construction sites), are brought together under the aegis of
> the occupational association in such a way as to minimize their
> differences and maximize their sense of common interest, concern,
> and destiny.

Even the casual observer of these meetings can readily detect the
outward manifestations of this process. Clusters of conversations
abound in and around formal programs that provide training for
younger members. Among purchasing agents, for example, "many
members exchange information and tricks of the trade in informal con-
versation around the bar before and after meetings" (Strauss 1972:236).
There are opportunities within these gatherings to seek elective office
or to seek out contacts that could pave the way to new and better jobs.

SUMMARY

This chapter described a variety of cultural forms by which the ideology of an occupational culture is conveyed to its members. An occupation's esoteric language, myths, stories, and songs symbolize what
it means to be a member. Occupational myths express the value of such
membership symbolically. Tales and songs of heroic deeds, tragedies,
and accomplishments dramatically illustrate the lives of the ideal practitioners of the occupation. These cultural forms exemplify the moral
order and highlight the boundaries between virtuous and inadequate
occupational behavior.

Even though cultural forms are distinct entities, they most often occur in clusters. While in occupational cultures, individuals are surrounded by and bombarded with a steady stream of these forms until they become taken-for-granted, everyday occurrences. They are often combined into complex ceremonies that express the occupation's values and beliefs. These ceremonies dramatically illustrate which behaviors are to be applauded or denigrated and where members stand in relation to one another, underscoring common values, reducing conflict, renewing commitment to the group, and enhancing solidarity.

In chapter 5 we will explore the process of becoming an occupational insider to illustrate how learning the cultural forms of a specific occupation constitutes a socialization process that teaches newcomers how to act like full-fledged members.

5. RITES OF PASSAGE IN OCCUPATIONAL CULTURES
LEARNING TO BE AN INSIDER

Entering upon a trade, marrying, growing old, and dying are also celebrated . . . After the phrase of Van Gennep, they have come to be called rites de passage, *rites of transition.*

—Everett C. Hughes

TO BECOME A MEMBER of an occupational culture, a newcomer must learn the group's distinctive ways of viewing and acting in the world; that is, he or she must become socialized by interacting with members of the culture. Socialization also occurs as people take on new roles and statuses. This chapter describes the specific processes by which individuals are socialized into their occupational roles.

ATTRACTION TO OCCUPATIONAL LIFE

Before one can become a member of an occupation, one must first be attracted to it and then recruited into it. Several factors contribute to whether an individual will be attracted to a particular occupation. Social class can set severe limits on both a child's knowledge about, and aspirations concerning, a given occupation. The education, income, and occupations of one's parents affect one's childhood fantasies and expectations about various occupations, so that children who come from families with high socioeconomic status learn about and aspire to many more occupations than do children whose families are of lower socioeconomic status (Shapiro and Crowley 1982; Brinkerhoff and Corry 1976). Similarly, gender has restricted occupational awareness, so that women have aspired to such traditionally female-dominated occupations as nursing, teaching, and social work and men have aspired to such traditionally male-dominated occupations as carpentry, plumbing, and mining (Sewell 1969). And race continues to be a powerful constraint on the aspirations of black youth, many of whom expect to be deadlocked in low-paying jobs or by chronic unemployment. A rural background can also restrict young peoples' opportunities to explore occupations to which they might be attracted.

Some observers insist that by the time race, nationality, family, area of residence, and sex are factored into the equation, the range of choices is severely restricted (Miller and Form 1980). Random factors such as military status, friendships, appearance, demand, and age further block and limit work possibilities. For that matter, the need to locate work may be the most severe restriction of all; that is, for many Americans, the chief determining force involved in their coming under an occupation's influence may be their need to avoid unemployment.

"The transformation of interests into occupation is rarely a simple or direct process," wrote Daniel J. Levinson (1978:101), a close observer of work lives. One may be attracted to specific members of an occupation with whom one has been exposed, to specific work tasks that one has seen performed, or to the extrinsic and intrinsic rewards that one perceives the members of an occupation receive for their work. Some make a "commitment by default" (Becker 1960:38); that is, because of ignorance, inertia, fear of failure, or reluctance to face decisions, they become committed to whatever work is available to them. Thus, attraction becomes a somewhat haphazard matter in which certain features of the occupation come to a person's attention, and, as this process continues and accelerates, it becomes increasingly difficult for the person to pursue alternatives. As a result, even if knowledge of other opportunities exists, the person is not apt to pursue them.

An initial attraction may lead to tentative commitment and attempted entry, provided immediate opportunities present themselves. College textbook editors, for example, are likely "to have embarked on a publishing career largely by accident. . . . Most of them entered publishing simply because they went looking for some sort of job, and publishing presented itself" (Association of American Publishers 1977: 38). Few editors planned a career in the publishing industry, and most believe they became editors by luck or accident. Likewise, Fred E. Katz and Harry W. Martin (1962) found that most nursing students enter training because of immediate situational pressures and for irrational, spur-of-the-moment, even impulsive reasons. Similarly, cocktail waitresses tend to "drift into the occupation without any long-range planning and preparation, but with positive attitudes toward the work" (Hearn and Stoll 1975:107). Like recruits to many other occupations,

they do not consciously set out to become members of a specific occupation.

An exception is police work. Van Maanen (1973:410) found that
"most policemen have not chosen their careers casually." At the same
time, their choice is restricted by the fact that "virtually all recruitment
occurs via generational or friendship networks."

Rothman (1987:267) has characterized the process of entry and first
exposure to an occupation as

> a social drama in which the participants play out social roles, en-
> gage in social rituals, and follow socially prescribed patterns. . . .
> The actual event can be an application for a job, or admission to a
> required training program such as medical school, a police acad-
> emy, or an apprenticeship program. . . . The preparation of re-
> sumes, searching out letters of recommendation, and filling out of
> forms are all elements of the process.

Thus, in the employment interview, social characteristics, such as socioeconomic status or group membership, may play a role in the selection process. According to Rothman (1987:268), interviewers use a
combination of objective criteria and stereotypes in selecting applicants. On the one hand, they regard sloppiness on an application blank
negatively, are less likely to choose women when they are as well prepared as men, are likely to favor blacks for custodial work, and rate
women who wear glasses as unattractive. On the other hand, they regard steady eye contact and smiles as positive attributes. Once accepted, an applicant has been, in effect, positioned to experience the
socialization forces of that culture.

SOCIALIZATION

After the initial period of attraction and recruitment, socialization
intensifies. Occupational socialization is the process by which one generation passes on to another the technical knowledge, ideologies, and
expected behaviors deemed necessary to perform an occupational role
(Applebaum 1984b:19). Through socialization, an outsider "learns the
ropes" and becomes an insider. As Barley has said (1983b:3), one learns
to interpret messages:

> To be an accomplished practitioner of an occupation one must be
> able to read meaning where a novice might misinterpret a message
> or see no message at all. In fact, occupational interpretations are

part of what we pay for when we purchase the services of practitioners as diverse as the physician, the plumber, the automobile mechanic, and the palmist.

Occupational socialization is based on the human capacity to change (Brim 1966). Psychologists suggest that personality traits can change over time and in different social contexts; consequently, the meanings that constitute "reality," and from which behavior flows, can be reconstructed in new situations. In American society, for instance, young girls are taught to be unassertive and when faced with a physical threat to seek a male protector. In the process of becoming a police officer, however, women must unlearn such behavior and learn to manage aggressively the physically violent and dangerous aspects of fighting crime (Martin 1982).

The occupational culture that is transferred from one generation to another is an inexact replica of the previous one because newcomers in pluralistic America are apt to bring to an occupation backgrounds that are quite different from, and at odds with, its ideologies (Bassis and Rosengren 1975). As a result, the prevailing culture is rarely a reproduction of the previous one. Rather, the prevailing culture bears both similarities and differences to the earlier one. To confuse the matter further, many occupations have high visibility, making for inaccurate expectations about the roles of its members. This is especially true of occupations such as police work, law, and medicine in which members' work lives are often portrayed inaccurately in the mass media. McCarl (1980:22) captures the inexactness of the socialization process among firefighters:

> Many of the more experienced firefighters feel as though the current influx of new recruits is not participating in this culture with the proper attitude; while the younger men and women on the job feel as though the formal and informal rules on the job are much too restrictive.

Occupational socialization, at best, is an incomplete process, subject to the constant forces pressing for change in the occupation's environment. There is, on the one hand, a passing on of the occupation's culture; on the other hand, there is resistance and a reformulation of it.

The degree of socialization ranges from relatively imperfect to quite thorough. During World War II, for example, millions of American males were temporarily socialized into the role of soldier, but once hostilities ceased, few opted to remain in the service; rather, most expressed a strong desire to return to civilian life (Lazarsfeld 1949). In contrast, the socialization of federal forest rangers is quite thorough: "The Rangers want to do the very things the Forest Service wants them to do, and are able to do them, because these are the decisions and actions that become second nature to them as a result of years of obedience" (Kaufman 1976:228). Similarly, socialization within the established occupations is generally very thorough, resulting in a permanent role change for recruits that persists across numerous transitions and situational changes. Medical students, for instance, experience medical school as a series of passages that gradually and incrementally makes them conceive of themselves as physicians (Becker et al. 1961; Merton, Reader, and Kendall 1957; Bucher and Stelling 1977). In their interactions with faculty, nurses, and other medical students, they learn to think and act like doctors. The potency of this experience is due in part to the fact that medical students actively shape their training by emphasizing some areas for study and ignoring other areas (Bucher and Stelling 1977). It is also due to the sheer amount of time it takes to become a doctor. Socialization in other occupations such as ballet dancing (Federico 1974) takes even longer and leaves a lasting impression on individuals' identities and sense of commitment.

Nightclub strippers, especially the features, receive "extensive training in stripping before they perform before an audience. . . . Many have been trained in 'Kootch Shows' by people whose job is specifically to train strippers" (Boles and Garbin 1977:234). But although barbers must complete 100 hours of classroom instruction, have 1,025 hours of practical training, complete written tests on the makeup of the skin and human nervous system, and pass performance examinations on the proper ways to cut hair and give shaves, the major source of their learning comes from helping one another (Woods 1972). In contrast, school teachers enter teaching after only a mild mini-apprenticeship, experience few ordeals, and learn little, if any, common technical culture. Consequently, they are largely self-made and individualized members of their occupation (Lortie 1975).

Although the basic processes are similar, the occupational socialization of adults is quite different from the socialization of children. The child acquires roles and values where none existed before. By contrast, occupational socialization frequently involves not only the learning of new roles but the unlearning of old ones and the distinct possibility of having to occupy conflicting roles. Susan E. Martin's (1982) study of the socialization of policewomen shows how women recruits need to learn aggressive attitudes, whereas male recruits tend to have them.

During socialization in childhood, the child has little or no control over the forces impinging on him or her. Day-to-day life in families and with peers has almost irresistible, unconscious influences. Schools, for example, exercise repeated influence that children cannot readily avoid. With their as yet unformed personalities, they are relatively inactive participants in their socialization experiences. In contrast, adults usually enter into socializing experiences voluntarily and usually retain some control over the process. Thus, compared with the socialization of children, the socialization of adults is more voluntary and more characterized by its freedom to escape if the process becomes intolerable.

Organizations, as well as occupations, socialize newcomers and those in career passages within an organization. Training and indoctrination are important aspects of this process of organizational control and coordination. According to Henry Mintzberg (1979:95), "Training refers to the processes by which job-related skills and knowledge are taught, while indoctrination is the process by which organizational norms are acquired." Both help transform new employees from one role and status to another. Both may also occur outside employing organizations. To the degree that this happens, or is controlled by the occupation in company-sponsored training, the occupation, rather than management, exerts control over the initial socialization of new members into occupational roles.

As they are learning technical skills, recruits are inevitably indoctrinated into the ideologies, values, and norms of the occupation. Sometimes, for instance, rites of passage occur sequentially within the occupation and the organization. Thus, separation rites may take place within the occupation, while transition and incorporation rites may occur primarily under the control and direction of the work organization.

RITES OF PASSAGE

Many, but by no means all, strategies for socializing newcomers into an occupation can be discussed under the general heading of rites of passage (Van Gennep [1909] 1960; Turner 1969, 1970; Haas and Shaffir 1982b). Rites of passage are ceremonies, "especially dramatic attempts to bring some particular part of life firmly and definitely into orderly control. . . . In the secular affairs of modern life [they are used] to lend authority and legitimacy to the positions of particular persons, organizations, occasions, moral values, views of the world, and the like" (Moore and Myerhoff 1977:3).

Three distinct rites—rites of separation, of transition, and of incorporation—make up the ceremony, and unless all three are completed, the passage is not completed. Rites of separation act to detach people, often physically as well as symbolically, from their former roles and move them symbolically into a transitional or "betwixt-and-between" phase. During the transitional period, their former status and roles are symbolically stripped away and they are in an ambiguous state in which their experiences have few if any features of their past or future experiences. Finally, rites of incorporation consist of collective actions that enable the newcomers to try out their new roles. Although variations on this sequence, and on the number of rites, occur frequently in occupational life, it nevertheless provides a general framework for beginning to analyze the socialization process.

Rites of separation, according to Meryl R. Louis (1980:231), facilitate the "unfreeing, moving away, or letting go . . . [that is a] . . . necessary preliminary step in effecting change at individual and group levels." They encourage recruits to let go of their current status and roles and symbolically move them into the transition phase, where they actually learn the technical performance of their tasks. During the separation phase, potential recruits must convince the gatekeepers of the occupation that they have what it takes to become successful members of the occupation. Within the well-developed occupations, this generally means convincing admission committees at professional schools that one has the basic qualifications to be trained to enter the occupation. Within the crafts, and to a degree in less developed occupations, it often means working as a laborer and convincing the people with whom one is working that one has the right stuff.

Aspirants to medical school begin to be separated out in secondary school (Haas and Shaffir 1982b). Well aware of the need to convince admission committees of their abilities, they consciously organize their lives around the idea of constructing a dossier that will provide evidence of their having appropriate and successful experiences, such as having done volunteer work, participated in research, demonstrated leadership, and garnered awards. In preparation for admissions interviews, they practice responses to anticipated questions and plan how they will make favorable first impressions.

If they are successful in overcoming these first hurdles and are admitted to medical school, they are rapidly plunged into a new system of ideas, beliefs, and practices that usually heightens their performance anxiety (Becker et al. 1961). Forced to learn everything from how to handle physicians' tools to the esoteric language of medicine, medical students are well aware that they are no longer part of the lay world and not yet part of the medical culture (Haas and Shaffir 1982b). As they don their white lab coats and identity tags, begin attending classes, tentatively use medical language and tools, and learn how to detach themselves emotionally from their patients, they are well on the way to separating from their prior selves.

Among pipeline welders, the rites of separtion are quite informal and simple compared with the entry process into medicine. Nonetheless, a separation phase does occur. Newcomers, or "broncs" who "break out" of the casual labor pool, must demonstrate that they are not "overbearing smart alecs" by cautiously participating in name calling, hitting, wrestling, and clod throwing (Graves 1958). When one newcomer, unfamiliar with the subtle cues of horseplay, tried to participate, "the welder neither answered nor looked at the worker. The worker stood with his foot on the truck's running board for a few minutes, then walked away" (288). When a "bronc" is able to comprehend the subtleties and successfully breaks out of the laborer's role, however, the skilled welders, supervisors, and inspectors recognize that he is entitled to learn the trade's secrets and that they are obligated to teach him. Similarly, the crews of fishing boats pay almost no attention to newcomers, often to the point of refusing to learn their names, until they have shown themselves to be worthy of recognition (Orbach 1977).

Rites of transition are characterized by liminality, a period "when the past has lost its grip and the future has not yet taken definite shape" (Turner 1970:354). The newcomers are neither their old nor their new selves but are eager to be transformed into the new. The term *liminality* refers to this state of limbo in which the neophyte is not in his or her old role or, for that matter, in the new one toward which the passage is leading. It is an ambiguous, unstructured state of in-betweenness. Many tribal versions of this period are marked by the initiates' names being taken from them; they are called by some generic phrase that identifies them merely as neophytes (Turner 1970:358).

In effect, "they are no longer classified, and not yet classified." They have physical but not social being. Among high-steel iron workers and tuna fishermen, newcomers are treated as scarcely being present at all. Victor W. Turner (1970:360) sees the liminal condition as being characterized by "a peculiar unity: that which is neither this nor that, and yet is both." In some occupations newcomers are actually physically absent. Some newcomers are assigned night duty, for example. According to Murray Melbin (1987:54):

> Many occupational careers start with assignments at night. Employment on evening and night shifts is a passage along which young people will advance toward the main social time table. The reporter's first salaried position on a daily newspaper begins on the 7 P.M. to 2 A.M. shift. In the post office and in the printing industry newcomers must accept after-dark schedules. ... The medical intern accepts a 36-hour span of duty in the hospital. Beginning law associates stay at the office late and even overnight to complete research reports.

Consequently, rites of transition are times when the occupation "seeks to make the individual most fully its own, weaving group values and understandings into the private psyche so that internally provided individual motivation replaces external controls" (Myerhoff 1982:112). Rites of transition are essentially a series of ordeals in which newcomers "learn the ropes" and demonstrate that they can perform the occupational role competently. Learning may occur in a variety of ways, and the ordeals may extend over either a comparatively brief period (e.g., months) or an extended period (e.g., years).

Medical students, for instance, face a series of ordeals in which they must convince several different audiences that they can play the part of doctor (Haas and Shaffir 1982b). Very early on in their educations they learn that, if they are to get through medical school and convince their teachers of their competence, they must develop a professional persona in which concern for the patient does not interfere with their responsibility to remain emotionally detached and objective. At the same time, the students are worried about learning massive amounts of technical jargon, making errors in matters of life and death, coping with the imperfect science of medicine, and performing intimate examinations. During this phase, the neophytes must convince an ever-shifting audience of patients, doctors, nurses, and hospital staff that they know how to perform their roles. Never knowing what medical problems to expect, the newcomers must always be prepared to improvise and convince those watching that they have adopted the symbolic, interactional, and ideological "cloak of competency" of a doctor (Haas and Shaffir 1982a).

Another ordeal in becoming a doctor is preparing for and passing the nationwide written licensing exam. Jack Haas and William Shaffir (1982b:199–200) have commented:

> When the ordeal has been completed, [medical students] can return to the interactional manipulation of professional symbols and anticipate enacting the role of "Doc" with full acceptance by client audiences. Ahead await internship and residency and more refining of the role as they seek to develop a reputation on stage as true and trusted professionals.

Among pipeline welders, the transition from apprentice to craftsman often takes as long as four years (Graves 1958), but the process is informal and unscheduled. Having broken out of their status as laborers, apprentices are allowed to participate as helpers in such physically demanding jobs as river crossings, which require many continuous hours of work with short naps in the truck. Being able to participate in such work means one has gained prestige because it "separates the men from the boys" (Graves 1958:11). During the transition period, apprentices observe the methods used on a given job and, when there are slack periods, practice welding on scrap pipe. Skilled insiders who have unimportant tasks to do are obligated to let the apprentices do the work, if they are available. During this period, master welders also humiliate, joke with, and generally harass the apprentices by withholding vital information and doling it out piecemeal.

Rites of incorporation signal to others that the novices have been transformed by their ordeals and training into members of the occupation. The novices are no longer considered ignorant of the ways of the world but capable of understanding the occupation's esoteric knowledge and implementing its essential skills. As such, they are to be accorded the rights and privileges of members of the in-group and are obligated to promote the occupation's welfare and defend it against intrusions from outsiders.

Within the established occupations, rites of incorporation are often staid affairs, as well exemplified by the sacred ceremonies of formal graduations. For medical students residency in a large hospital is a form of incorporation into the medical fraternity. In effect, the students are now junior physicians, treating patients under the watchful eye of senior physicians.

Among pipeline construction workers, rites of incorporation are less clear-cut because there is no ritual as such that marks the transition from bronc to full-skill status (Graves 1958). Instead, the reasonably skilled are urged to go look for work elsewhere and not to remain with the companies where they "broke in." In sharp contrast to the relationship criteria (whose boy is he?) used during the transition period, production criteria are now applied to their performance. Consequently, as their skill increases, productivity takes on increasing importance, and the newly trained are encouraged to enter the competitive labor pool and to incorporate themselves into completely new companies and new gangs.

Rites of incorporation for smoke jumpers include completion of training and inclusion on the jump list (McCarl 1976). All summer the old hands closely observe and monitor initiates' behavior. Full acceptance is withheld, however, until the season is practically over and the new smoke jumpers have proven themselves.

Despite the general erosion of rites of passage in modern secular society, there are, as we have just seen, still instances in occupational life of the classical sequences described by Van Gennep ([1909] 1960). In some cases, such as that of the pipeline welder and the smoke jumper, the three phases of separation, transition, and incorporation are not formalized into explicitly defined stages but rather unfold informally. Nevertheless, the stages are quite distinct. For the physician, all three of the stages are quite formal.

Because rites of passage constitute an ideal prototype around which socialization can be examined, it seems appropriate to provide two other empirical examples from occupational cultures. Since the formal pattern exemplified in medical training makes it rather easy to imagine how the classical rites of passage might function in other established occupations such as law and the clergy, it seems appropriate to turn to instances in which there are less formalized rites of passage. Studies of municipal firefighters, underground miners, and police provide such examples.

In the case of municipal firefighters, the rites of passage unfold within the organization's hierarchy and involve the preparation of elaborate food events (McCarl 1984). After a rookie finishes his probationary year, he prepares and serves a dinner to other members of his company. This dinner is a rite of separation, signaling a clear-cut severance with past identities and the beginning of his career as a firefighter. He prepares additional meals as he learns more details and takes more tests, to signify he is in transition to the ranks of officer. These meals symbolize incorporation into and status in the cultures of both the occupation and the organization.

An elaborate ceremony at the time of retirement, serves, in effect, as a rite of separation from both the occupation of firefighting and one's engine company. Its most prominent feature is a verbal "roast" during which the audience and various speakers confront the retiree with many of his misdeeds and indiscretions and generally review his overall performance as a firefighter. He responds to these accusations in any manner he chooses. These "roasts" are intermingled, however, with compliments and expressions of respect and appreciation. At the end of the dinner, the former firefighter appears publicly in front of his fellow firefighters as a retiree. He is forced into isolation and made to realize the inevitable and irreversible change that is happening before his, and others', eyes.

Among underground miners, the separation phase is symbolized by the "portal" to the mine, which marks the boundary between the old life on the outside and the new one far below. Passing through it, the newcomer journeys from his customary social world into another that "people outside just don't understand" (Vaught and Smith 1980:164). Because miners return to the surface each day, separation occurs repeatedly. Aboveground, miners prepare to enter the mine by putting on their work clothes, during which much camaraderie takes place. Within this milieu, the new recruit puts on new, standard overalls, a mining belt, and boots and carries accoutrements of the occupation, including a bright orange hat, a dinner bucket, and a lamp. The newness of this equipment spotlights the newcomer, and during the first trip down the "slope"—and for a period thereafter—he is subject to a variety of indignities; other miners beat his hat, pulling his lamp cord and belt, kick dents in his shiny new dinner bucket, and generally call attention to his trappings of the occupation. These actions remind the new worker that he is not yet a member of this "select" group. Charles Vaught and David L. Smith (1980:166–67) describe this situation as follows:

> Crowded into the man-trip, personal space invaded and freedom
> of movement restricted by the close proximity of other workers,
> they are lowered into an environment that is noisy, dark, dusty,
> and illuminated only by shifting beams from miners' cap lamps.
> They are in truth "new men." . . . [The newcomers] are now de-
> pendent upon these boisterous strangers to lead them around and
> show them what to do.

The separation phase also includes three or four shifts during which the
newcomer is ignored but occasionally discussed as if he were not
present.

During the transition period, miners learn on the job by performing
whatever work is required, under the close scrutiny and degrading
remarks and stinging rebukes of senior miners. Recruits are given nicknames during this period. These names are typically derived from
gaffes or personal traits and symbolize that the recruits are in a new
world where their old names do not apply. Among the more colourful
and derogatory of these names are "Maggot Mouth," "Plunger Lip,"
and "Big Coon."

Male miners become incorporated into the culture of mining via
a series of blatantly gross, body-centered games (Vaugh and Smith
1980). During "greasing," for example, several miners grab a novice
unannounced, remove his trousers, coat his genitals with grease,
and throw handfuls of rock dust on his greasy genitals. Apprentices
are also forced to engage in "pretty pecker contests," during which
mock judges choose who has the prettiest pecker. These games cul-
minate in "the making of a miner," which consists of asking the
apprentice if he has been made a miner. When he says "No!" the
miners grab and hold him down and administer several swats to
his behind. This process is repeated until all the miners are satisfied
that they have "smacked him pretty good." These games of degradation graphically confront the new miner with the group's solidarity and impress upon him that he must always defer to its will.
He now belongs to the fraternity of miners.

A lengthy screening process, often taking as long as six months and
consisting of a series of qualifying examinations, serves to separate out
aspirants to police work. This "arduous screening procedure" (Van
Maanen 1973:410) engenders feelings in the rookies of having been selected for employment in an elite organization. Rookies typically go

through additional rites of separation as well as transition in a police academy but experience incorporation in a police department doing patrol work. Nurses tend to experience separation through formal education in centers outside the work setting, whereas incorporation occurs in the "work setting and its agents [and] . . . its structure and situational demands are the most powerful socializing agent" (Lurie 1981:46).

Van Maanen and Schein (1979:238) note that "recruits in police academies are . . . assessed quite thoroughly by staff members as to their loyalties not only to the organization, but to their fellow recruits as well." Similarly, the workers in Donald Roy's (1952) machine shop refused to tell him about how to make money on difficult piecework jobs until he had demonstrated that he would be loyal during secret skirmishes with management.

Police training emphasizes a vocabulary of defensiveness, professionalization, and depersonalization (Harris 1973). Recruits are trained to be constantly alert to the possibility of danger and to be very suspicious of most situations. The term *professional* is used to instill a positive image of responsible, independent commitment, while *depersonalization* imparts a view of one's occupational self as seeing the public in a detached and categorical manner, rather than individually and emotionally.

Incorporation into the police officer's role entails graduation from the academy and the rookie's first experiences as an officer, during which the newcomer must convince other members of the force that he can manage dangerous assignments (Van Maanen 1973; Harris 1973; Jermier 1982).

Ideally, rites of separation, of transition, and of incorporation should all take place in an occupational culture. Van Gennep's original work on rites of passage emphasized, however, "just how similar are the beginnings, middles, and ends of an extraordinary wide range of rites. . . . These similarities are not random analogies, but part of a single, general phenomenon" (Huntington and Metcalf 1979:8). Some occupational cultures, as we have seen, follow the classical sequence (i.e., those of pipeline welders, doctors, underground miners). Many others, however, do not. Here the assessment made by Terence S. Turner (1977:69) of rites of passage in modern societies applies: "Often one or more of the three rites seem to be missing entirely, or at least cannot be identified as such."

INCOMPLETE RITES OF PASSAGE

Members of some occupations experience only one, or two, of the three rites of passage. In other instances, one, or two, of the rites are feeble, while others may be well formed. Thus, although rites of incorporation have been clearly evident in tribal cultures, they often seem to be missing or ill formed in modern occupational life. Among the Andaman Islanders (Radcliffe-Brown 1964:94), for instance, rites of incorporation for young males consisted of a series of intricate dances performed by all members of the tribal groups, during which the initiate was saluted with bundles of twigs to which he had to respond by performing a vigorous dance. Slowly, under close observation, he assumed his adult role, but only after weeks of monitoring by adults. Richard Pascale's description (1984: 30) of how successful companies put new managerial recruits into the field and give them "carefully monitored experiences" following rites of transition bears a distinct similarity to A. R. Radcliffe-Brown's account of the Andaman Islanders.

One reason that rites of incorporation appear to be missing in modern occupational life is that they often occur in multiple locations before a number of audiences; consequently, they are not easily observable as a whole. I (1987) found, for instance, that graduating seniors from a Northeast professional school experienced occupational rites of passage both within the university and within their first employing organizations. Within the university, a series of events acted as separation rites in the freshman year, and a series of placement activities, "senior day," and commencement exercises signaled the student's transformation into being a "professional." Their first roles in a company, complete with their initial orientations and probationary periods, signified their final incorporation into their occupational roles. Similarly, nurses who attend university-based programs go through separation rites as a part of their freshmen-induction events and their course work and graduation act as rites of transition, but their actual incorporation occurs in the organizational setting within which they are first employed. We can think of these rites of passage as being incomplete within the occupation but as being completed in the organization. Even in these cases, however, separation and incorporation rites may at times be weak, while the transition rites may be relatively potent.

An occupation that entails the first two rites but not the third is that of high-steel iron work. Members of this occupation must learn to manage the anxiety and trauma produced by working high above a pandemonium of activities, "protected from certain death only by their skill in balancing on slender beams . . . a skill threatened by swirls of weather and wind" (Haas 1977:148; see also 1972 and 1974), and they must convince their veteran co-workers of their dependability and trustworthiness, especially when "running the iron." Recruits, or "punks," first serve as "fire watchers." This job entails standing below on the ground and watching for falling bits of welding material. It enables the punks to learn by watching experienced iron workers perform their tasks. But then, without any orientation or training, they are asked to "punk for the journeymen." This is the only practice they get in walking the steel (Haas 1974:99). In this role, they must respond to various demands from the journeymen to locate and bring them tools, equipment, and materials.

During this period, the punks are subjected to "binging," blistering personal attacks and verbal degradations. They are constantly questioned about their personal lives and activities and are reviled for the slightest shortcoming; at the same time, the journeymen are imparting technical information to the apprentices. Binging allows the journeymen to evaluate the apprentices' trustworthiness, self-control, emotional reactions to the "punk" label, and whether the apprentices' confident front will break down under crisis. The punk label is never removed ceremonially; rather, the apprentices must live it down by consistently demonstrating that they know how to behave technically and emotionally.

In contrast to medical students, workers attempting to enter the trades often do so casually and indirectly, and they often must convince the craftsmen with whom they are working that they are fit recruits. Except for the few comments necessary to perform the work, experienced workers studiously ignore newcomers to fishing (Orbach 1977), mining (Vaught and Smith 1980), railroading (Kemnitzer 1973, 1977), and the building trades (Silver 1986; Applebaum 1981). This "silent treatment" and lack of direct interaction heighten the newcomers' anxiety about being able to perform and being accepted, thus forcing them to distance themselves from their old roles and preparing them to learn the new one.

Within the crafts, learning to behave like a member of the occupation often entails intensive on-the-job socialization during the transition period. Newcomers learn by performing whatever work is required under the watchful and critical eye of older, experienced members.

Compared with the separation period, this transition period is well formed and studded with unique argot and caustic nicknames, along with complicated information about practice. According to William W. Pilcher (1972:105), nicknames are the "most colorful part of the entire linguistic repertoire of the longshoremen, and they are nearly always insulting in tone, although their derogatory nature is not always apparent to outsiders."

Newcomers are also aided in learning to perform their roles to the extent that occupations possess unique argot, costumes, and tools (Loeske and Cahill 1986). Apprentice electricians, for instance, discover that tools reflect ability and maturity (Riemer 1977). Newcomers carry a large number of tools of varying quality, but master electricians carry only a few well-worn tools of very high quality. As apprentices move toward journeyman status, they wear "bib" overalls, display their names on their increasingly scratched and dull hard hats, and demonstrate their mastery of such technical jargon as "red head," "funny paper," "mule," "mouse," and "rabbit gun." Similarly, railroaders must learn distinctive languages (Kemnitzer 1973, 1977). They must learn the technical terms to carry out the skills they are learning. They must also learn a complex communication system to perform these skills.

INFORMAL AND UNORGANIZED SOCIALIZATION

Accompanying practically all entry experiences are events that are unplanned, that differ from workplace to workplace, and that happen freely or naturally within limited locales. Thus, occupations tend spontaneously to create "local knowledge . . . shared information, which is not formalized, but . . . is used by group members to support the performance of work tasks . . . and transmitted to new members through informal communication networks" (Baba 1988:1). Such knowledge may be acquired in conjunction with formal education and continue to be acquired as members work within their occupations, or it may take the place of formal apprenticeship training, as is often the case in the building crafts (Silver 1986). Such knowledge is necessary because formal knowledge is rarely adequate to the tasks required. The more sophisticated the technical expertise and the more skilled the work group, the more complex and valuable is the local knowledge. Consequently, such information becomes part of the occupation's trade secrets. Even the extensive socialization of lawyers into the role of federal district judge is almost entirely an informal process. There appears to be an absence of any structure or typical process whereby newly appointed judges "learn the ropes":

> The data indicate that the socialization process, even within the formal boundaries of the federal judiciary, is a highly unstructured, ad hoc phenomenon . . . While the federal judiciary system does perform and endure because of the socialization of its new members, the heart of such socialization is primarily in spite of, and in addition to, any conscious or structured teaching process in the system (Carp and Wheeler 1972:390).

Informal socialization tends to happen in situations "where the newcomer is accepted from the outset as at least a provisional member of a work group" (Van Maanen and Schein 1979). Virginia L. Olesen and Elvi W. Whittaker (1968:296), commenting on the importance of informal socialization among nurses, observe, for instance:

> It was not in the high councils of the curriculum planners, nor in the skill of the most sophisticated and understanding instructor, nor in the late night cramming for exams that professional socialization occurred. Embedded in the frequently banal, sometimes dreamy, often uninteresting world of everyday living, socialization was of the commonplace. In the mundane, not in the abstract or exalted, occurred the minute starts and stops, the bits of progress and backsliding, the moments of reluctant acquisition of a new self and the tenacious relinquishing of the old.

Likewise, even though firefighters attend formal schools, the most effective method of learning takes place "when an officer or experienced firefighter takes an inexperienced probationer under his wing in an attempt to provide her/him with an inside perspective" (McCarl 1980:7).

MENTORS

Within some occupations, becoming a member involves a mentor or sponsor (Kanter 1977). Van Maanen and Schein (1979:247) refer to this process as "serial socialization." They write that "in the police world, the serial mode—whereby rookies are assigned only older veteran officers as their first working partners on patrol—is virtually taken for granted"

Many construction workers learn the trade because close relatives get them part-time jobs during school holidays and summer vacations. This enables the newcomers to break into the industry early, especially into the informal "social networks that later will be necessary to making a living as an adult. The younger relation can ride the coattails of his or her sponsor while establishing connections of his or her own" (Silver 1986:114).

Likewise, some women become truckers because they are sponsored by another driver, usually a husband or boyfriend who teaches them the ropes. Muriel F. Lembright and Jeffrey W. Riemer (1982:457) obtained data from ninety women truckers and supplementary information from one hundred male truckers at three centrally located truck stops. Fully 80 percent of the women drivers were sponsored by another driver—either their husband or boyfriend. The authors concluded that novice women drivers face many of the same problems encountered by women attempting to enter other male-dominated occupations. In this case, however, "these tensions were less than expected, due largely to male support, sponsorship, and protection." In this regard, the findings are similar to those of Kanter (1977:183), who concluded that sponsors are in effect teachers and coaches and went so far as to write that for women entering the work world, sponsors seem essential.

A sponsor is also valuable in the building trades, even though it is commonly believed that formalized apprenticeship training is the major socializing device. From his study of building craftsmen, Marc L. Silver (1986:112) concluded, however, that "a significant proportion of trades people do not go through formalized training for their craft. . . . Personal relationships with friends and relations play the key role."

Mentoring is especially important in those situations in which conformity to norms within the occupation is viewed as deviant behavior by outsiders. For example, traveling salesmen, cab drivers, waiters, and bartenders often "fiddle"; that is, they manipulate their work roles to generate extra income (Mars 1982). For instance, they learn to short-change customers.

Because fiddling is viewed by outsiders as "stealing," socialization into it is subtle and indirect. During training, mentors use a joking tone and the excuse of "anyone can make mistakes" to introduce newcomers to the idea of fiddling. Eventually, the newcomers accept that it is necessary because of the impossibility of keeping accurate books and the ever-present pressures from employers for greater productivity.

Learning to fiddle takes about six months. Then trainees either accept the inevitable nature of the fiddle or, finding it too repugnant, terminate their training. If the training has an effect, they slowly but surely come to realize that they will have to devise their own fiddling system.

Similarly, prostitutes are introduced to their calling, including theft from their "Johns," by informal sponsors (Bryan, 1966). So too some factory workers learn to circumvent management's guidelines, thereby increasing their pay, from informal mentors on the "Q.T." (Bensman and Gerver 1963).

Overall, mentoring can either supplement or replace various rites of passage. In the building trades it appears to substitute to a considerable degree for all three rites; for police recruits, however, mentoring seems to add meaning to the rites of incorporation as newcomers move from the academy into full-fledged membership.

RELATION OF RITES OF PASSAGE TO ROLE COMMITMENT

By transforming individuals' identities, rites of passage make members of occupations one of their own. This is a practical necessity if an occupation is to pass on its cultural heritage even partially from generation to generation and to defend its position against interlopers. Consequently, it is important to ask whether rites of passage do increase individuals' commitment to their occupational roles.

Generally, those occupations in which becoming a member is an ordeal generate more commitment than those in which becoming a member is easier. Becoming a university professor or a physician, for instance, entails a greater ordeal—that is, it probably requires greater nervous energy—than becoming a school teacher or a social worker because professors and doctors have larger and more complex roles to learn and to perform and many more audiences to satisfy before they are accorded membership in the occupation (Lortie 1968; 1975; Loeske and Cahill 1986). Whereas professors and doctors must learn to play their well-defined characters according to the well-worn expectations of their audiences, because they do not have well-defined scripts to follow, teachers and social workers virtually end up creating their own characters. It therefore seems reasonable to assume that teaching school and social work generate less commitment than do medicine and university teaching.

Progress for professors and doctors calls for them to satisfy a series of hurdles in graduate school and later in their first professional positions. Like the medical students described earlier, aspiring university professors face a series of ordeals in graduate school and their first positions before they are fully incorporated into their occupational roles (Lortie 1968). Thus, they must pass examinations in their courses, demonstrate knowledge of a specialized field, and pass examinations in their general academic disciplines before they are even allowed to begin and complete the last ordeal in their graduate education: their doctoral dissertation. Furthermore, in their first academic positions, they must teach the courses senior professors eschew and publish in competitive research journals. At the same time, they must develop a teaching style for communicating with students. Finally, five or six years into their careers, the senior members of their academic department decide whether their teaching and research merits giving them tenure—the final ordeal in becoming incorporated into the occupation (Trice and Beyer 1984).

By contrast, entry into school teaching (Lortie 1968) or social work (Loeske and Cahill 1986) is not an ordeal. In both instances, individuals are admitted to the occupation upon completing only a few requirements, typically practice teaching or a fieldwork practicum and the bachelor's degree. In contrast to the collective experiences of medical students, these experiences are essentially ones in which the novices must work out their own roles. Social workers, for instance, find that their practicum experiences are so different from one another's that they no longer speak the same language and do not "sustain a common identity" (Loeske and Cahill 1986). Similarly, novices perceive student teaching as an individual "sink-or-swim" experience and speak of their training as "Mickey Mouse" (Lortie 1968, 1975). In both cases, newcomers have few props to rely on in perfecting their performances and experience little or no peer pressure to perform in a certain way. In addition, from their first day on the job, they essentially work alone, as responsible for their student loads or clients as are twenty-five-year veterans.

Finally, as a consequence of their sink-or-swim socialization, teachers and social workers tend to discover that they must devise their roles largely on their own. Teachers who initially think of their role as instructing students in a particular subject may gradually come to see themselves as counselors (Blase 1986). As they come to know their students' personal lives and problems, they may also begin to perceive of themselves as role models for living "good" lives.

Similarly, novice social workers, lacking "the benefit of clear directorial cues, a distinctive set of identifying symbols, or receptive audiences for their occupational performances," come to believe that "a certain constellation of personal qualities [are] the defining characteristics of an authentic social worker" (Loeske and Cahill 1986:252). These are "responsible," "pleasant," "patient," and "optimistic" (Clearfield 1977:26). These traits are not unique to social work but are claimed by other "helping professions" (Morales and Sheafor 1983) and are possessed by loving mothers and good friends as well. Consequently, social workers claim that these defining traits are not acquired through training but develop "naturally" (Loeske and Cahill 1986). In short, social workers experience weaker and more diffuse rites of passage and, in general, learn few cultural forms, such as myths, symbols, and stories, to delineate their cultures.

INDIVIDUALIZED PASSAGES

Three-phase classical rites of passage are generally identified by their occurrence between youth into adulthood. In current American occupational life, however, there are many other passages following initial entry into the labor force. The early-middle and middle-age periods of work life, for instance, are replete with migration out of one occupation and into another. Abbott (1989:280) observed:

> We know that even among professionals outmigration is extremely high. Electrical and chemical engineers, operations researchers, accountants, clergy, and college teachers all face probabilities of more than 50% of leaving by age 40 the census categories in which they began their careers. If this is the case among professionals, how much greater is it among other workers!

According to Nigel Nicholson and Michael West (1989:193), "It seems that most companies act as if their responsibility for managing transitions begins and ends with recruitment procedures." Further, a study of job changes in four departments of a large corporation produced the following: "Formal socialization is almost exclusively limited to new hires who enter organizations in cohorts. Employees in our job transfer and job changes samples report few experiences that can be characterized as formal socialization" (Brett 1984:175).

Under these conditions, it seems reasonable to presume that a significant percentage of workers may well be learning, unlearning, and relearning sets of occupational tasks during large parts of their life spans (Wallace 1989). Further, it seems likely that nothing approaching rites of passage attends these changes, since work organizations themselves seem to be practically devoid of any organized effort to initiate them. True, socialization may occur informally, in bits and pieces, but this is accidental and quite uneven. As a result, the experience of passage may be individualized. For example, waiters, fishermen, and overland truck drivers, who experience only weak or partial rites of passage upon entry into the work force, may find their experiences at least as random and individualized as they go through outmigration.

Occupations such as engineering, human resources, finance, and accounting are ideologically close to management, and it is a natural sequence to move from these occupations into general management. In this context, socialization becomes imbued with competition and is also experienced alone and randomly. Van Maanen and Schein (1979) observe that there is little, if any, sequence by which workers rotate through various positions and departments in preparation for becoming a general manager. Indeed, in some organizations, these moves are totally random. For example, some managers begin their careers as accountants, then work in marketing or personnel, and then become general managers. Others start out in engineering, then work in marketing, and eventually become managers.

Barney G. Glaser and Anselm L. Strauss (1971) have observed that many persons going through midcareer passages seem to do so alone. By midcareer, occupational life has often become so enmeshed in organizational structure that careers are inevitably entwined within both the occupation and the organization. Accountants, for example, whether in general management or not, advance in prestige, experience, and authority within a highly competitive company hierarchy, marked by the erosion of their chances of upward mobility (Faulkner 1974b). Van Maanen (1978) and James E. Rosenbaum (1989) liken this situation to a tournament or contest between individual aspirants, and it is just the opposite of rites of passage in signaling a role transition. This process symbolizes individual accomplishment, informal and political manipulation, and competitive endurance. There are no intimations of success as in the completion of a rite of passage, only an impersonal winning of a bureaucratic position, accompanied by the increasing likelihood of losing in the competition for upcoming positions: "Even among the 'high potentials' once you are dropped from the fast track you can't get back on it" (Van Maanen 1978:24).

Rosenbaum (1979, 1984) analyzed the career paths of an entering group of managers over thirteen years. Employees who were promoted early had much more elevated career paths, in contrast with employees who did not receive early promotion. In brief, midcareer passages are likely to be highly individualized modes of socialization. As a consequence, rites of passage, especially in an ideal form, seem to be rare.

There is also evidence that within work organizations careers may as often be characterized by immobility as by mobility. Based on their study, D. A. Schrier and F. D. Mulcahy (1988:148) state that middle managers "often do not make it to top management and resign themselves to a career of being 'betwixt-and-between': A guy is sixty years old and has lost every battle along the way and says 'fuck it' and waits until retirement."

Similarly, Robert R. Faulkner (1974b:167) insists that "occupational age" plays a crucial role in the career patterns of fashion models, professional fighters, lawyers, scientists, strippers, dancers, and actresses, as well as of engineers and astronauts. Persons in these occupations must "recognize and face up to the career dilemmas of becoming occupationally and biologically older." Referring to the careers of symphony orchestra musicians, he writes that "most performers find themselves stranded in the middle levels of the orchestra structure"(154).

Early-middle and middle-age newcomers to an organization may also be socialized by an "investiture" mode (i.e., through "processes that ratify and document for recruits the viability and usefulness of those personal characteristics they bring with them. . . . 'We like you just as you are'") (Van Maanen and Schein 1979:250). In these instances, neither the occupation nor the organization seeks to change the recruit; "rather it wishes to take advantage of and build upon the skills, values, and attitudes the recruit is thought to possess." When an organization recruits nuclear physicists or organic chemists from academia, for instance, they often urge them to start out in the same field of research in which they were engaged while they were in academia. In much the same manner, computer programmers in the 1960s and early 1970s "hopped from job to job with impunity. . . . They [were] wined and dined, coddled and humored, promoted and pampered" (Sullivan and Cornfield 1979:186) as their careers unfolded. In these cases, rites of passage were nonexistent; rather, passage into the role was highly personalized. If rites of passage are thought of as "divestiture socialization"—that is, "organized explicitly to disconfirm many aspects of the recruits' entering self image" (Van Maanen and Schein 1979:251)—then individualized passages (i.e., investiture) represent the virtual absence of these rites.

A revealing example of investiture can be found among employee assistance program (EAP) workers. Although there is a tentative and growing consensus in the EAP movement about what constitutes the core tasks of the EAP worker and how to perform them, there is nevertheless much conflict, diversity, and "babble of voices." Discussions and interviews with EAP workers indicate that they often learn to do their work "by the seat of their pants" and through sink-or-swim and on-the-job experience. Even though a certification program has been set in motion and an examination is being administered, fully three-quarters of those who have taken the test have been admitted. As an emerging part of the personnel occupations, EAP workers seem only too willing to improvise on the general EAP role as they believe appropriate to meet their immediate individual needs and for their work settings. Their entry and subsequent adaptation to their work bears little if any trace of the traditional rites of passage.

Individualized passages may also be a function of the ill-defined nature of the tasks that members, and outsiders as well, attribute to an occupation. Thus, social workers tend to experience individualized entry into their occupation, a theme that appears to generalize into mid-career. Recall that their practicum training experiences vary significantly, making for an individual mode of socialization. Social work may well be an example of an occupation that has yet to define its boundaries clearly, with the result that its socialization of newcomers, as well as of recruits in midcareer, is more random and individualized than that of many other occupations (Loeske and Cahill 1986). In the same vein, Judith R. Blau (1984:7) notes that architects "have never agreed about the profession's core or specialized domain . . . [and] continue to resist a definition of its boundaries and internal specialization." Having such an undefined set of core tasks can only make for an individualized entrance and progression into the occupation's culture since numerous variants and alternatives are possible.

Finally, even when there are no rites of passage, they can be created. Barbara G. Myerhoff (1982:132) suggests that "if they [rites of passage] are not provided for us we may provide them for ourselves . . . What is required is a small community of friends or family, some symbolic and traditional sources of inspiration, a clear formulation of the change involved and its significance, and courage." Within this framework, status changes can be viewed as opportunities through rites of passage to transform otherwise disorienting and lonely experiences "into commemorations that acknowledge change."

There is some evidence that midcareer rites of passage take place in Japan. A *60 Minutes* broadcast (1987), for instance, showed Japanese midlevel managers in their thirties, forties, and even fifties with occupational backgrounds as accountants and engineers undergoing a thirteen-day "self-improvement" program. The program resembled a rite of passage into more advanced roles in the organization. Such career rites *could* occur among accountants, engineers, and staff personnel such as psychologists in American workplaces. Similarly, within law firms, police departments, and architectural firms, career rites of passage could and may take place.

SUMMARY

Attraction and entry into an occupation are often characterized more by caprice than design. Once entry takes place, however, youthful newcomers may experience some rites of passage, typically separation, transition, and incorporation. Both high-status professionals such as physicians and blue-collar workers such as pipeline welders go through these phases. Others experience only one or two of these rites, most usually the transition phase.

Many occupational changes and shifts occur during the early-middle and midlife periods of work, but these tend to have few rites of passage attached and often none at all. Those passages there are tend to become increasingly lone journeys in which informal and local forces account for what little socialization there is.

Passages also become individualized as one's occupation is more absorbed into the hierarchical structure of one's organization. In this context, passages are the rewards for individual competitiveness and political shrewdness. With increasing age, however, rites of passage of any kind into new, meaningful work roles become practically nonexistent.

PART II. OCCUPATIONAL CULTURES INSIDE WORK ORGANIZATIONS

S O FAR WE HAVE examined the basic elements of cultures and have concluded that, to varying degrees, these features apply to occupations. To the extent that distinct ideologies, and the cultural forms necessary to deliver them, can be identified, an occupation is a culture. But cultures rarely, if ever, function in isolation from other cultures. This seems to be especially true of occupational cultures. Members routinely practice inside formal work organizations. Even physicians increasingly tend to be involved in organizations such as large clinics, health maintenance organizations, and hospitals. Members of occupations practice "inside" an organization as a result of either importation or internal development or a combination of both.

Regardless of members' origins, however, being inside makes for new cultural dimensions. Members of occupations form subcultures, for example, that interact with, and must adapt to, members of a variety of other subcultures, including members of other occupations. In part II I examine the nature of subcultures in general and of occupational subcultures in particular (chapter 6). Next, I construct a typology of the prominent adaptations that occur between occupational and administrative subcultures (chapter 7). I then look at the modes of adaptation between occupational subcultures (chapter 8). Finally, I reflect in some detail on the implications of this analysis in light of the three themes set forth initially, paying particular attention to a suggested subcultural analysis of organizational culture (chapter 9).

6. OCCUPATIONAL SUBCULTURES AND COUNTERCULTURES

What is deviant organizationally may be occupationally correct (and vice-versa).
—John Van Maanen and Stephen R. Barley

ORGANIZATIONAL SUBCULTURES subscribe to clusters of understandings, behaviors, and cultural forms that characterize them as distinctive groups within an organization. Differing noticeably from the core culture in which they are embedded, subcultures may exaggerate the core culture's ideology and practices or deviate in some way from them. By contrast, countercultures are in intense conflict with the core culture. Before applying this notion directly to occupations, it would help if we consider the concept of subcultures in general.

NATURE OF SUBCULTURES

Subcultures exist in practically all cultures. Even in simple pastoral cultures, secret societies, clans, totems, and people who are close in age form distinctive subcultures (Sapir [1915] 1966; Warner 1937). In modern industrial societies, most individuals are subjected to the tugs and pulls of different subcultures. Indeed, Geertz (1983:161) writes that the "hallmark of modern consciousness . . . is an enormous multiplicity [of cultures] . . . and the first step is surely to accept the depth of the differences." Likewise, Ward H. Goodenough (1978:119) states, "Multiculturalism is the normal experience of most individuals in the world today, for they are perforce drawn into the microcultures of administrators, teachers, physicians, and others who have power over them."

In many studies, the concept of subcultures is expressed through such terms as subsets, subgroups, subunits, splinter cultures, cultures within cultures, cultural pluralism, many in one, multicultural, and "the management of diversity." These terms suggest that few, if any, formal organizations have single homogeneous cultures. Rather, there are more likely to be many cultures that, because of their heterogeneity, are potentially conflictual systems of meaning or in some fashion differ from the core culture. As Kathleen L. Gregory (1983:359) puts it, "Many organizations are most accurately viewed as multicultural." In this sense, work organizations reflect their environments.

Although occupations can be distinct subcultures within organizations, students of organizational culture have tended to overlook them. In part, this oversight stems from earlier attempts to view organizational cultures as relatively monolithic and homogeneous (Peters and Waterman 1982; Davis 1984). Other observers (Trice and Morand 1989; Riley 1983; Gregory 1983; Louis 1983), however, tend to see organizational cultures, including occupations, as made up of diverse internal systems of meaning—subcultures. In some instances, they have gone so far as to suggest that there is no core organizational culture and that work organizations should be seen primarily as intermingling subcultures that have a modest amount of overlap between them (Van Maanen and Barley 1985). According to this view, this relatively small overlap constitutes the overall culture, while all other beliefs and activities reside in the subcultures (Gardner 1946; Dalton 1959; Gregory 1983; Arnold 1970).

Proponents of this view are not suggesting that social scientists should abandon the concept of an organizational culture. Rather, they are saying that work organizations are especially multicultural, that their subcultures cluster around a few cultural elements that are widely shared, and that, to understand organizational behavior, one must examine the "differences in objectives and preferences of subunits and concentrate on [the] processes by which these differences get resolved" (Tushman 1977:207).

Subcultures may be found even in tightly controlled organizations such as the military. George C. Homans (1946:295), for instance, reports, "The crew of a small war ship is actually more differentiated than its numerical size might suggest." Similarly, Wilensky (1967:48) describes how military subcultures contributed to the Pearl Harbor disaster:

> In the armed forces, intense rivalries between services and within
> services—among supply and procurement, plans and operations,

research and development, intelligence—led to intelligence failures. . . . In 1941, the signals of pending attack on Pearl Harbor lay scattered in a number of rival agencies; communication lines linked them, but essential messages never flowed across the lines, let alone at the top. The Army and Navy presented a picture of cordial, respectful communication, empty of solid substance.

Like cultures, subcultures have cultural forms that carry ideological messages from which come collective understandings and patterns of behavior. At the same time, these messages differ noticeably from the common core of ideologies. Subcultures either intensify or deviate from these ideologies, generating a unique set of understandings, behaviors, and cultural forms of their own.

The degree to which subcultures conflict with the core culture varies widely. In some instances, a variable such as gender may separate out a particular group of individuals so that they interact more frequently among themselves but the set of beliefs that is generated is not significantly different from that of the core culture. In contrast, in some groups, the ideologies may be so sharply in conflict with the ideology of the core culture that they become countercultures. The majority of subcultures probably lie somewhere in between.

A basic ingredient for the development of a subculture is differential interaction, either on or off the job or both. Subcultures form because their members interact face to face more frequently with one another than with other people. For example, many jobs encourage friendliness so that complementary tasks can be done smoothly. If persons in the interaction cluster share similar problems and uncertainties, an identity as a distinct group with a shared milieu forms. Should this group transmit its ideology to newcomers so that it plays a part in their socialization, the group has yet another feature of a distinct subculture. The employees in this group probably share something among themselves—information, friendship, favors, resources, even enmities—further identifying themselves with one another. This bonding loosens members' commitment to the common core culture, permitting them to generate shared rationalizations that, in turn, allow them to violate significant aspects of the common culture.

Although there must be at least some interaction for subcultures to form, work by Fine and Kleinman (1979) has shown that they may include large groups of members. In cases where there is no face-to-face interaction, however, there must be "communication interlocks" to connect the small interacting groups with one another and to diffuse information and ideologies. Interlocks create a variety of connections. Often there is overlapping membership in a few groups in which elements of the culture are accepted and practiced. There may also be significant "weak-ties" (Granovetter 1973) among acquaintances who have an affinity for one another and who maintain infrequent but warm contact, often over great distances. Fred Katz (1958:53) described such casual yet ongoing relationships between widely dispersed members of well-established occupations. Their friendships remained on a "low simmer" via such mechanisms as Christmas cards and occasional encounters at professional meetings.

Elements of the culture can also be diffused via roles that require intergroup relations (i.e., publishers' representatives, guest lecturers, salespeople, and consultants). In addition, diffusion occurs via the mass media, which simultaneously transmit cultural information to hundreds, even thousands, of small groups and isolated individuals. Through these interlocks, subcultures transcend the need for face-to-face interactions, and thus membership is not necessarily determined by spatial or temporal closeness. For example, distinct subcultures emerged in a large office products firm as a result of the electronic mail being distributed to both work-related and extracurricular lists. Even though they shared no physical space and had no face-to-face interactions, subcultures such as the Computer Science Group and the Captain Developers (work related) and the Cinema and the Rowdies (extracurricular) were readily identified (Finholt and Sproull 1990:49, 53).

OCCUPATIONAL SUBCULTURES

In modern work organizations, occupational cultures constitute a distinctive and often the most well-organized source of subcultures. Employees are often as committed to their occupations as they are their employing organizations (Ritzer and Trice 1969a; Hebden 1975). The essence of occupational life automatically makes these occupations subcultures. This essence consists of the fact that occupations come into existence whenever their tasks come to be the nucleus "around which groups can be formed as their members seek autonomy and control over their particular and distinctive work" (Freidson 1982:54). These groups can have a life of their own outside of the organizational setting (Child and Fulk 1982:156).

As noted in chapter 2, individual employees experience occupations

as reference groups (Pavalko 1971) and sources of personal identity—
a "ready made me" (Goffman 1961b:88)—both inside and outside organizations. This is because, as pointed out in chapter 5, occupational
cultures socialize persons into specific ways of performing a series of
tasks, as well as into the values, attitudes, interests, skills, and knowledge that accompany and justify them. Thus, as we have seen, occupations produce ethnocentricity in their members.

According to Van Maanen and Barley (1985:41), members of well-
developed occupations are imported into workplaces in the first place
because organizations

> alter their structure when the cost and uncertainty of engaging in
> an exchange relation with groups outside the organization's
> boundaries outstrip the cost of providing the desired resource in-
> ternally. . . . Structural inclusion becomes more likely when serv-
> ices are seen as having a potential to evolve into an
> "organizationally specific asset."

For example, corporations develop in-house legal staffs and public
schools hire psychologists because of "structural mimicry." Managers
become acutely aware of what other organizations in their role set are
doing and, to signal that they too are modern and progressive, they
import members of occupations similar to those hired by the other
organizations (Tolbert and Zucker 1983).

Occupational groups can also be "foisted on organizations by outside
agencies" (Van Maanen and Barley 1985:42; DiMaggio and Powell
1983). Thus, police organizations may be urged, even required, to bring
in artists, statisticians, lawyers, doctors, and psychologists.

Because members of occupations seek autonomy and control over
their work, they pose a threat to the power and authority of management in work organizations. One way to describe this situation is in
terms of the distinction between the occupational principle and the
administrative principle (Freidson 1973). As I explained in chapter 2,
members of occupations believe that they should exercise control over
their work. That is, ideally, members of the occupation should direct
how, when, and where its distinctive tasks should be performed and
only they should decide who is qualified to perform those tasks. This
overarching ideology is reflected in attempts by occupations to professionalize and unionize.

According to the administrative principle (Freidson 1973), however, management ought to control these basic features of work. It ought to decide how tasks are to be performed, who is qualified to perform them, and how performance should be evaluated and rewarded. Occupational cultures are often able to constrain management in making such decisions because the occupations provide the basic training that members need to perform their work. Consequently, management may have no direct control over the work procedures that workers learn or over the values and ethical principles that are inculcated during training. Furthermore, because workers may not need to depend on work organizations for their training, they may enter employing organizations as relatively independent agents who have allegiances to occupational groups outside the organization.

Occupations can also become organizational countercultures in which the basic ideologies deny, or even reverse, those of the dominant culture of the organization. Under these conditions, they can be thought of as "out of cultural and psychological contact with either their traditional culture or the larger society" (Berry 1980:15). Occupational countercultures generally deny the organization's managerial culture of rationality.

Two factors influence the formation of countercultures: infinite aspirations and the deauthorization of authority. As protesters make demands on the overall system, their aspirations and expectations tend to rise. According to Raymond Boudon (1982:105):

> Greater equality tends to produce envious comparisons: as they become more equal, individuals find their inequality harder and harder to bear. . . . Dissatisfaction and frustration may grow when each person's opportunities begin to open out and improve. . . . Individuals may well grow discontented with the social system to which they belong as it offers them, on the average, better opportunities for success and promotion.

In sum, the more equal Americans become, the more they seek inequality.

Originally, deauthorization meant questioning the legitimacy of the older generation's established administrative position. The potential of age groups to generate countercultures was commented on by Ralph Turner (1969:398) during the cultural upheavals of the late 1960s and early 1970s. He wrote: "The major readjustments which are being made in society no longer concern socioeconomic classes, but concern *age groups.* The most striking phenomenon of the last quarter century has been the increasing authority, independence, and recognition accorded the youthful generation." Viewing the matter from the 1980s, Milton J. Yinger (1982:58) concluded that countercultures are "much more likely to occur" when conditions encourage a sense of "my generation" rather than a sense of belonging to a family or community.

Deauthorization has increasingly come to mean the questioning of the legitimacy of expertise as well. Phyllis Stewart and Muriel G. Cantor (1982:274) refer to this process as "the deprofessionalization of almost everyone." Increasingly, lay groups and clients questions the expertise of professionals (Haug and Sussman 1969; Hall and Engel 1974). In the process a climate for the persistent questioning of authority comes into being.

Because the conflict from which they emerge generally has involved less worker resistance than one might expect, countercultures are usually neither frequent nor potent enough in the workplace to disrupt ongoing production significantly (Edwards and Scullion 1982). For instance, one study of youth committed to the counterculture estimated that only about 15 percent of all youth were committed (Horn and Knott 1971). In addition, a work organization will in all likelihood "get the counterculture it deserves, for [counter-cultures] do not simply contradict, they also express the situation from which they emerge—pushing away from it, deploring its contradictions, caricaturing its weaknesses, and drawing on its neglected and underground traditions" (Yinger 1978:496). Many work organizations, as a result, are attempting to "take the edge" off countercultures through such programs as quality of work life, organizational development, and employee assistance programs. These programs act as rites of renewal, even rites of conflict reduction, by symbolically putting the company's "respectable" people in a good light (Trice and Beyer 1984).

Nevertheless, distinct occupationally based countercultures do emerge. Joseph A. Raelin (1987:25), describing cultural values that became enormously popular during the 1960s and that remained so into the 1980s, writes that "defiance of authority" begins from a base of sharp, even cynical, attacks on and challenges of the status quo. He goes on: "In journalism young editors began to clash with older editors and challenge the very policies of the news organizations. Staffs were reported to have bought advertising space for editorials to counter their own paper's position!" In this instance there was not only sharp alienation from the managerial culture but considerable alienation from the occupational culture as well.

In analyzing the differences between jazz musicians and "squares," Becker (1951:139) wrote that "their rejection of commercialization in music and squares in social life was part of the casting aside of the total American culture by men who could enjoy privileged status, but who were unable to achieve a satisfactory personal adjustment within it." Roy (1954) provided an example of machinists who resisted and violated company-promulgated rules governing production procedures because they thought they made no sense. As an occupational group they joined together with various informal groups and blocked a series of attempts by management to implement a new production-control program.

Similarly, peers can constitute a cohesive group and socialize newcomers into norms of behavior that are in direct opposition to the goals of the organization. Nursing students, for instance, exert pressure on their more able peers not to excel and make training more difficult for the other students (Olesen and Whittaker 1968).

A striking example of regularly practiced countercultural behavior is the pilfering of cargo by Newfoundland longshoremen (Mars 1982). A work gang of twelve to twenty men self-select themselves to unload a specific freighter. They then cooperate in systematically pilfering the most desirable parts of its cargo. Their pilfering involves an elaborate division of labor and requires complete cooperation and trust among members of the group. First, certain members who work in the hold and have unlimited access to the cargo identify certain crates as desirable to steal. Next, other members of the team "accidentally" drop and damage these crates. The damaged crates are then routed to special teams in the sheds who sort through the crates, taking out some of the contents. At the same time, the forklift drivers stack the cargo so that the supervisor is prevented from witnessing the pilfering process. The longshoremen are so well organized that they have a "fitting room" where members can try on a pilfered suit and other garments. The loot is distributed at after-work drinking celebrations in which older members reinforce the group's behavior and socialize new members by telling stories of other particularly successful lootings. Gerald Mars's findings confirm Pilcher's (1972:100) earlier description of longshoremen:

Liquor, transistor radios, and other relatively small and desirable objects are always subject to pilfering, and the longshoremen are more then ingenious in obtaining them. . . . Recently competition has greatly increased the zeal with which these companies protect their cargo, bringing them into direct conflict with the established habits of the longshoremen.

Kanter's (1977) description of "stuck" office workers and secretaries in a large corporation also provides a good example of a counterculture. Because they were very frustrated in their hopes of achieving higher status and increased responsibility, the office workers sought to block and thwart the work efforts of others. Thus negativism, malicious gossip, stalling tactics, and other forms of passive resistance marked their behavior toward outsiders. In this example, as in the others, on-the-job behaviors that were explicitly forbidden or highly improper were approved by the occupational group.

ADMINISTRATIVE SUBCULTURES

In sharp contrast, subcultures of managers, especially high-status ones, embrace the administrative principle. These subcultures of rationality are typified by "the organization of life through a division and coordination of activities on the basis of an exact study of men's [sic] relations with each other, with their tools, and their environment, for the purpose of achieving efficiency and productivity" (Freund 1969: 18).

Max Weber (1947) saw rationality as the principle moving force in Western civilization and on the basis of historical comparative analysis predicted that increasingly larger and larger spheres of life would be organized hierarchically and guided by rational rules of conduct. Weber captured this emerging culture of rationality in his ideal-typical description of bureaucratic administration, which he saw as supplanting traditional administrative forms in Western society. He characterized bureaucracy as having the following features (Weber 1947:196–204, 329–36; Scott 1981:68–69):

- A fixed division of labor among participants in which the regular activities required of personnel are distributed in fixed ways as official duties.
- A hierarchy of offices in which each lower office is controlled

and supervised by higher ones. Lower offices enjoy a right of appeal, however.

- An intentionally established system of abstract rules governs official decisions and actions. These rules are relatively stable and exhaustive and can be learned. Decisions are recorded in permanent files.
- The "means of production or administration"—for example, tools and equipment or rights and privileges—belong to the office, not to the office holder, and may not be appropriated.
- Officials are selected on the basis of technical qualifications, are appointed to the office, not elected, and are compensated by salary.
- Employment by the organization constitutes a career for the officials. After a trial period, he or she gains tenure of position and is protected against arbitrary dismissal.

The culture of rationality has been well articulated by traditional systems theorists (e.g., Taylor 1911; Gulick and Urwick 1937; Fayol [1919] 1949; Simon 1957; March and Simon 1958), who view organizations as instruments for attaining specific goals. As they use the term, *rationality* refers to the extent to which a series of actions is organized in such a way as to lead to predetermined goals with maximum efficiency. It refers, then, to the implementation of goals, not their selection. As W. Richard Scott (1981:32) has said, "Rationality resides in the structure itself—not in the individual participants—in rules that assure participants will behave in ways calculated to achieve desired objectives, in control arrangements that evaluate performance and detect deviance, in reward systems that motivate participants to carry out prescribed tasks, and in the set of criteria by which participants are selected, replaced, or promoted."

Underlying the administrative principle are deeply held beliefs that only management possesses the right to decide how to organize work and that workers should be excluded from exercising discretion or control over their behavior. Sometimes these beliefs are boldly stated; often, however, they are cloaked in science. Taylorism (Taylor 1911), for example, promotes the belief that managers can increase productivity by "scientifically" studying what workers do and redesigning the way they do it. Human relations theory, which grew out of interpretations of the Hawthorne experiments, instructs managers to pay attention to employees' feelings to increase productivity (Roethlisberger and Dickson 1946). Contingency theorists tell managers that how work should be organized depends on the nature of the environment to which the organization must relate (Lawrence and Lorsch 1967). Behind each of these philosophies stands the belief that management knows, or can know through "scientific reasoning," the best way to organize work and that if the organization is to prosper, management must be free to use that knowledge.

The administrative principle is a conceptual construct designed to highlight important elements in the empirical world. Its empirical reference is the owner-entrepreneur and his administrative and technical staff, who were responsible for the radical transformation of work during the course of the Industrial Revolution (Freidson 1973). The belief was that, because the owner-entrepreneur risked his capital to make a profit, he had the right to organize work. "Seen historically, bureaucratization may be interpreted as the increasing subdivision of the functions which the owner-managers of the early enterprises had performed personally in the course of their daily routine" (Bendix 1956: 211–12). Such functions included supervision, personnel selection and management, accounting and financial management, recordkeeping, job design, and long-range planning.

The bureaucracy is a relatively new organizational innovation. According to Weber, it was fully developed only in "the modern state" and "in the most advanced institutions of capitalism" (1947:196). By virtue of their place in the bureaucratic hierarchy, managers are thought to have the legitimate power to dictate to their subordinates how work is to be performed.

In modern America, large-scale organizations are a taken-for-granted aspect of everyday life. They deliver water, gas, and electricity to American homes; they make federal, state, and local governments possible; they provide health care and social services; and, of course, they dominate most people's working lives. Consequently, Americans tend to take for granted the rules, hierarchy, and paperwork of bureaucracies, and they are surprised when they encounter an organization that lacks the characteristics. Although bureaucracies are criticized by some theorists (e.g., Bennis 1966), they seem to remain for many Americans the expected way to organize work.

Conflicts between Occupational and Administrative Subcultures

The traditional crafts provide an excellent example of how occupational control can powerfully constrain administrative rationality. Craft unions do more than bargain with management for members' welfare and rights. Through the "jurisdictions" they set up, through their hiring practices, and through their training programs, they actually do some of the administrative work needed to coordinate and control work processes that are done by management in mass-production manufacturing firms. One result is that the administrative structures tend to be smaller and less elaborate in the construction industry, for example, than in manufacturing firms. Another is that decision making is more decentralized: "Decisions, which in mass production were made outside the work milieu and communicated bureaucratically, in construction work were actually part of the craftsman's culture and socialization and were made at the level of the work crew" (Stinchcombe 1959:180).

One symbol of a craft union's determination to exercise control over its work lies in the ownership of its tools. Plumbers and electricians, for example, typically own their own means of production and thereby enhance their control (Riemer 1979; Silver 1986).

Similarly, journalists in media organizations seek to evade administrative control:

> The journalist wants to select his own stories, to treat them as he feels appropriate, and to avoid being rewritten and edited by members of the organization. The sheer size of a mass media organization creates a division of labor and a set of supervisory officers who impinge on autonomy; journalists in the United States have been more concerned with their professional autonomy than with mechanisms for auditing their performance (Janowitz 1977:92).

Scientists provide many examples of how occupations constrain management control. In the 1960s, scholars studying scientists in industry and research laboratories documented the conflicts that arose between the demands of employers and the expectations and values instilled during scientific training (Kornhauser 1962; Marcson 1960).

During the same period, members of other established occupations also got considerable attention: lawyers in corporations (Smigel 1964) and physicians and nurses in hospital settings (Strauss 1972). Physicians provide the extreme example; they have established control—for a period of time, at least—over their own work, hospitals, medical schools, and licensing procedures. Their hegemony, however, is not without limit insofar as recent concern over rising medical costs has prompted increased public scrutiny of medical practice and new government controls. How successful these attempts will be remains to be seen.

Other occupations—university teaching, accounting, engineering, and architecture—also enjoy substantial control not only over their immediate work but also more generally within the organizations in which they work. Freidson (1977:24) has summarized the ability of such occupations to control the work activities of their members, whether they be in private practice or in an organizational context:

> The effectively organized professional occupation controls even the determination and the demarcation of tasks embodied in jobs supported by employees. . . . Through their influence on regulatory agencies, the organized professions (and the crafts) are often responsible for writing job descriptions for their members and determining the employer's training and educational requirements as well as the kind of special skill imputed to the qualified worker.

In U.S. society, which values individualism and autonomy so highly, such control is a prize that many seek. Thus, many occupations that lack the standard requirements for professional status try to claim its benefits by calling themselves professional. The word itself has come to have a very favorable connotation and is applied to activities as diverse as cleaning septic tanks, dry-cleaning clothes, and advising people about investments.

A dramatic instance of the clash between the occupational principle and the administrative principle occurred during the prelaunch, decision-making period for the ill-fated Challenger spacecraft in January 1986. The senior engineer at the Kennedy Space Flight Center in Florida who represented the manufacturers of the booster rockets "argued long and hard against proceeding out of concern that seams of the craft's booster rockets would not hold because of the frigid weather" (Eckholm 1986:137). His opinion as an expert engineer was challenged by NASA administrative officials as appalling and disruptive. Yet the engineer maintained his position throughout the launch and the ensuing disaster. Not so, the vice-president of engineering for the company. In a classic instance of the clash between the occupational and the administrative principle within one individual, "[the vice-president] reversed himself after being asked by Mr. Mason [senior vice-president] to shed his role of an engineer and take the role of a management person." In his role of engineer he had joined other engineers in unanimously opposing the launch. Yet in his administrative role, he had decided to support it.

A less dramatic clash between occupational and administrative principles occurred during the reorganization of a midwestern state's Department of Health and Environment. Traditionally, physicians and engineers had dominated the department. They emphasized "expert control over political accountability; freedom from political interference, belief in the innate power of science, and a commitment to do whatever was needed without regard for political consequences became the core values of this dominant subculture that controlled the department from 1904 until 1983" (Maynard-Moody, Stull, and Mitchell 1986:308).

A reorganization in 1983 created a second potent subculture of bureaucrats. In contrast to the physicians and engineers, the bureaucrats felt responsible primarily to elected officials and legislative intent. They insisted on following formal chains of command, as well as many written policies and procedures. Their reference groups were other state and federal administrators. In contrast, the physicians and engineers saw their relationship with elected officials as a necessary evil and their expertise as more valuable to the public interest than the decisions of politicians. Consequently, they were willing to use money as they deemed necessary and to ignore the chain of command if they thought their judgments warranted it. Their reference groups were the professional (occupational) associations to which they belonged. Via a series of ritualistic and procedural changes, the bureaucrats dislodged the physicians and engineers and scattered them throughout other state agencies.

Occupational influence is not confined to the established occupations. Rare is the manager who is not aware of "secretarial power" and the anger that "scut work" can produce (Winston 1984). Equally rare are those observers who deny that secretaries constitute a subculture. Thus, when secretaries are in steno/typing pools, dependent on the same resources—copying machines, word processors, and supplies—

and unattached to any one office, there is fertile ground for an occupational subculture to grow and thrive. And even when these conditions do not exist, a sense of ethnocentrism tends to emerge (Kenyon 1982). Occupational associations for secretaries strengthen this sense of "weness" and aid those in them to develop identities and definitions of their role that transcend organizational boundaries (Kiechel 1981).

At the same time, too much influence can be attributed to occupational specialties. The specific organizational context in which members of an occupation practice can have pronounced effects on the amount of tension that is created between the goals of administrative authority and of one's occupational socialization. One study found, for instance, that hospital pharmacists identified with physicians, chain-store pharmacists identified with clients, and neighborhood pharmacists identified with other pharmacists (Kronus 1976a:303). In this case, situational forces in the work organizations were obviously competing for the pharmacists' loyalty and source of identity.

Finally, it is important to remember that the occupational principle and the administrative principle are not incompatible in all situations. Ritzer (1975:627), for example, insists that "professionals are becoming a part of bureaucracies and indistinguishable from them." In addition, both administrators and professionals use universal standards, value specialization, and insist on the importance of technical qualifications (Scott 1981:156).

EFFECTS OF OCCUPATIONAL SUBCULTURES ON ORGANIZATIONS

When organizations employ members of a diverse mix of occupations, subcultures will inevitably have to compete for resources and power. Organizational researchers have investigated these tendencies under the rubric of organizational complexity. They have found that in organizations where relatively large numbers of highly trained craftspersons or professionals control their own work operations, there tend to be significantly more supervisory levels to coordinate their efforts (Hage and Aiken 1967; Meyer 1968). Thus, the complexity that arises because of the diversity of the occupational mix tends to occur in larger rather than smaller organizations (Beyer and Trice 1979; Blau and Schoenherr 1971).

The ideologies and vested interests of occupational cultures and their subcultures are likely to surface when collective decisions in organizations become necessary, making for complex internal negotiations. Among various university faculties, for examples, there are at least four issues over which occupational subcultures usually emerge: (1) hiring decisions, (2) tenure decisions, (3) curriculum changes, and (4) resource allocations. Of these, curriculum changes may be the most revealing of cultural diversity derived from occupational mix since they either enhance or threaten the access of members of each occupation to the major raw materials in a university—students. Severe internecine conflicts are thus to be expected and taken for granted, and the curriculum changes made usually reflect power shifts among occupational groups of faculty rather than changes in the needs of students.

Since occupations command allegiance from their members, the question naturally arises whether the presence of occupational cultures dilutes the allegiance of members of those occupations to the organizations that employ them. Alvin Gouldner (1957) has argued, for example, that professionals belong to either of two camps—"cosmopolitans," whose main orientation and presumably allegiance are to their profession, and "locals," whose main orientation is to their employing organization. Robert Blauner's (1964) account of printers as an autonomous occupational community concluded that they derived their work satisfaction largely from their craft and had little if any loyalty to the companies that employed them. Later research (Ritzer and Trice 1969a) questioned the underlying assumption that members of occupations could not be committed simultaneously to both their occupations and their organizations.

Actually, multiple loyalties are common among members of work organizations. Employees may have allegiances to various degrees to their occupation, the management of their organization, their company, their labor union, and their "working-class" identity. Theoretically, an employee could feel no loyalty to any of these collectivities and identify only with his or her self-interests. Although no studies have attempted to examine all of these loyalties, Ken Fidel and Roberta Garner (1987: 20) have reported that among computer workers "attachment is lacking to all three of the traditional bases [their company, their occupation, and their union]." In an earlier study of programmers and systems analysts, the systems analysts showed "a significantly lower identification with their occupational group and a stronger orientation toward their employing organization than [did] the programmers" (Hebden 1975:116).

Data collected from in-service training courses for executives in an Italian management institute produced similar results: "In our population, at least, a person who has two equally stable and consolidated reference cultures at his disposal (his organization and his occupation) will tend to identify with the organization rather than his occupation" (Gagliardi 1989:170). These findings may be influenced, however, by whether the organization offers employees opportunities to be promoted. Offering such opportunities tends to weaken occupational loyalties (Van Maanen and Barley 1984).

Blau and Scott (1962:69) offer evidence that among social workers and nurses "a professional orientation is inversely related to organizational loyalty. Professionals tend to be cosmopolitans and not locals." They found that those social workers who identified more strongly with their occupations were less likely to conform to administrative procedures to deliver what they believed to be the best possible service to clients. In contrast, those social workers who identified less strongly with their occupation adhered more strictly to the organization's standard operating procedures.

Commitment to one's occupation and to one's organization can be correlated yet not interfere with each other. Ritzer and Trice (1969a, 1969b) found, for example, that personnel workers' occupational commitment was slightly, but not significantly, stronger than their organizational commitment. They interpreted their results to mean that this dual loyalty arose because the personnel occupations are relatively undeveloped and historically are management-oriented and thus lack sufficient status, or meaningful enough tasks, to predominate over organizational loyalty. Somewhat similarly, Sim Sitkin and Kathleen Sutcliffe (1991) found in their study of pharmacists that, even though they were loyal to both their organizations and their occupation, neither occupational nor organizational forces dominated in influencing the performance of specific tasks.

Several recent studies have looked at dual union and organizational commitment (Fukami and Larsen 1984; Angle and Perry 1986; Magenan, Martin, and Peterson 1988). Although their methods vary somewhat, the results of these studies agree substantially. Dual commitment is not unusual and is most likely to occur in situations in which union-management relations are good and job satisfaction is high. Only when these relations are bad, or job satisfaction is low, do employees commit themselves to their union only.

Another obvious question that arises is how much control occupational subcultures exert over their members compared with organizational cultures. Two simple structural indexes of the relative potency of an occupational subculture are the number of members of the occupation who are in the organization and the multiplicity of cultural forms that convey the occupation's ideologies. The number of members is important insofar as only one or two members cannot provide one another enough support to form a potent subculture. Given how isolated they are, these members are likely to be treated as tokens by upper management. At the same time, a group that includes more than a handful of members of the same occupation can usually provide enough support to its members to form a viable subculture. Further, the more their roles enable them to interact with other members of the occupation who are relatively isolated from the organization, the more powerful their occupational identity and subculture will be.

It also seems that occupations that have many different cultural forms have greater effects on their members than those that do not. Having well-defined rites of passage and numerous and popular myths, heroes, jargon, rituals, and taboos are all evidence of the presence of a relatively potent occupational subculture. This is especially true of potent socialization practices and clear-cut rites of passage into the occupation. The presence of these cultural forms usually means there is more potent commitment and a common identity. For example, some occupations (as discussed in chapter 5) require much longer and more arduous training than others, and other occupations (as discussed in chapter 1) require members to face constant danger. When members increase their investments by meeting arduous demands, they experience increased commitment to the entity that made those demands.

SUMMARY

Since members of occupations typically practice inside organizations, occupations can be thought of as subcultures. They differ from the core organizational culture in that they either overemphasize its ideology or deviate significantly from it. In some cases, the deviations become so pronounced that a subculture becomes a counterculture.

The basic ingredients from which subcultures grow are differential interactions, although membership does not require face-to-face relations. For instance, the mass media, go-betweens, electronic mail, and "weak-ties" formed among dispersed members act to connect small clusters with one another.

Occupational groups can be significant influences in organizations. Such groups adhere to the occupational principle, in one way or another. Although its strength varies, this principle has the potential to become the basis for significant differences between members of the occupation and management. Moreover, environmental forces can pressure organizations to import members of occupations to ensure the organization's legitimacy. Finally, although occupational countercultures seem to be infrequent, there are, nevertheless, prominent instances of their existence.

In contrast, managers form subcultures around the administrative principle. They embrace the ideologies of rationality and claim they are its practitioners. Because of their position in the organization's bureaucracy, members of administrative subcultures become defined as having the power to instruct subordinates in what to do and how to do it. Historically, administrative subcultures are a recent invention; nevertheless, they are now a taken-for-granted aspect of everyday life in modern America.

The potency of the clash that can occur between the occupational principle and the administrative principle was illustrated during the launching of the ill-fated Challenger spacecraft. The clash was embodied within one individual: the vice-president of engineering. As an engineer, he opposed the launch; as a high-level manager, he supported it.

7. Adaptations between Occupational and Administrative Subcultures

Most occupations perform their distinctive work within an organizational setting where they must negotiate with managers who believe in the administrative principle: only management knows how to act rationally.
— William J. Sonnenstuhl and Harrison M. Trice

IN THIS CHAPTER we will review and expand on the four types of occupational subcultures introduced in chapter 2. We will explore further how these subcultures generate various adjustment patterns in organizational settings as they interrelate with administrative subcultures.

Broadly speaking, occupational and administrative subcultures disagree on the content of work and the terms of employment. By content of work, we mean who will be permitted to perform a specific set of tasks and with what degree of autonomy. By terms of employment, we mean how workers will be compensated for their efforts and the general conditions under which they will perform those tasks. Although both concerns are of interest to most workers, because it goes to the heart of what it means to be an occupation, a prominent issue for occupations is the maintenance of a sizable measure of control over their distinctive tasks (Freidson 1985). As important as issues of compensation and resources may be to members of occupations, there is nothing about this issue that is distinctive to occupational life. Consequently, it is more important for occupations to protect their degree of control over the content of their work. Relative to the well-established occupations, this point can be illustrated as follows:

> The inherent conflict between managers and professionals results basically from a clash of cultures: The corporate culture, which captures the commitment of managers, and the professional culture, which socializes professionals. Both cultures are further sustained by the wider social culture. Briefly, professionals who are

salaried, namely scientists, engineers, lawyers, accountants, teachers and the like who work in organizations rather than private practice, are socialized through their disciplines and culture to carry out their technical responsibilities as members of a professional group. . . . Managers, on the other hand, undergo a different kind of socialization. Their formal education . . . emphasizes interdisciplinary and practical approaches to problem solving. Managers are further expected to learn the bulk of their craft on the job (Raelin 1985:2).

Since occupational and managerial subcultures tend to clash over the content of work, they must develop ways of adapting to one another. That is, as they negotiate about how to structure their interactions and relationships, they must work out some form of adaptation. It is worth repeating at this point that each of the occupational subcultures described in chapter 2 typically must adapt to management subcultures operating within an administrative hierarchy. Managers from this hierarchy represent the administrative ideology that seeks to control not only the terms of work but the content of job roles (Kraft 1979; Shaiken 1984). That is, they seek to influence decisions about who will be deemed qualified to do the work and to direct how it will be done. Although the levels of bureaucratic and administrative control may vary depending on the size of the organization, the extent of centralization, and the number of formal rules (Scott 1965), the administrative principle nevertheless seems to operate rather consistently (Jackall 1988; England and Lee 1974; Guth and Taniuri 1965).

GROUP-GRID ANALYSIS OF OCCUPATIONAL SUBCULTURES

As reviewed briefly in chapter 2, group-grid analysis (Douglas 1978, 1982) provides a framework for constructing different ideal occupational subcultures within organizations.[1] Recall that, according to group-grid analysis, all cultures can be classified on two dimensions: the group dimension and the grid dimension. When combined, these variables describe the shape of a culture's internal social relationships.

When applied to occupations, the group dimension assesses the degree of collectiveness among members. It provides a measure of the pressure members place on one another to conform to collective expectations and the protection membership bestows on members (Mars

1. These adaptations are from Sonnenstuhl and Trice 1991.

1982). In occupations at the strong end of the group dimension, the boundary between insiders and outsiders is tightly drawn and members are encouraged to relate primarily to one another. In occupations at the weak end, members may interact with whomever they choose, free of group restraints. Cultures with strong group pressures are rich in cultural forms that emphasize the collective life and separate it from others, thereby establishing clear social boundaries and underscoring who is, and who is not, a member (Mars 1982).

The grid dimension assesses the ordering of occupational life in terms of roles and positions within the occupation, that is, in terms of social structure. In occupations at the strong end of the grid dimension, individual behavior is tightly constrained by formal rules; in occupations at the weak end, individual behavior is constrained by few if any rules, so that group members have a great deal of freedom to behave as they choose toward one another. Cultures that are strong on the grid dimension are rich in cultural forms that emphasize one's place and role relative to those of other members; they emphasize hierarchical authority, formal rules, impersonal relations, differential rewards, and the division of labor (Douglas 1982; Mars 1982).

ACCOMMODATIVE OCCUPATIONAL SUBCULTURES
(STRONG GRID/STRONG GROUP)

To maintain their cultures, accommodative occupational subcultures (strong grid/strong group) compromise the occupational principle by balancing (accommodating) their definitions of their culture and procedures against those of the managerial administration so that neither subculture prevails. Mutual toleration and agreed-upon working arrangements enable both sides to keep their ideologies and cultural forms intact.

Typically, members of strong grid/strong group occupations practice in large-scale, bureaucratized organizations. To fit their occupation's practice into such an organizational context, they cannot avoid the formal rules and hierarchical structures that exist. At the same time, they retain their distinctive occupational cultures and maintain their own internal administrative arrangements (i.e., their own grid arrangements). A rather fine-tuned equilibrium between the two subcultures results.

Corporate physicians, who have managed to accommodate themselves to both management and union concerns, express the struggle to maintain balance as follows: "Physicians accept production as a priority too; we do work in that situation, and that priority to a lesser or greater degree takes priority over health. You just have to bargain to sort of push health a bit; they push production, and you bargain" (Walters 1982:2).

Within organizations, members of strong grid/strong group occupations have a rank vis-à-vis the members of the other occupations with whom they interact, as well as a ranking system within their own group (i.e., their grid dimension). At the same time, the boundary around the group is drawn tightly according to definitions of who is an insider, and members interact primarily with one another in performing their tasks. The managerial administration generally controls such terms of employment as salary adjustments, but the occupation retains firm control over the actual content of its work. For instance, administrators determine a corporate physician's salary, but the physician, in the privacy of his or her consulting room, decides whether or not to prescribe drugs, patients' recuperation times, and such. Thus, even though members of well-established occupations work for organizations, they often retain a substantial degree of independence.

At the same time, a corporate physician's decision concerning, for example, whether an employee is fit to work often must be justified to the company's management and union as well as to outside arbitrators (Walters 1982; Walsh 1986). Accommodative subcultures must often incorporate into their tasks chores that their colleagues in other settings might regard as anomalous, even deviant, behavior. For instance, corporate physicians are responsible for assessing employees' excuses for absenteeism, for certifying employees' fitness to work, for reviewing workers' compensation claims, for evaluating occupational health hazards, and for operating health-education and disease-prevention programs. Their colleagues working in other milieus would probably regard these tasks as outside the practice of medicine.

Meat cutting represents another occupation that has achieved accommodation with management (Walsh 1989). Unlike industrial physicians and corporate attorneys, but like unionized crafts workers in the construction industry, meat cutters have achieved this accommodation through unionization rather than licensure. Meat cutters have a body of knowledge, training programs, and occupational associations. Further, they have retained considerable control over their domain by enlisting support from customers who prefer special cuts, by taking control of new technologies (i.e., power saws, wrapping machines) as they have been introduced into meat departments, and by compromising with their administrations on the establishment of new classifications of workers (e.g., seafood clerks and deli clerks). At the same time, however, they have preserved their traditional three-year apprenticeship program. As John P. Walsh (1987:13) has said, "As a result of the cutters' enclosure of their department, . . . [they] . . . are given only loose guidelines and output requirements and are free to do the rest in the most efficient or convenient way." The accommodation between the administration and the meat cutters is graphically illustrated by the following description:

> I asked a union leader for permission to interview some members. He called them at work and set up appointments for me to see them while they were working. I asked if I should ask the store manager's permission to interview in the store. He said, "No, just tell the head cutter I sent you." In fact, I interviewed a cutter in the back room, while he was working. A co-manager came back during the interview and used a nearby phone, saw me and my tape recorder, but said nothing about it (Walsh 1987:13).

A study by Arthur L. Stinchcombe (1959) suggests that skilled craftspeople in the construction industry can perform their various tasks without much direction and control from supervisors or clerical support because their work is guided by the standards of a well-defined body of knowledge and the craftsmanship that comes from it. Career commitment is to the occupation, not to a construction company, making for a relatively strong grid dimension as well as a strong group dimension. These features are underscored by the large seasonal fluctuations in both the volume of the work to be done and its product mix. In all three of these occupations—corporate medicine, meat cutting, and construction work—members perform many of those functions that might normally be performed by management: planning, directing, and controlling work processes (Freidson 1986; Stinchcombe 1959).

Corporate law is another example of an occupation with a strong grid/strong group pattern that has accommodated to bureaucratic administrations. Like industrial physicians, in-house lawyers have achieved such accommodation because of their culture. Corporate lawyers share with lawyers everywhere a belief in the rule of law, a common body of knowledge (e.g., legal jargon, rituals of jurisprudence) that is not readily intelligible to laypersons, common training experiences, and a powerful occupational association to represent their interests (Spangler 1986).

Although corporate attorneys worry about compromising their autonomy, they nevertheless retain control over the day-to-day content and administration of their work. Like corporate physicians, they have accomplished this through state licensure, which ensures that only attorneys can practice law. The structure of legal departments reflects this mandate. It is typically headed by a corporate general counsel, who is a lawyer, and is staffed by lawyers who are mentored in corporate practice by senior colleagues and whose performance is scrutinized regularly by their peers. The law department is a self-contained entity for purposes of evaluation and reward even when its members are physically dispersed among divisions or subsidiaries of the company. This arrangement protects the autonomy of the department and ensures that the business activities of executives are adequately monitored.

Companies routinely require managers to seek legal clearance for business projects; the attorneys review the legal implications of every deal in light of the environment, product safety, Securities and Exchange Commission laws, labor laws, antitrust laws, and fair trade standards. Business executives frequently view their company's lawyers as "deal killers" and sometimes refer to the law department as the "Department of Profit Prevention." Nonetheless, by most accounts, staff lawyers rarely have to veto a suggested business project insofar as executives rarely ignore the attorney's estimate of legal risk. When executives do ignore legal advice, the decision is referred to higher management levels both within the law department and the business division: "The lawyer says to the manager, 'I am bumping your decision up one level, so that my manager goes to your manager.' And that continues all the way up to [the general counsel] talking to the president if the issue is strong enough" (Spangler 1986:94). Lawyers claim that when this happens "the problem goes away" (Spangler 1986:99). Corporate attorneys are thus able to protect their autonomy, control the content of their work, and claim that they seldom are pressured to compromise their professional judgment. Lawyers claim that the administrators are forced to accommodate the deal killers.

In reality, however, the complete insulation of corporate law departments from administration is impossible because management controls the terms of the attorneys' employment. For instance, management dictates the number of staff, their salary range, and the length of their career ladder. Law departments are often understaffed, and the attorneys receive less salary, enjoy less prestige, and have fewer chances for advancement than their counterparts in law firms. These conditions prompt many attorneys to leave their occupation and seek management positions, a decision reinforced by law professors' admonitions to learn from business and by the encouragement of the department's general counsel. Although the terms of employment prompt attorneys to leave their occupation, these conditions do not appear to erode their control over their work (Spangler 1986).

Another example of an accommodative subculture is composed of military psychiatrists whom Arlene K. Daniels (1969) describes as "captive professionals." According to her account, they are frequently pressured to make diagnoses that legitimate the decisions of commanding officers or military courts. In addition, she argues, their judgments are given consideration by only a few commanders, while others ignore them and demand conformity to the military hierarchy. Because of their marginal and insecure position within their occupation, military psychiatrists are probably more vulnerable to cooptation by a managerial subculture than are corporate physicians. Consequently, they frequently experience conflict about making independent decisions within the context of their military responsibilities. Nevertheless, the military hierarchy and psychiatrists have worked out accommodations with one another. The psychiatrists retain control of the content of their work because the military hierarchy cannot appoint just anyone that it wants to do psychiatric work. Further, the psychiatrists still control entrance to the occupation and still decide how its major tasks will be carried out because only they are deemed qualified to decide who is capable of doing psychiatric work.

ASSIMILATED OCCUPATIONAL SUBCULTURES (WEAK GROUP/STRONG GRID)

As occupations of the weak group/strong grid type interact with company managers the mode of adaptation is assimilation. That is, members take on the ideologies and administrative forms of bureaucratic managers, thereby making for a strong grid but weakening the occupation's culture. In effect, the administrative principle prevails. This absorption may occur either because the ideologies of the subculture are compatible with those of management or because of management's aggressiveness and forceful efforts to fracture, redistribute, and control the occupation's tasks and body of knowledge. In either case, management is able to exert control over both the task content of the occupational role and the administrative terms of employment surrounding it. From management's perspective, thorough assimilation is the goal. This amounts to deskilling (Braverman 1974) or deprofessionalizing (Rothman 1984) of the occupation and, as in the case of printers, leads to the erosion of the occupation's culture.

The experience of printers stands in contrast with that of meat cutters, construction workers, corporate lawyers, and physicians, for example, and underscores the ever-present determination of some managerial subcultures to assert the managerial principle aggressively. Printers were once considered the epitome of skilled blue-collar craftsmen (Wallace and Kalleberg 1982). They had an occupational community (Lipset, Trow, and Coleman 1956) that served them well in resisting the introduction of computerized typesetting. In the United States, however, the International Typographers Union signed a historic agreement allowing publishers to automate composing rooms as quickly as possible while guaranteeing the printers lifetime job security. Since then, the union's culture has been dramatically assimilated, and today the union exercises little control over printers working conditions and entry into their craft.

In Britain, by contrast, printers have retained control of their domain because they continue to set journalists' copy into type—albeit on computer terminals rather than linotype machines. From the perspective of the British trade unionists, the American unions bargained away the interests of their members far too cheaply, failing to build the links with other unions that would have enabled them to control new technology as it was introduced.

Engineering is another example of an assimilated occupation. Unlike printers, however, engineers readily become assimilated by management because their ideologies are quite compatible with those of management. They convert easily to the administrative principle, readily accepting management's bureaucratic arrangements. Thus, they acquire a strong grid system but a culture vulnerable to absorption by management. Indeed, Robert Perrucci and Joel Gerstl (1969), underscoring the lack of cohesiveness in engineering, refer to it as an occupation without a community of shared values, and Reginald Carter

(1977:125) concluded from his study that "engineers in industry are probably more like managers than different from them."

A second set of findings confirms this tendency: "Engineers who hold staff positions over a decade are less involved in their work than are those whose jobs include managerial duties" (Bailyn 1977:116). According to David F. Noble (1977), the modern occupation of engineering was created and supported by corporate capitalism. Not surprisingly, E. Layton (1971) and Monte Calvert (1967) call it a "business profession," one dominated by the interests it serves. Noble (1977: 44) notes, "As they increasingly tended to identify their professional status with their corporate status, their pursuit of professionalism became, at the same time, a crucial aspect of the corporate management of technical knowledge and technical people: The corporate control of technology."

Engineers do perceive of themselves as craft workers, however, and do enjoy a great deal of autonomy in their jobs, but these occupational characteristics do not create a capacity to resist managerial authority (Zussman 1985). Although some observers (Veblen 1921; Bell 1973) argue that the concern of engineers for technical efficiency brings them into conflict with management's efforts to maximize profits, engineers themselves see no such conflict:

> [The engineers] argue that their work is inherently economic in character; *cost is itself a criterion of a technical efficiency*. Cost is a parameter of their work, no different in principle from the physical properties of a metal. They do not experience a tension between the logic of efficiency and the logic of profit maximization precisely because their very concept of efficiency is shaped by consideration of profitability (Zussman 1985:120–21, emphasis in original).

Engineers readily seek managerial positions, manifesting little regret for the loss of their occupations. According to R. Zussman:

> Engineers are not notably loyal to their employers or their occupation. . . . They [do not] feel an obligation to remain with the company or in engineering against the logic of careers. Rather, most of the young engineers . . . are prepared to leave their employer in search of better pay or more rapid promotions (1985:157–58).

Accountants, as we have already seen, also hold occupational ideologies akin to those of managers. They view themselves as "designers of order" (Montagna 1973:142) and assume a conservative function in which they play a role as a reducer of ignorance and a preserver of order and the status quo. Thus, they believe that accounting functions to generate consensus and governance over systems by means of rational knowledge and that there is no inherent conflict between the basic stance of professionalized occupations and bureaucratic, hierarchical management systems (Ritzer 1975).

Two additional studies have also made this point: J. Sorensen and T. Sorensen (1974) and R. Lachman and N. Aranya (1986) point out that over time the occupational orientation of new accountants entering work organizations is increasingly replaced by an organizational orientation that reflects managerial ideologies and administrative procedures. That is, accountants come to prefer managerial priorities over the occupational preferences they learned during their formal education. Like engineers, they readily adapt, and fit into, management's administrative apparatus and make it their own. Thus, there is a strong grid dimension, but, again, they did not create it and this weakens their group dimension.

The various personnel occupations—often referred to as human resources management and its specialties—also fall into the strong grid/weak group category. Like accounting and engineering, their early history is closely associated with the history of management. In the early twentieth century, managers embraced welfare work and scientific management as a specialization within their ranks (Eilbert 1959). Many writers agree that modern human resources work grew from these two early movements (Miller and Coghill 1961). From them originated the traditional personnel functions: selection and placement, job analysis, wage and salary administration, safety and hygiene, and employee training. These functions called for personnel workers to follow the same formal rationality that dominated the work lives of those in management subcultures (Watson 1978).

Until World War II, these management practices were rather uncommon. The war, however, produced unprecedented federal intervention in personnel practices: "Government agencies fostered a widespread diffusion of personnel innovations . . . by mandating specific models of employment, by providing incentives for organizations to create or expand personnel departments and bureaucratic controls" (Baron, Dobbins, and Jennings 1986:378). This widespread diffusion of personnel practices and bureaucratic procedures ensured that a cluster of personnel occupations, whose members would soon claim to be professionals, would emerge. But, like engineers and accountants, the members of the personnel occupations are responsive to and relatively compatible with the managerial interests they serve. Their grid system is, in fact, a vital part of the administrative procedures of management itself.

Computer programming is another example of an occupation that has been assimilated into managerial subcultures (Orlikowski 1988), providing it with a strong grid but weakening its group dimension. Computing as a technology is relatively young; consequently, the occupation that has grown up around it is still developing. It has a growing body of knowledge (e.g., technical jargon, organizing myths, academic courses and programs), but

> the profession lacks an organizational means of internal mobilization or communication. The absence of organizations and publications that effectively define the nature of professionalism and the standards of work and ethics by default places those functions in the hands of firms that hire EDP (Electronic Data Processors) workers (Fidel and Garner 1987:17).

In the early days of computing, computer programmers effectively used a number of strategies to retain control over their work, including norms that denied outsiders' competence, protective myths, norms of secrecy, and control over training and recruitment practices (Pettigrew 1973). During the rapid spread of computers, however, corporate managers quickly demystified the work, leaving members of the occupation in semiautonomous control over day-to-day activities but nevertheless characterized by significant amounts of bureaucratic structure and supervision (Fidel and Garner 1987). As systems analysis and computer programming became separate clusters of distinct tasks, members of the former occupation tended to identify with their employing organization significantly more than the latter did because they believed they were furthering the objectives of senior managers (Hebden 1975). Computer programmers, in contrast, appear to lack a commitment to or an identity with either their occupation or their employing organization (Fidel and Garner 1987).

DOMINATING OCCUPATIONAL SUBCULTURES (STRONG GROUP/WEAK GRID)

Strong group/weak grid subcultures embrace the occupational principle, tenaciously retaining control over the content of their work and how it is administered. They follow somewhat the pattern of the guilds of the Middle Ages (Kranzberg and Gies 1975) and craftlike occupations with strong grid dimension of today (Smigel 1964; Montagna 1973; Nelson 1988). Dominating occupations

> are characterized by strong group relations because they are able to restrict full membership to those who have completed occupationally prescribed training and exclude those who are not bonafide insiders. Consequently, members frequently interact within a mutually interconnecting network with others with whom they share a consciousness of kind, and their occupational roles become a blue print for guiding their behavior outside of work (Sonnenstuhl and Trice 1991:300).

Members of these occupations tend to believe they must be vigilant about defending the boundaries of their occupation so as to prevent the uninitiated from performing their distinctive tasks. At the same time, of necessity, a grid system of administrative rules and hierarchical authority comes into existence within the culture to routinize and implement the work in which the occupation specializes. The occupation, in effect, generates its own administration to which it must adapt. Because the group dimension is so strong, however, the grid dimension tends to be weak. Usually the hierarchy is relatively flat and has roughly three ranks that, in one way or another, reflect those of traditional crafts: apprentice, journeyman, and master. Because all members have experienced the required occupational training, few members direct other members' work. Rather, members have internalized the rules about how to perform and therefore can be given a great deal of autonomy over the content of their work.

Nonetheless, "the rank and file have to take orders just as clerical workers have to, [but] these orders are given by a subordinate colleague, not by someone trained in management or some other field" (Freidson 1984:1, 12) The question, as always, is who performs the administrative function: a member of the occupation who is obeyed because of his or her expertise or an outsider who must be obeyed because of his or her position within the organization? The mode of adjustment by the occupational community becomes one of dominating and permeating this administrative apparatus.

Within law firms (Smigel 1964) and accounting firms (Montagna 1968), for example, management functions are performed by members of the occupation who bring their occupational ideology to the task of administration. Rank-and-file members of the organization exercise autonomy over the technical aspects of their day-to-day work, accept some but not all administrative constraints, and accept technical supervision so long as it is carried out by a respected member of the occupation (Baldridge 1981; Nathanson 1971; Smigel 1964; Spangler and Lehman 1982; Montagna 1974; Reeves 1980). As a result, persistent conflict seldom arises between the rank and file and managers as long as the occupation remains in control of the content of its work (Freidson 1986). If members of the occupation believe that their administrative colleagues have the group's interests at heart, they usually show goodwill toward them; however, if these colleagues are perceived as pursuing the interests of administration at the expense of the group, there is likely to be a deterioration of the goodwill that will eventually lead to a change in the hierarchy by the members of the occupation (Feldman 1987). Such instances are reaffirmations of the proper order of things: survival of the occupational community comes first.

Large law firms are guildlike organizations that have a hierarchy of partners (i.e., the masters) and associates (i.e., the journeymen) in which the partners own the business and make the administrative decisions (Spangler 1986; Smigel 1964; Tolbert 1985). They decide from which law schools to recruit newcomers, which senior partners will mentor which newcomers, when associates will begin work on their own cases, and on which teams associates will work. Throughout the socialization process, the partners strive to strengthen the skills of their junior colleagues; successful mentoring produces autonomous craftspeople who believe that the essential task of an attorney who provides legal advice to corporate clients is to "think like a lawyer" (Spangler 1986:66). Virtually all the rules are made by the partners, and the associates must adhere to them if they wish to become partners too. According to Eve Spangler (1986:66), "Associates seem to be blinded to the manipulative quality of bureaucratic rule-making in part because the rules enshrine domination by fellow professionals rather than by business people, and in part because their daily experiences depend less upon the rules than upon their relations with mentors and sponsors."

One major change that has affected some of the rules is the decreasing dependence of corporations on law firms. Another has been the accelerated growth in both the size and numbers of these firms. As Pamela S. Tolbert and Robert N. Stern note (1988:4): "Between 1960 and 1986, the number of firms employing more than 100 lawyers grew from less than a dozen to over 250. Both the average number of lawyers in a firm and the number of firms with more than 50 lawyers have increased dramatically." In spite of these profound changes, however, based on a study of two hundred large law firms, Tolbert and Stern report that promotion decisions for young lawyers, by and large, remain under the control of the firms' partners. In contrast, compensation decisions have come more and more to be separated from professional control and to be tied to the administrative hierarchy (i.e., to concerns for profitability).

Law schools, however, still appear to be dominated largely by faculty lawyers. Steven P. Feldman (1987) reports on a case in which a dissident group of faculty at a large law school were able to force out a dean even though two outside evaluations had supported him. Indeed, a detailed case study of four law firms revealed little direct evidence of centralized control by the administrative side. If anything, power was more evenly distributed among more members rather than in the hands of a few partners (Nelson 1988).

Employees of secondary schools also perform administrative functions. School systems, for instance, can be viewed as two subcultures, of superintendents and of teachers, of a larger occupational community, education. Many contemporary writers (e.g., Lortie 1975) argue that the administrative subculture of superintendents dominates that of teachers. This, however, misses a historically relevant fact. During the latter half of the nineteenth century, the state moved to bureaucratize schooling, and, to maintain control of the education process, teachers established within schools of education an administrative track based on the then prominent ideology of scientific management (Larson 1977; Meyer and Rowan 1977). Viewed from this perspective, school administration is advancing the interests of the occupation in the face of state demands.

Similarly, police and social welfare agencies may be seen as attempting to maintain and advance the interests of their particular occupational communities in the face of state pressures. Pressed by the state to bureaucratize, the police and social workers established administrative tracks within their own schools. Courses in criminal justice administration and social work administration may include heavy doses of management theory, but that theory is intended to be used in the service of preserving the occupation's control over the content of its work, even if the terms of its employment may be in the hands of the state and local legislatures who control the purse strings.

The weak group/weak grid mode of adaptation emerges when an occupation, or a group of occupations, attempts to abandon both the administrative principle and the occupational principle. Members make a conscious attempt to construct a work organization in which everyone has a voice in formulating what tasks need to be done and how these tasks are to be performed. Prominent examples of these organizations are free schools where neither the teachers nor the administrators have strong influence because the norms and values favor individuality and shifting preferences over structured effort. Mars (1982:28) characterizes this mode of organization as follows:

> This is the type [of organization] that emphasizes entrepreneurality, where the individual's freedom to transact on his own terms is highly valued; where individual flair is at a premium . . . along with resistance to external constraints and the high value placed on independence.

Health collectives often contain doctors, nurses, and dieticians who seek to demystify medical practice by teaching nonprofessional volunteers to perform some services and patients are taught to take care of themselves as much as possible (Rothschild and Whitt 1986). And at alternative-style newspapers, the entire staff tends to become involved in reporting on and writing stories, rather than individual reporters and editors. Such ideologies and practices greatly weaken the occupational principle. The administrative principle is also weakened by the tendencies of these organizations to view decisions as "morally binding only if they reflect the will of the collectivity and are arrived at through a process of democratic consensus" (Rothschild and Whitt 1986:50).

In their pursuit of egalitarianism, occupations in this mode purposefully devise weak group/weak grid relationships. As a result, the occupations involved often have weak boundaries because they employ members on the basis of friendship, political attitudes, and informally acquired knowledge rather than membership within the occupations (Sonnenstuhl and Trice 1991). Further, since rules are based on group consensus and members have the right to veto decisions, members of the organization have considerable control over each other. Consequently, members spend a significant amount of their time debating what it is they should be doing and who should be doing it (Rothschild and Whitt 1986; Jackall and Crain 1984).

In one such organization, the Midwest Community Mental Health Center, made up of social workers, psychologists, and vocational and motivational counselors, meetings and storytelling constituted the cultural forms that enabled some ongoing definitions of roles to emerge in the organization. Helen B. Schwartzman (1984:91) described the dynamics:

> Meetings in this context are a form for group interaction, for interpretation, construction and reconstruction of events; stories are a form for individual interpretation, construction, and reconstruction of events. Both of these forms provide individuals and the organization with a way to create and then discover the meaning of what it is they are doing and saying. In an organized anarchy these activities are essential because they are the only way available for the organization to constitute itself to its members and for members to legitimate their actions to each other.

These organizations are organized anarchies (March and Olsen 1976) that are characterized by their (1) ambiguous and inconsistent goals, (2) unclear and fuzzy technologies, (3) fluid participation of members, (4) unpredictable environments, and (5) confusing histories. According to J. F. Padgett (1980), individuals working in organized anarchies do not have a clear view of what they are trying to do, how they should do it, who should be doing it, where they are doing it, or what they have already done.

Although the ideology of a democratic workplace is appealing to Americans, there are relatively few cultural forms available to communicate it to workers. Since the basic ideology, in effect, is that everyone is often free to make his or her own way, there are few collective representations of such organizations and those there are are ambiguous. Consequently, members of such organizations must continually invent new ways of making sense of what they are doing. For instance, Schwartzman (1984) found that almost all participants in the Midwest Community Mental Health Center characterized it as a "crazy house" because everything about its operation was ambiguous: What were its goals and mode of operation? Who represented the community? Who was in charge?

Democratic communities can be found in a broad range of work enterprises, including producer cooperatives, alternative schools, food cooperatives, rape crisis centers, feminist health collectives, and free schools (Jackall and Levin 1984; Case and Taylor 1979; Swidler 1979). They tend to be in special niches of the economy, such as custom and craft production, services where they are not in direct competition with capitalist enterprises, and relatively labor-intensive fields where the costs of entry are low (Rothschild 1986). Licensed occupations, such as medicine and law, are often instrumental in setting up collectives, but their services are generally limited to clients who cannot afford to pay for the services of established professionals. They are therefore not in competition with these professionals.

Rothschild and Whitt (1986) provide a number of excellent examples of democratic communities; the Haight-Asbury Free Clinic is one. Initially established by professionals at the health department in San Francisco to provide alternative health services to black, Chicano, and counterculture youth, the clinic has been successful in prompting participants to organize other free clinics to provide "health care for the whole person, mind, and body."

Under California State law, the Haight-Asbury clinic had to have a board of directors, so it recruited prestigious members from the community. Its first director was sympathetic to worker participation but did not wish to have the clinic organized as a collective; rather, he designated six coordinators to head up the administrative, medical, educational, and counseling components. Decisions were made at meetings of the members of each component, at weekly staff meetings, and at monthly board of directors meetings.

The first director resigned, and the staff had to struggle with the board of directors to reassert its collective principles (e.g., equal pay, staff control). Eventually, the staff forced those board members who wished to develop an administrative hierarchy to resign and appointed new ones who were sympathetic to their principles.

Medical, counseling, and health-education services were performed by trained volunteers. The medical component, for instance, was staffed by two physicians, a medical coordinator (who was also a nurse), and six to eight volunteer advocates. The advocates, who completed a two- to three-month training program, attended component meetings, at which issues were decided relevant to the medical component and new medical information was disseminated. They also took medical histories and attempted to ensure that the doctor understood the patient's problems and that the patient understood the doctor's diagnosis and treatment. Generally, they worked to demystify medical practice and teach the patients to take care of themselves.

Other democratic communities, such as law collectives, share the characteristics of the free clinic. All strive to protect the democratic process of decision making and to demystify the organization's enterprise by teaching its secrets to all members and clients.

Although collective democratic organizations create a great deal of commitment in members, they are also very stressful because of the inordinate amount of time spent in meetings and arguing about what is "right" (Rothschild and Whitt 1986). For some members of the Midwest Community Mental Health Center, for instance, working there "was undignified, unprofessional, just plain craziness, but it was fun in a way." For other staff, it was often frustrating, sometimes "unreal," and in some instances very traumatic. One ex–staff member reported having nightmares about the center two years after he resigned (Schwartzman 1984:90).

Although the ideology of an egalitarian workplace is appealing, democratic communities are difficult to maintain (Rothschild-Whitt 1979; Rothschild and Whitt 1986; Whyte and Whyte 1988). Believing that the Iron Law of Oligarchy (Michels 1949) applies to all organizations, many theorists have predicted that collective democracies eventually yield to administrative rationality and evolve into new organizations based on that ideology. Rothschild-Whitt (1979) suggests a number of factors that work against collective democracy and push toward administrative rationality: the large amount of time required to reach consensus, the homogeneity of group members, the emotional intensity of decision making, prior nondemocratic socialization, bureaucratic demands made by outside funding and licensing agencies, and inevitable individual differences in talents, skills, knowledge, and personality. Katherine Newman (1980) argues that environmental constraints force collective democratic organizations to yield to administrative rationality. Once they apply to and become dependent on traditional funding sources for financial support, they are forced by agencies to become bureaucratized. In some instances, this may lead to organizational collapse if members refuse to develop a bureaucratic hierarchy; if members are willing to compromise their egalitarian principles, however, the organization may continue as a "bureaucratic collective."

Similarly, Schwartzman, Anita Kneifel, and Merton Krause (1978) document how the community board of a large mental health center pressed the staff to behave more bureaucratically and professionally than egalitarianly. After a new director was hired, staff meetings became more bureaucratized administrative functions instead of communal therapeutic events. According to one staff member: "You'd really be surprised at the Center now. . . . Staff meetings are really short and it's not heavy like it used to be, it's much more positive. Maybe people have negative feelings, but they keep it to themselves" (107).

In other cases, collective democracy may give way to the occupational principle. This is likely to occur in collectives that provide "professional services," such as free medical clinics, law collectives, and alternative schools. According to Rothschild and Whitt (1986:121): "The collectivist organization is facilitated . . . by having a professional base in its community. The local environment most favorable to the development of participatory-democratic organizations would combine a vulnerable target institution, which leaves significant local need unmet, with a large and supportive professional population."

Such alternative institutions appear to survive as long as the members of the occupations who normally deliver such services are willing to tolerate their existence. But even in these cases, the occupational principle seems always ready to assert itself. In the law collective studied by Rothschild and Whitt (1986), for example, attorneys freely shared their expertise with members who were not attorneys and encouraged them to practice law, but the state of California restrained the use of their knowledge, asserting that only licensed lawyers could plead cases before the bench. Similarly, one woman at a collective newspaper quit rather than rotate out of reporting into another function (Rothschild and Whitt 1986), and the associate director of a community mental health center could not stop acting like a social worker: "She is a group worker and that is the way she functions. She was constantly being the group worker while *she was saying to the group we must all be open, we must all equally participate as we share our guts so we know ourselves*" (Schwartzman et al. 1978:105; emphasis in the original).

According to Jackall and J. Crain (1984), those democratic collectives that survive must deal creatively with three contradictions: (1) deprofessionalism versus the need for expertise; (2) freedom versus cohesion, and (3) spontaneity versus the need for permanence. Deprofessionalism, which has been a hallmark of democratic collectives since the 1960s, has often produced antirationalism, even antiintellectualism, which promotes a search for simple answers to complex questions. Those collectives that survive must recognize that

> business today requires more expertise than ever before. Markets are more segmented and complicated; competition is more intense; and the need for long-term rational planning is a necessity. . . . Cooperatives have to find better ways to integrate experts or at least expert structure and ideology. . . . Some cooperatives are beginning to recognize that the goal of deprofessionalization may depend on a judicious reliance on professionals (Jackall and Crain 1984:99).

DYNAMIC NATURE OF ADAPTATIONS

Although the types of occupational subcultures described above capture some of the major features of their adaptations, they do so in a static fashion. Adaptation is a dynamic process that takes place over time. Such a perspective places less emphasis on occupations as communities pursuing control over the content of their work and moves toward a more complex notion, that occupational subcultures are dynamic forms that are constructed and reconstructed in their interactions and ongoing negotiations with management. Adaptation is an interplay of in-place arrangements with ongoing dynamic actions (Strauss et al. 1964). A striking example of this point is the rapid change that can occur in *egalitarian subcultures (weak group/weak grid)* that are pressured to become more bureaucratic. For instance, they may become increasingly assimilated by a management hierarchy. Writing about alternatives in community mental health organizations, Gordon P. Holleb and Walter H. Abrams (1975:146) state:

> The transformation from a consensual to a hierarchical organization occurs through numerous minor reforms and policy changes rather than one massive reorganization.. . . [It] can happen without the conscious intent of the staff. Soon the staff begin to realize that they have, little by little, lost many of the values upon which they were founded. . . . The staff can either assert their initial goals of

equality and consensus, or . . . move on to a more bureaucratic and hierarchical structure.

This swing to bureaucracy does not necessarily mean a total rejection of egalitarian beliefs (Jackall and Crain 1984). Even if the swing is pronounced, it may well be followed by a return to the ideology of organizational democracy tempered by an awareness of the necessity for some administrative arrangements (Ingle 1980). That is, a "bureaucratic collective," tempered by the administrative ideas it has encountered in dealing with marketplace economics and labor conditions, may well result over time.

Despite substantial differences in national cultures, this trend toward becoming a bureaucratic collective may be in keeping with some of the features of the thirteen highly successful cooperatives in the Spanish Basque town of Mondragón reported on by Davydd Greenwood (1988). These cooperatives were a subgroup of the 161 labor-managed producers' cooperatives in the province of Guipúzcoa, first formed in 1956. Commenting on the complex interdependencies of hierarchy and equality in these cooperatives, Greenwood writes:

> Outside observers often compare the cooperatives with an abstract model of the capitalist firm. From this vantage point, the cooperatives are egalitarian. . . . However, if the comparison is made with cooperatives worldwide using some sort of ideal-typical hierarchy/equality continuum, Mondragón's acceptance of hierarchical staff structures and compensation systems would place the cooperatives toward the hierarchical end. At the same time, outside observers quite reasonably put emphasis on egalitarianism and solidarity held by cooperative members themselves (1988:60).

The members of these cooperatives embrace an ideology of group solidarity rather than equality. They accept that complex processes of production require a complex division of labor and diverse skills. They, in essence, believe that "some degree of differentiation and hierarchy is inevitable. . . . They strongly emphasize solidarity, by which they mean a commitment to one set of social rules for all members and a style of interpersonal relations that asserts the equal worth of individuals at any level of the organization" (Greenwood 1988:58, 64).

The dynamics of *assimilated subcultures (weak group/strong grid)* suggest that they will be characterized over time by a further weakening of the occupations' cultures. Since the ideologies of many occupations of this type tend to be compatible with those of administrative authority, the increasing absorption of these occupations into managerial systems seems highly likely. The absorption of computer programmers and engineers into the ranks of management are examples of this trend (Shaiken 1984). But even when there is scant ideological compatibility with administrative authority, the members of some occupations, such as machinists (Littler 1982; Shaiken 1984; Jones 1982) and clerks and secretaries (Crompton and Jones 1984), have been deskilled as a result of managerial determination, making for a weaker group dimension and more absorption by management. Ronald G. Corwin (1986:226), for instance, concludes that "typing, accounting, bookkeeping and filing have all been mechanized and routinized, and the workers in those occupations subjected to cost accounting and bureaucratic modes of supervision that have encroached on their autonomy."

Management's sustained and powerful thrust toward tighter control probably will act to weaken further the group dimension of numerous other weak group/strong grid occupations, making for their absorption into managerial subcultures. Recall that the printers had at one time a strong group dimension in their occupational culture. But this once accommodative occupation has been pressured by management into a more assimilative mode. Managers and employers in the printing industry, by the introduction of new production technology, amassed the power necessary to overcome the resistance of a craft labor union (Corwin 1986).

Recent studies of air traffic controllers, printers, and teachers, as well as of clerical occupations in postal work and the insurance industry, have all revealed a similar trend toward deskilling (Cornfield 1987). Similarly, Shoshana Zuboff (1988) found that management in the telephone company she studied used a work force supervisory system that set production quotas, closely monitored each employee's output, and, most important, fragmented craft skills and allocated specific tasks to specific employees.

Even the strong group/strong grid (accommodative) subculture developed by the longshoremen has been sharply eroded over the last decade on the West Coast. The skills and knowledge necessary to load and unload cargo no longer depend on human labor. Cranes, containers, and computers have made the longshoreman largely obsolete (Betcherman and Rebne 1987).

Daniel Cornfield (1987) has argued that the destruction of occupations such as longshoring has been facilitated by factors relatively unique to these specific American industries. Their favorable market conditions have aided change, including the provision of severance pay ("buyout") for displaced workers. Further, there have been comparatively high rates of turnover among employees who had little vested interest in their employer's survival. Regardless of the causes, however, one fact is clear: distinctive occupational cultures such as printing, longshoring, and air traffic control have been dramatically deskilled and eroded.

The dynamics of *accommodative* occupational subcultures (*strong group/strong grid*) suggest that over time these occupations will seesaw back and forth between a stable and an unstable relationship with management. Evidence of this seesaw relationship comes from additional studies of deskilling efforts by management hierarchies. In these cases, management attempted to reduce the body of knowledge mastered by the given occupation to a computerized, rationalized program that could basically function even if the practitioners of the occupation did not perform the skilled tasks. But although such efforts at deskilling have been mounted vigorously, they have not been uniformly successful. John Child and colleagues (1984), for example, contrasted the impact of microelectronic technologies in banking, health care, and retail occupations. The outcomes varied relative to the occupational resources available to resist deskilling. Form (1987:44) has summarized the relevant research findings:

> Skill degradation theory found most support in early case studies of dying crafts. Later historical research into a wider set of occupations demonstrated that these early findings could not be generalized. . . . Increasingly, research has shown that skill changes depend on type of technology, industrial organization, product and labor markets, labor union strength, business power and many other factors.

As a result of these findings, it seems reasonable to assume that ongoing negotiations, bargaining, and give and take, often on a daily "touch-and-go" basis, will come to characterize the adaptations made by accommodative occupations. In brief, these adaptations are negotiated and renegotiated over time (March and Simon 1958; Bacharach and Lawler 1981). At times, and under certain conditions, they result in a weakening of an occupation's control; at other times, they result in a stalemate, and under some conditions, they result in a strength-ening of the occupation's control. A study of the recently modernized General Motors assembly plant in Linden, New Jersey, for example, found that "the skilled trades workers experienced skill upgrading and gained enhanced responsibilities, while production workers under-went deskilling and became increasingly subordinated to the new tech-nology" (Milkman and Pullman 1991:123). Apparently, adaptations are a result of numerous variables combined with bargaining, negotiating, and the effective use of resources.

Cornfield (1987) argues that specific features of the industry within which an occupation is embedded set the stage for whether the rela-tionship will be accommodative. For example, accommodative rela-tionships exist in coal mining, where miners and managers have worked out formal ways to achieve labor-management cooperation; in aircraft manufacturing, where machinists and managers have imple-mented a joint committee on technological change; and in the telecom-munications industry, where electricians and managers have similar joint labor-management committees in an attempt to foster cooperation relative to technological change. Such industries are (1) characterized by long employee tenure, (2) a high percentage of unionized workers, and (3) the presence of an external threat to the industry that jeopard-izes both job security and profits. As these conditions moderate, or worsen, the occupations accommodative stance may be eroded by an increase in management's efforts to further deskill the occupations, as has occurred among machinists and miners, thereby moving the rela-tionship toward an assimilative mode.

These insights may not be applicable to occupations such as medi-cine, law, and science, which also have strong group/strong grid cul-tures. Some scholars have suggested that the deprofessionalization of medical work is about to happen and may even be taking place and that computerized programs set up to diagnose diseases will deskill the work of physicians by codifying their knowledge (Haug 1975, 1977; McKinlay 1982). Apparently this automation has largely involved pa-tient history taking, however, and not, even in experimental settings, actual decision making. Although some experimental work has been done toward the development of programs that depend on artificial intelligence, they are still in the early stages of development, and they apparently remain largely simulated prototypes (Pople 1984). To the extent that current programs record, retrieve, and otherwise store patient records, they may have changed some aspects of medical work. Nevertheless, whether to accept these changes is still largely controlled by doctors. Rather than deskilling physicians, technological developments may actually enhance their expertise by relieving them of clerical tasks that in the past were a drain on their time and effort.

Over time, some *dominating occupational subcultures (strong group/weak grid)* come to resemble accommodative ones as they interact with administrative subcultures. Ideally, occupations of this type have powerful group features, and the administrative structures they set up are weak. When they practice within organizations where they do not dominate numerically, however, they tend to become accommodative. This process is perhaps most apparent and advanced within medicine, and it appears to be propelled by efforts to make medicine just another "big business." Originally, medical work, whether in solo practices or hospital settings, was geared toward satisfying the physicians' needs, and those individuals who were hired to manage hospitals and clinics were trained in health administration (Starr 1982). As it has become profitable for entrepreneurs to buy hospitals and other health-care organizations, however, the interests of physicians have come under attack by managers who are less sympathetic to the ideology of health care and more sympathetic to the ideology of bureaucracy and profit making. This trend has accelerated in recent years as employers, employees, insurers, and state and federal legislatures have become preoccupied with strategies for containing health-care costs.

Concerned with improving their profit margins, health-care administrators have had little choice but to put constraints on physicians. Although these efforts have prompted some to observe that doctors are becoming wage earners (Derber 1982), the constraints have largely concerned the terms of physicians' employment rather than the control of their work. That is, doctors may be constrained to accept lower fees, to use fewer diagnostic tests, and to forgo the latest in medical technology, but they have not been forced to relinquish control over their distinctive tasks of performing surgery and prescribing drugs. They retain control over these critical tasks. In adapting to corporate management, physicians appear to practice more and more in an accommodative mode. In the future, like other employees, they may have to accept reduced terms of employment. They probably will continue to exercise control over the content of their work because of the cohesiveness of their occupation, but, as physicians move out of solo and group practices and become increasingly swallowed up by large medical organizations, they may come to resemble their corporate brethren, who, as we have seen, have already assumed an accommodative mode.

SUMMARY

Viewed from inside organizations, occupations are subcultures that must relate to, and adapt to, other subcultures. One of the principal "other subcultures" they must adapt to is the managerial hierarchy, especially its upper levels. In this chapter the units of analysis were the modes of adaptation that characterize the relationships between occupational and administrative subcultures. I constructed four ideal types,[2] expanded from their definitions as presented in chapter 2, and examined some empirical instances of each.

One mode of adaptation is accommodation—each subculture adapts to the other, and there are no major changes in either one. In this mode, neither the administrative principle nor the occupational principle dominates. Another mode is assimilation—the occupational subculture is absorbed into the managerial culture. In this case, the administrative principle prevails. In the third mode, this is reversed and the occupational principle prevails: an occupation dominates over the administrative apparatus, which grew up around the occupation's practice of its distinctive body of knowledge. The fourth mode is an egalitarian one: a collection of workers reject both the occupational principle and the administrative principle, producing a democratic organization.

Occupational subcultures are dynamic entities. Thus, even if an occupational subculture currently approximates one of the ideal types, it will probably be pushed and pulled toward another type later on (Sonnenstuhl and Trice 1991). Classic examples are egalitarian subcultures. Although they initially manage to replace both the occupational and administrative principles, the passage of time and environmental conditions force them into becoming more bureaucratic and professional.

---

2. These ideal types were constructed with William Sonnenstuhl. See Sonnenstuhl and Trice 1991.

8. Adaptations between Occupational Cultures

Perhaps the unit of observation should not be individual occupations, but clusters of interdependent occupations that appear in different types of work organizations.
—William Form

A S PROMINENT AS the adaptions between occupations and management may be, numerous other arenas of adaptation remain. One is that between occupational cultures themselves.

This chapter examines some of the processes by which occupational cultures adapt to one another. Although these processes may take numerous forms, the chapter is concerned with only three prominent ones: chronic clashes, accommodation, and assimilation. By chronic clashes, I mean those intermittent conflicts that occur, typically in the immediate community, between occupational cultures. In the short term these conflicts result in continued clashes with little if any change in the cultures involved. Over time, however, drives for state licensure, professionalization, or unionization may set the stage for some accommodation or even assimilation.

By accommodation, I mean the relationships occupational cultures negotiate with one another with respect to their boundaries so that both occupations can practice side by side. Unable to dominate one another via competition and conflict, they work out arrangements that enable them to tolerate, even respect, each other's ideologies, task knowledge, and cultural forms.

Finally, as occupational cultures inside organizations come into contact, competition for task control emerges and one culture comes to dominate over one or more others. As a consequence, the subordinate culture or cultures tend to take on the ideologies and cultural forms of the dominant occupation. That is, they become assimilated.

CHRONIC CLASHES

Chronic clashes between occupational cultures are fueled by the "oughts" of their respective ideologies and signal that the cultures involved are strong enough to exert influence over at least some aspects of their claimed tasks. The outcomes of such clashes are rarely clear, and they tend to remain volatile for considerable periods of time. Such clashes often occur in the community surrounding a work organization.

CLASHES IN THE COMMUNITY

On May 2, 1988, a helicopter crashed in New York's East River, trapping its pilot and passengers under water. Emergency rescue squads from New York City's police and fire departments rushed to the scene. The police, following established protocol, took charge and refused to let the fire department's scuba divers into the water. After one of the passengers died, the firefighters charged that the death was attributable to the police's failure to permit the divers from the fire department to join in the search. The commissioner of the fire department insisted that divers were on the scene, were badly needed for the search, and excluding them from the rescue made no sense. In response, the police insisted that the two groups of divers spoke "a different language . . . [and that the firefighters] should not have been on the scene because they were not called and they were not needed" (Lyall 1988).

Another example involves biologists and fundamentalist clergy. Scientists constantly construct boundaries between science and nonscience and between themselves and "pseudo-scientists." For example, as Thomas F. Gieryn (1983:783) has documented, litigation over "creationism" suggests that "for some Christian fundamentalists, religion and science continue to battle for the same intellectual turf. To the victors go the spoils: Opportunities to teach one's beliefs about the origins of life to biology students in Arkansas public schools."

A bill introduced into, but defeated by, the Wisconsin legislature in 1991 reflected a clash between the claims of social workers and family counselors, on the one hand, and clinical sociologists, on the other. The former insisted, via the bill, that they be allowed to construct tests that would have determined whether practicing sociologists could work in counseling and social service areas. Had the bill passed, practicing sociologists "would have been required to take a social work, marriage and family therapy, or counseling section test—all of which would be constructed by members of those groups" (Billson 1992:2). In all probability this clash will continue in other states for years to come.

The long-standing and acrimonious conflict between chiropractors and medical doctors is yet another example. Although significantly reduced in recent years by state legislation favoring certification of chiropractors, community-based clashes still occur in some states over which occupation is exclusively mandated to perform specific therapeutic tasks.

Similarly, clergy and funeral directors have conflicted repeatedly over who can conduct religious services during funerals. Again, considerable accommodation between the two groups has occurred in recent years, although flare-ups still occur in local communities and regions.

A final example involves the long-standing conflict between optometrists and ophthalmologists over the use of therapeutic drugs. A "turbulent historical relationship between optometry (the practice of testing eyes in order to prescribe corrective lenses or exercises) and ophthalmology (a specialization in medical practice that deals with the anatomy, function, and diseases of the eye) supports the view that conflicts over task boundaries can be a protracted struggle for task control" (Begun and Lippincott 1987:84). Two forces, among others, in the environment of these two occupations led to the challenge posed by optometry to the tasks claimed by ophthalmology (Begun and Lippincott 1987). One was that the supply of members of both occupations grew significantly during the 1970s. The other was that third-party insurance companies favored ophthalmologists over optometrists when making payments, and the former fought strenuously against the inclusion of latter.

As early as the 1930s, ophthalmologists had insisted that optometrists had a deficient educational base and were lacking in the knowledge necessary to treat the eyes. Optometrists had a long-term strategy, however, and had gained university affiliation and accreditation based on an expanded curriculum. Thus, beginning in the 1960s, optometry claimed that specialized courses in pharmacology, pathology, and biochemistry gave optometrists the knowledge base to do the tasks ophthalmologists do.

A drive by optometrists in North Carolina to be certified to prescribe drugs has been quite successful. In contrast, optometrists in Maryland have been much less organized and effective. Both cases have been marked by "protracted conflict" (Begun and Lippincott 1987:381), however.

Clashes can also occur between members of occupations within the same organization. In one construction company engineers and geologists who are building an underground repository for radioactive wastes are feuding over what physical conditions will be like in the Nevada desert ten thousand to one million years from now (Wald 1989). And corporate purchasing agents often engage in running battles with engineers over who will control the decisions about what supplies to buy (Strauss 1964).

In other instances, members of occupations go about their distinctive tasks without ever encountering one another until they are in a particular organizational setting. Thus, when prosecution attorneys, as well as defense attorneys, call psychotherapists as expert witnesses to testify in court on a defendant's state of mind, they may try to exploit differences in psychotherapeutic diagnosis and treatment to make their case. In the process, psychotherapeutic expertise is opened to question and its practitioners subjected to ridicule. Stanley Mosk (1986) attributes such conflicts to misunderstandings of roles and unrealistic expectations of the law, while Louis Everstine and Diana S. Everstine (1986:xi) put the matter squarely in cultural terms:

> A meeting of minds between lawyers and mental health professionals occurs too rarely. This lack is partly one of communications, because the two disciplines speak different languages. Moreover, they inhabit different cultures and thus have different aims. The legal enterprise, for example, seeks to discover truth, while psychotherapy and the other helping professions seek to promote health . . . profound ideological differences.

When a legal question of insanity or dangerous behavior is raised, these two occupations can be quite opposed. Psychotherapists belong to associations that insist members are incapable of making predictions based on their assessments of patients, while lawyers and the courts ignore these disclaimers and insist that psychotherapists have a professional obligation both to diagnose and to predict. The plethora of laws now governing mental health practitioners in any given state attest to the fact that, although lawyers and mental health workers still may go about their work without much interaction, the likelihood of a clash seems to have recently increased at an exponential rate.

CLASHES BETWEEN EMERGING AND ESTABLISHED OCCUPATIONS

Freidson (1985:xvii) suggests that as new needs arise, new occupations develop to meet them. At such moments, occupational disputes and clashes are likely to occur as new turf is carved out and new occupations lay claim to tasks performed by older occupations. According to Freidson (1985), there is a broad area of indeterminacy that allows for a number of combinations of tasks to crystallize into the bundles of roles we call jobs, occupations, trades, or specialties. Funeral directors, for instance, combined tasks previously performed by embalmers, midwives, and clergy to develop their distinctive trade (Mitford 1963). Athletic coaches drew from the tasks of gymnastic teachers and physicians in developing their occupation (Ball and Loy 1975). As these occupations have established their niches in the labor market, they have appealed to their clients by displaying symbols of professionalism.

The personnel occupations are a good example of an occupational group that has borrowed heavily from other occupations and encountered considerable conflict as they vigorously pursued the label of professional. Initially—early in the century—the personnel occupations were a "dumping ground" because "every time something comes up that [management] want[s] handled and they don't know exactly where else to put it, they give it to personnel" (Ritzer and Trice 1969a: 42). Historically, personnel administration grew out of the work of industrial welfare secretaries. At the turn of the century, industries hired welfare secretaries to perform such tasks as arranging for immigrant workers to learn how to speak English and providing them with essential health and social services. Later in this same period, some employers also hired psychologists to interview, screen, and hire new employees. Many employers could not afford such specialists, however, or discovered that they did not require full-time psychologists. In many of these instances, welfare secretaries took on the tasks of interviewing, screening, and hiring new workers (Tead 1934).

Eventually, as welfare workers became known as personnel workers, they also took on such tasks as the supervision and maintenance of parking lots, reception desks, in-company telephone services, firefighting and plant security, and festive company events. And, in the process, they borrowed from other occupations. From industrial engineers and statisticians, they acquired the tasks of developing job descriptions and performing job analyses, and these tasks were integrated into wage and salary programs. From teachers, they acquired teaching techniques, which they incorporated into their training and performance appraisal programs. From police, they learned to set up plant security systems. And from lawyers, they acquired skills in negotiating with labor unions, devising internal grievance and arbitration procedures, and implementing local, state, and federal laws.

As early as 1912, some personnel workers began performing these tasks on a full-time basis. Shortly thereafter, they established an occupational association to promote themselves to their clients—the business community—and to set up schools to bring together and teach newcomers the diverse skills necessary to be a personnel administrator. Eventually, they established through their association certification and credentialing procedures for identifying those among them who were qualified to perform personnel work. Over the years, these procedures have been put forward as the legitimate ones for hiring individuals to do personnel work. Gradually, then, businesspeople have come to see social workers, clergy, teachers, police, psychologists, and lawyers as less appropriate for doing personnel work because they no longer have legitimate claims to perform the diverse tasks that now comprise modern personnel work and industrial relations.

Similarly, employee assistance work is an emerging occupation that has borrowed tasks from other occupations: psychology, social work, sociology, community health nursing, personnel work, and training and benefits specialties. From personnel work, they have borrowed the idea of using job performance to identify alcoholic and other troubled employees and the notion of progressive discipline as a way to encourage such employees to change their behavior. From psychology, social work, and nursing, they have borrowed the idea of providing alcoholic and other distressed employees with counseling services and skills in referring such employees to community resources. From sociology, they have borrowed knowledge about the adoption, implementation, and evaluation of company policies and procedures. More recently, they have increasingly borrowed from benefits and services specialities the skills to manage health-care plans.

Employee assistance work has some, but by no means all, of the accoutrements of an established occupation: an occupational association, a nucleus of persons who claim to do EAP work, and a slowly accumulating distinctive body of knowledge (Quick, Sonnenstuhl, and Trice 1987). Although some observers (Roman and Blum 1988) see employee assistance work as being made up of a number of distinctive core tasks, there is still a great deal of dispute about what they are and who should perform them. Some social workers, for instance, see employee assistance work as a natural extension of social work and argue that it should be performed by licensed social workers (Akabas and Kurzman 1982). In the state of California, the insurance industry and health maintenance organizations have complained that employee assistance workers have intruded on their turf and have lobbied the state legislature to bar them from competing with these established entities. Similarly, some members of Alcoholics Anonymous argue that employee assistance "counselors" are attempting to make a living doing what Alcoholics Anonymous members do for free.

Such disputes indicate that employee assistance work as an occupation is still in an early stage of development and that if it is to become a full-fledged occupation with a distinct ideology, it has a long way to go before it will have differentiated itself from psychology, personnel occupations, social work, and Alcoholics Anonymous in the minds of prospective business and union clients. Until employee assistance workers can display the appropriate professional symbols and convince their clients and state licensing boards that they, and not their competitors, have the appropriate expertise and values, the conflict will remain unresolved. Even if they do come to display symbols of professionalism, EAP workers will probably be easily assimilated into administrative subcultures, along with other satellites of personnel, such as benefits and services administrators, selection and placement specialists, wage and salary administrators, and training officers. Along the way social workers may increasingly attempt to lay claim to the tasks now being performed by EAP workers.[1]

In the next section I describe how occupational cultures can partially resolve chronic clashes by carving out a secure niche for themselves within the larger labor market (Freidson 1982). Doing so involves an elaborate rite of conflict reduction in which members of the occupation attempt to convince both their clients and ultimately the licensing au-

---

1. EAP workers currently perform many diverse tasks, *but there seems to be* a developing consensus about their core work (Hathaway and Trice 1992).

thorities of the state that only they have the competence necessary to perform the disputed tasks.

PROFESSIONALIZATION AS A RITE OF CONFLICT REDUCTION

As discussed in chapter 3, unionism and professionalism are ideologies used by occupations to attempt to maintain control over their distinctive lines of work. In modern times, professionalization has become the dominant organizing myth for doing so (Meyer and Rowen 1977; Wilensky 1964a).

Professionalization may be viewed as an elaborate rite of conflict reduction in which the members of an occupation, usually through their occupational association, enact a series of rituals to convince their clients and ultimately the state that they should be granted a monopoly to perform their work. For an occupation's attempts at professionalization to be successful as a rite of conflict reduction, however, the occupation must demonstrate more than its expertise. It must also demonstrate that its ideology complements the dominant values of American society.

According to Robin M. Williams, Jr. (1977:37), "The stock of common beliefs, knowledge, experience, norms, and values that are shared by millions" is a critical cultural resource for resolving conflict in America. Among these values are a belief in individuals' freedom to compete, in the use of democratic processes to resolve conflict and ensure equal opportunity to achieve, and in the need to help the "little guy," whose freedoms may be trampled by "big business" and "big government" (Williams 1970).

Attempts by occupations to professionalize speak to these dominant American values. For instance, the largest wave of state licensing in America occurred during the latter quarter of the nineteenth century when members of such diverse occupations as plumbing, barbering, blacksmithing, and pharmacy feared that large businesses would put them out of work and sought professional licensure to shelter themselves from corporate influence (Freidman 1965). State legislatures tended to support occupations in this effort (Parkes 1947).

Attempts by occupations to professionalize lead practitioners to display symbols such as their licenses as a way to gain the trust of their clients and access to their particular market. Such symbols convey the notion of expertise and trustworthiness. Knowing that a physician has learned the extensive curricula of medical school or a craft worker has gone through an apprenticeship program, for instance, conveys to clients that members of these occupations possess a unique knowledge that is not easily learned and that is based on scientific rationality rather than mere opinion.

Occupational associations also symbolize a conformity that is valued by Americans. Occupational associations such as the American Medical Association and the Air Line Pilots Association convey to users of the services of their members that the members are generally all alike in their practices; all members know what constitutes "good" practice, and clients need not fear being taken advantage of. In addition, the presence of occupational associations underscores that what is being sold is not mere opinion but a standard product whose mysteries are not easily understood and grasped.

Finally, occupational codes of ethics provide evidence of a commitment to public service. The codes of ethics espoused by, for example, nurses, sociologists, lawyers, doctors, accountants, engineers, and architects state their intention to pursue the public good and to discipline members who violate that trust. Winning the public's confidence, and eventually the state's as well, in the occupation's ability to perform its tasks may require the use of such symbols.

BOUNDARY DISPUTES

LAW

Although state licensure provides an occupation with monopolistic control over its work, it does not by any means resolve all boundary disputes. Perhaps one of the best documented and historically most contested arenas of licensed occupational work is law. Barlow F. Christensen (1980) has traced in detail the "unauthorized" practice of law from colonial times to the present. Over this span of time, lawyers have experienced both successful and unsuccessful attempts to prevent the unauthorized practice of their occupation.

During the prerevolutionary colonial period, there were no professional associations of lawyers that could be called the "bar." Rather, there was an informal bar made up of traders and land speculators as well as minor court officials such as deputy sheriffs, clerks, and petit justices. Charges of "unauthorized practice" against these "pettifoggers" included encouraging lawsuits for their own gain, incompetence, and excessive fees.

After the American Revolution, the economy expanded rapidly, spawning a need for trained lawyers who called practice according to the principles of English common law. An American bar emerged, fashioned by its members, that exaggerated the evils wreaked upon society by uneducated practitioners and that proceeded to develop higher standards for admission to practice, including a college education.

From 1800 until approximately 1870, the status of lawyers declined as they became identified with the collection of debts and the imprisonment of debtors. Populist Jacksonian democracy argued for opening up the practice of law. Educational requirements were generally eliminated, and applicants were admitted to the bar without previous training (any citizen over twenty-one years of age could practice law).

Between 1870 and 1950, lawyers again consolidated their hold over the practice of law. Local bars increasingly filed lawsuits against those who attempted to practice law without the benefit of a legal education, arguing that members of corporations who were practicing real estate and corporate law did not possess the necessary qualifications. The American Bar Association established the Special Committee on Unauthorized Practice of Law. Representation before administrative agencies by nonlawyers came to be considered unauthorized practice. And by 1940, all states required professional training to be admitted to practice.

Despite the legal profession's gains, other occupations continue to challenge the tight boundaries drawn by attorneys around their domain. In Arizona, for example, real estate brokers and sales people may draft legal instruments that deal with property ownership, and laypersons for organizations such as the National Association for the Advancement of Colored People and representatives of labor unions may act as intermediaries between their members and staff lawyers. The tax practices of accountants, the estate planning activities of insurance agents, the activities of title insurance companies, the drafting of wills by banks and trust companies, and the drafting by realtors of legal documents in real estate transactions all pose continuing challenges to the occupational domain of lawyers.

MEDICINE, PHARMACY, AND DENTAL WORK

Boundary disputes may also occur among closely allied occupations such as medicine and pharmacy. According to Rothman (1984:

195), even "professional monopolies must be protected constantly from threats of encroachment by closely allied occupations." For instance, physicians have held a monopoly over the prescribing of drugs since the late nineteenth century (Starr 1982), but since the colonial era pharmacists have contested this exclusive right (Kronus 1976b).

During the colonial period both pharmacists and doctors prescribed, mixed, and sold drugs. During the American Revolution, however, physicians began a concerted effort to regulate and limit the right of pharmacists to prescribe drugs for the treatment of illnesses. Arguing that their university training was superior to the pharmacists' apprenticeship, physicians claimed that only they were qualified to prescribe medications. By 1821, this claim was widely accepted among clients. After the pharmacists established their first schools of pharmacy, however, they once again attempted to assert their right to prescribe as well as mix and sell drugs. The pendulum of power once again swung in favor of the physicians during the 1880s, when they were granted state licensure, providing them with a monopoly over the right to prescribe drugs. During the 1920s, pharmacists voluntarily adopted a code of ethics, limiting their tasks to the preparation and sale of drugs, but physicians continued to press for legal reassurances that the dispute was totally resolved.

Apparently the dispute remains unresolved. In 1986, Florida pharmacists "gained the right to prescribe 30 different medicines for the treatment of minor illnesses" (Rothman 1987:88), and nationally they are seeking to "reprofessionalize" pharmacy by committing themselves to "clinical pharmacy." This new role would involve patient and drug counseling and thereby "reconstitute a relationship of interdependence between pharmacist and physician" (Hornosty 1989:123).

Similarly, dentists have had a long-standing professional monopoly over the right to prescribe dentures, and denturists, the technicians who actually make the dental plates, are challenging this exclusive right (Rosenstein et al. 1980). Because of the shortage of dentists in low-income areas and a chronic need for dentures in these communities, dental technicians began to lobby vigorously for the legal right to work independently of dentists (Waldman 1980). As David Rosenstein and his colleagues report (1980:614), "In 1978 supporters of denturism in the state of Oregon succeeded in passing an initiative which allows denturists to provide dentures directly to the public."

PSYCHOTHERAPY

A third contentious boundary dispute in the medical arena concerns the provision of psychotherapy (Hogan 1979). This is a particularly conflictual area because it has been difficult—if not impossible—to define what constitutes diagnosis and treatment. Until World War II, psychiatrists held a monopoly over the provision of psychotherapy because of their medical license to perform all things related to the human body. During and following the war, this monopoly was challenged, first by psychologists, then by social workers. It is now being challenged by a virtual army of marital, family, and substance abuse counselors who are battling "over which professional groups ought to be allowed to perform psychotherapy independently" (Hogan 1979:27).

Responding to the shortage of qualified psychiatrists, psychologists claimed that they were competent psychotherapists and that they could perform the same roles as psychiatrists. Consequently, in 1945, psychologists began to lobby for state licensure. By 1955, only four states had licenses for psychologists, however, because "the medical profession, headed by psychiatrists, was putting up stiff opposition. . . . [They] claim[ed] . . . that no one but a psychiatrist had the requisite training to properly diagnose and treat mental illness" (Hogan 1979: 28). Psychiatrists insisted that psychotherapy was a kind of medical treatment and did not call for a separate occupation operating on its own, unsupervised by physicians.

The struggle continued, but by the 1970s all fifty states had passed laws licensing psychologists with doctoral degrees to perform psychotherapy and forbidding unlicensed persons from using the title of psychologist or performing psychological services.

As time has gone by, the challenges to the jurisdiction of psychiatry have increased, and its control over psychotherapy has further declined. According to Abbott (1988:313) "Psychiatry has virtually conceded the psychotherapeutic world to its competitors," and psychologists, via state legislation, now have the legal right to practice psychotherapy independently, without the supervision of a physician. Psychiatry lays claim to the pharmacological and biological aspects of major mental illnesses such as depression.

In the mid-1970s, social workers and marriage and family counselors entered the psychotherapeutic fray, "striving to establish parity with psychologists and psychiatrists" (Hogan 1979:27). Desiring to be considered primary health-care providers for insurance purposes, social workers lobbied for state licensure on the grounds that they were as well qualified as psychologists to provide therapy and had been offering their own brand since the mid-1940s. Social workers had been able to offer psychotherapy because the early laws licensing psychologists denied to nonpsychologists only the designation psychologist, not the right to practice as psychotherapists (Wardwell 1979). Social workers' claims of having equal qualifications have been challenged, however, because numerous social workers possess only bachelor's degrees whereas licensed psychologists must have doctorates. Indeed, social work laws have frequently allowed for licensing without any advanced academic credentials, giving credit for work experience and job-based training. Moreover, in 1972, California actually lowered the requirements for becoming a registered social worker. According to L. T. Zuckerman and R. A. Savedra (1972:93):

> These changes, approved by the Board, represent a precedent shattering break with historical tradition. No other professional certificate or license in history has undergone a similar *lowering* of minimum requirements. . . . The fact is, there are no mental health professions in the U.S. with entry level professional degrees pegged at the bachelor level (emphasis in the original).

Consequently, insurance companies have been reluctant to reimburse patients who consult bachelor-level social workers because the insurers do not believe that such workers are really "professionals."

ACCOMMODATIONS BETWEEN OCCUPATIONAL CULTURES

While conflicts between occupational cultures are frequent and may lead to the domination or elimination of one occupation by another, members of occupational cultures often accommodate to one another and work closely together. The cultures of both occupations become interrelated in such a way that neither comes to dominate the other; both cultures exist side by side.

CRAFT UNIONS

A classic instance of accommodation is found among the craft unions that make up the construction industry. According to Applebaum (1981:54), carpenter journeymen, mason journeymen, operating engineers, ironworkers, electricians, and plumbers "must accommodate one another, not only as different crafts, but as individuals. Personal conflict on these bases is a recurring activity, but so is horseplay and verbal joking. This serves as a means of blunting and controlling hostility." Similarly, Riemer (1979:22) observes that tradespeople recognize and respect the installation requirements of other crafts and strive for harmony; "they work together to build buildings."

Members of craft unions reduce conflict through membership in the Building Trades Council, a loose confederation of local unions from the various building and construction trades (Silver 1986). Having no power over the affairs of individual member unions, the council serves as a forum for regular discussion, as a mechanism for resolving interunion conflicts, and as a liaison for member unions with local government and economic and political agencies. Its meetings function as information-sharing sessions about local conditions, ongoing projects, and interunion politics. Overall, the council reinforces members' commitment to solidarity and common values.

The members of construction trades also share several common values that promote adaptation on the job, including (1) getting to work on time, (2) performing work correctly and efficiently (i.e., having knowledge of the craft), (3) performing tasks unsupervised, (4) being honest about one's work, (5) being willing to perform difficult or dangerous work, and (6) taking pride in one's work and taking care of tools and equipment (Applebaum 1981; Steiger and Form 1991). Workers who live up to and exceed these expectations win the respect, trust, and admiration of their co-workers inside and outside their craft, and they are generally rewarded by being given the choicest work assignments. Those who do not conform to these standards become the subject of contempt and ridicule, are given the least desirable assignments, and may ultimately be discredited for incompetence.

Most of the construction trades value cooperation between crafts because

> the fluid nature of construction work, with its constant change, requires adaptive ability on the part of construction workers. In many cases a man does not know who may be working next to him until he arrives on the job. On large-scale projects, where there are larger numbers, there is a greater chance men working together will not have had previous contact. This requires some difficult adjustment. If a man cannot adjust he will be laid off. Foremen and superintendents do not judge the effectiveness of a journeyman

solely on his output. He must also cooperate with others. Experienced construction workers know they must adjust their behavior to fit with other members of their own and other trades (Applebaum 1981:28).

Cooperation with members of other crafts is expressed in specific behaviors (Applebaum 1981). For instance, workers are expected to perform a task at the request of another worker or a foreman if it will make someone else's work easier, and workers are supposed to permit other workers to complete their work before beginning their own. When disputes about the sequence of tasks arise, the workers discuss the sequence and work out a compromise, so that some tasks may be held off or slowed down. For instance, when a job calls for installing a drop ceiling where electricians have to put in lighting, a plumber has to lay sprinkler lines and other pipes, and a sheet metal worker has to put in heating, a compromise will be worked out.

> The ducts will have priority since they are difficult to modify. Next the plumber will receive priority since his pipes are more difficult to bend and "run" than those of the electrician. The electrical work will be left until last, and the conduits (electrical pipe) would be "snaked" around the other installations.... Compromise, "helping out," and mutual consideration are the typical taken-for-granted rule (Riemer 1979:22).

The cooperation among the members of crafts extends to managing mistakes, a common occurrence on construction jobs (Riemer 1979). Indeed, crafts workers who take responsibility for their mistakes and correct them are regarded as particularly trustworthy and have good reputations (Applebaum 1981). Many mistakes are the result of faulty negotiations between crafts workers and consequently are resolved by renegotiating the situation (Riemer 1979). Hold-ups occur, for instance, because two groups get their "signals crossed," and circumstantial errors occur when workers are under too much pressure. To correct these mistakes, members of the different crafts must work together and share the blame.

Accommodation between crafts workers is facilitated if they learn the languages of the other crafts workers with whom they most closely interact. Plumbers, electricians, and sheet-metal workers all need to understand one another's work to negotiate a reasonable sequence of tasks. According to Silver (1986:69), such workers need to have at least a secondary knowledge "of some aspects of other trades.... Such secondary knowledge can make the difference for workers between being able to do their work easily and efficiently or having to continually refigure plans."

Finally, the laborers at construction sites often facilitate cooperation between crafts (Silver 1986). When new workers come onto a site, they seek out the laborers who are already there to learn such things as the location of running water and supply shanties and the whereabouts of other workers. Such information saves the new workers many steps and much time in becoming acquainted with the new site.

CONCERT MUSIC OCCUPATIONS

The concert music world is composed of members of a large number of occupations who collaborate to create a harmonious sound (Gilmore 1987; Faulkner 1973, 1974a). Among these people are composers, a variety of musicians, conductors, critics, managers, and financial specialists. Unlike complex organizations such as universities and mental health hospitals, the concert music world lacks a formal structure or organizational authority that coordinates the activities of participants. Rather, the glue that holds the members of these diverse occupations together is conventions. Conventions are tacit agreements that have become part of the customary way of doing things, and people conform to these agreements because they expect others to conform to them as well.

Within the music world, these conventions include agreements about compositional forms, notation, instrumentation, and the skills used to play instruments. In combination, these conventions constitute the "concert world."

Musicians are highly independent individuals who tend to view the directives of the conductor with the bias of an expert worker. According to Faulkner (1974a:243), the musician "tends to emphasize his [sic] own expertness and unique talents in making judgments about how things are to be played." Thus, "doing it his [the conductor's] way can be viewed as forced compliance which is outside a player's zone of acceptance." Consequently, within the concert world, performers must find some method of accommodating to the conductor and to one another to play their music.

Samuel Gilmore identified three distinct concert worlds in New York City: the Midtown, the Uptown, and the Downtown. As Gilmore says:

"To organize collective events, collaborators adopt identities provided by a social world to locate and be located by compatible partners. New-comers use social worlds to identify and learn appropriate conventions. Both processes serve to integrate individuals into the ongoing collective activity" (Gilmore 1987:212).

The conventions of the three concert worlds Gilmore identified vary. The Midtown world is highly organized; its musicians are represented by a union, work for scale, and have well-established avenues for searching out work. Its conventions are evident in the well-known repertoire of classical composers' works that Midtown orchestras perform. Within this arena, playing music is often regarded as factory work, and musicians are expected to follow the conductor's lead (Gilmore 1987). To a great extent they do so if they believe that the conductor knows what he or she is doing musically and permits them to play the music they are capable of performing. If they do not respect the conductor's interpretation, they will ignore his direction, misread notes, play parts correctly but up or down an octave, play soft passages loudly and vice versa. Finally, they end up "merely playing," rather than enthusiastically "making music" (Faulkner 1974a).

In contrast, in the Downtown concert music world, the musicians play more avant-garde works, which generally call for them to be knowledgeable about new forms of notation and instrumentation. There are few composers and performers in this world and few places and opportunities for them to perform. Often, composition and performance become blurred because composers play their own music or performers end up collaborating with composers on new pieces. Downtown composers and performers make great economic sacrifices for their art so that when they do perform it is with gusto. As one performer stated: "I've played with Pxxxx for twelve years. So have most of the group. That develops ensemble, which is rare down here. We know what each other are doing" (Gilmore 1987:220).

The Uptown concert music world has a moderately complex production organization. The composers and performers respect the musical conventions of the classics but also strive for originality. Many of the composers are part of academic music departments, and they often find one another through professional and campus channels. When professional musicians are used in Uptown performances, they are paid according to union scale, but it is not unusual for them to put in more time than that for which they are paid. As one performer stated: "I believe in the music of our time. That's why I play it.... I don't know why others do it, but if you ask me, new composition is what keeps this job interesting" (Gilmore 1987:223).

Other music worlds, such as rock and jazz and other art worlds, such as the theatre, have their own conventions that enable the members of these diverse occupational cultures to come together without a strong administrative unit to create their art (Becker 1982).

UNIVERSITIES AND COLLEGES

In organizations with an extensive mix of occupations whose work is not closely intertwined, adjustment between members of the occupations may be facilitated by a formal authority system augmented by an informal system of "open, free lance interactions" (Gilmore 1987:210). That is, the formal system may allocate resources to members of each occupation on the basis of the formal structure, and intermittent, informal communications may hold the various members together. Universities, for instance, are composed of mathematicians, psychologists, chemists, historians, astronomers, economists, linguists, physicists, anthropologists, biologists, and lawyers. The cultures of these groups vary widely in their internal consensus about the content and specific tasks of their occupations and about how to organize their time relative to teaching and research. Physicists and chemists, for example, tend to have more internal agreement than do sociologists and political scientists on their basic tasks (Lodahl and Gordon 1972). Most of the persons in these diverse occupations rarely have cause to interact directly, yet they are interrelated indirectly via a common administrative system that produces uniformities in matters of overall policy.

Thus, a central administration provides academic departments with general guidelines on hiring, promotions, retirements, and salaries and coordinates the hiring and general management of nonacademic personnel who work with the academics. At the same time, each department decides on specific hirings and promotions relative to its own discipline, jealously guarding these prerogatives against intrusion by the central administration. An overall uniformity pervades hiring and promotion because departments throughout universities pay attention primarily to the same criteria: the candidate's university and department affiliations and the reputations of recommenders on her or his behalf (Long, Allison, and McGinnis 1979:828).

MENTAL HOSPITALS

Similarly, mental hospitals may be complicated organizations composed of a wide variety of occupational groups. A mental hospital studied in 1972–73, for instance, had on its staff three psychiatrists, two psychologists, two internists, two pastoral counselors, six social workers, one physical therapist, one vocational therapist, one speech therapist, one dentist, and two pharmacists. Although the psychiatrists were in charge, the members of the other occupations carried out their work independently. The study revealed many instances of informal, indirect, and independent cooperation between the members of these occupations. For example, pastoral counselors negotiated a procedure with psychiatric social workers whereby patients could attend church services either on the grounds or in the community, and the vocational counselor, in conjunction with the internists, developed a joint program with a nearby physical therapy clinic. These observations are consistent with the finding that "organizations having the highest number of occupations have the most joint programs" (Aiken and Hage 1968:918), and they complement those of Strauss and his colleagues (1964).

Strauss and his colleagues (1964) observed the daily interactions between physicians, nurses, social workers, and psychologists at a mental hospital. The social workers and psychologists had "much in common" because they were jointly opposed to traditional medical methods of treating the mentally ill; consequently, they did not compete with one another for status or resources. In treatment teams, the social workers and psychologists clashed rather markedly with the nurses and physicians, who especially disliked granting psychotherapeutic functions to social workers. Working together, however, the social workers and psychologists were able to exert considerable influence over the nurses and doctors about what constituted appropriate therapy. Conflicts between social workers and psychologists were further minimized because they focused their energies primarily on the delivery of psychotherapy, making traditional tasks such as working with patients' relatives and administering psychological tests minor efforts.

ASSIMILATION BETWEEN OCCUPATIONAL CULTURES

In this section we will examine how task disputes among occupations may be resolved because the subordinate occupational culture takes on many of the ideologies and cultural forms of the more dominant

culture. I refer to this process as assimilation; the assimilated occupation may be thought of as a satellite orbiting around the dominant
culture that controls its work. Freidson (1977:25) refers to a

> growing corp of technical workers . . . organized around the delin-
> eating and supervising authority of key professions. . . . They are
> thus bound into an occupationally subordinate position even
> though many have organized themselves into occupational asso-
> ciations and trade unions and have claimed many of the attributes
> ascribed to professions.

According to Richard Simpson (1985:420), "Some professions . . . establish dominance over an entire division of labor, including control
over the work content of subordinate occupations." Lawyers, for instance, have created paralegals, legal secretaries, and legal assistants to
perform much of their routine tasks (Spangler and Lehman 1982), and
electrical engineers have a bewildering array of occupational offshoots,
differing in pay, prestige, and opportunities for mobility (Kraft 1979).
One of the satellites spun off from electrical engineering is computer
programming. Graduates of elite science institutions that train computer programmers become research specialists or entrepreneurs who
design computer systems and languages. A second group graduate
from engineering schools and become applied mathematicians and
middle-level managers (Rothstein 1969). Finally, engineering technicians receive training in junior or community college programs and
enter jobs as technicians in local industries.

Computerization has also led to the creation of satellite occupations.
The use of computers in medical diagnosis (Shuman 1988) and legal
work (Calhoun and Copp 1988), for instance, has spawned satellite
occupations within medicine and law respectively. In both cases, the
dominant occupation retains control over the work and assigns routinized tasks to its satellites. Computerization has thus created the base
for the satellite occupations and, as computer assaults upon occupational tasks continue, may ensure an increase in the number of
satellites.

The most impressive set of satellite occupations center around physicians and make up the allied health delivery system. Glenn Gritzer
and Arnold Arluke (1985:1) estimated that by the 1970s "well over 500
allied health care occupations had arisen. Many of these specialties, like
their physician counterparts, have created subspecialties." Nurses, os-

teopaths, dentists, podiatrists, and optometrists, for example, are all allied with physicians, and nursing itself has subspecialties in psychiatry, geriatrics, and pediatrics. All of these occupations pattern their approach to health care after that of the physician, but physicians have been able to restrict the practice of these specialists to specific parts of the body and to a limited range of therapies. Meanwhile, the physicians retain a monopoly over the central medical tasks of performing surgery and prescribing drugs.

Walter Wardwell (1979) provides a typology of medical satellites: (1) limited practitioners, (2) marginal practitioners, and (3) quasi-practitioners. Limited practitioners, such as osteopaths, are limited to treating particular parts of the body; marginal practitioners treat practically the entire body but use unorthodox methods; and quasi-practitioners are nonmedical and largely pseudoscientific. To the category of limited practitioners, Wardwell adds pharmacists, but as a special case because pharmacists practice in hospitals as well as in retail stores. Despite these differences, the pharmacist is still an adjunct to the physician, who retains the authority and judgment in the doctor-patient relationship. But the "entrepreneurial role and his frequent contacts with the public put [the pharmacist] in a position of some strength vis-à-vis physicians" (Wardwell 1979:230).

Among limited practitioners, dentists have the most stable relationships with physicians. The educational curriculum of dental students reflects the same biological emphases as does that of medical students, and dentists receive training to perform complex surgical and rehabilitative procedures, sometimes closely coordinated with medical and speech specialists. Although these operations are performed relatively rarely, other procedures for the treatment of oral diseases require highly skilled treatment and are performed nearly universally (Young and Cohen 1979).

Dentists are also the center for two well-defined satellites that act as direct supports to dentistry: dental assistance and dental hygiene. Hygienists are, however, the more technically skilled and "are probably of most concern to dentists as other countries witness the rise of technicians as independent entrepreneurs, prescribing and selling dentures directly to the patient" (Young and Cohen 1979:197).

Podiatrists and optometrists have also been partly assimilated into the physician's network, apparently in a more limited fashion than dentists. Podiatrists do not have medical degrees, but they do treat the feet in a way quite similar to that of physicians. They administer drugs, use staples and casts, and occasionally have hospital staff privileges; however, "they may not treat systemic disorders or (in most states) perform amputations" (Wardwell 1979:235).

Optometrists are a well-established occupation within the allied health system. They are skilled in the science of optics but may not diagnose or treat pathological conditions or use medications to dilate the pupils of the eyes. They may prescribe corrective exercises for strengthening the eyes, however.

Increasingly restive in their satellite role, optometrists have attained a high degree of public acceptance despite the limitations physicians have put on them via state licensing. From the perspective of physicians, the chief problem with optometry is its practice in department and jewelry stores. Within the medical profession these practices have caused optometrists to be viewed as more commercial than professional, resulting in much ambivalence and continued limitations.

Osteopaths and chiropractors are examples of marginal practitioners within the physician's sphere of influence. The two groups have had quite different assimilative patterns, however, vis-à-vis physicians. In the case of osteopaths, their assimilation seems to be almost complete, rendering them less marginal. According to Wardwell (1979:242):

> Apparently organized medicine had decided to absorb osteopathy. The lines of distinction between the two groups have become blurred as more and more privileges come to be shared with osteopaths, e.g., eligibility for internship and residence training in medical institutions, enabling young osteopaths to obtain the prescribed board certification as medical specialists.

In contrast, chiropractors are "not likely to follow osteopathy toward fusion with medicine" (Wardwell 1979:243) because of their hostility to drugs and to surgery. These antimedical positions have earned them the contempt and rejection of physicians. Chiropractors could become limited medical practitioners, however, if they confine themselves to a very narrow range of therapeutic techniques. Hence, they could possibly be assimilated into organized medicine in a satellite role, as podiatrists and optometrists have been. It seems unlikely that this will happen soon. There are signs, however, that chiropractors are slowly becoming recognized by physicians for their skills in spinal manipulation, especially in cases of acute back trouble (Haldeman 1992).

In the early 1970s, a new occupation called physician's assistant (PA) was created by physicians in an effort to alleviate the alleged shortage and maldistribution of physicians. The role was patterned on that of the military corpsman and was created to provide employment for male medics who had completed their armed service. PAs were expected to complete a two-year training program distilled from the specialized knowledge of medicine. From this education, they were expected to know enough about medicine to do routine tasks for the doctors under whose supervision they were to work.

Despite their early support from doctors, the occupation of physician's assistant has not become a well-established medical satellite. Indeed, Eugene S. Schneller (1978) found that their use by doctors has declined for two reasons. First, their training is rather elaborate, approaching that of a mini-medical school education. As a result, many PAs view themselves as M.D.s; yet, they are not accorded any appreciable autonomy, causing considerable defection. Second, physicians express greater anxiety about working with male PAs than about working with female certified nurses, midwives, and pediatric nurse practitioners because the men are less willing than the women to take on a subservient status (Record and Greenlick 1975).

In a related study, Kenneth F. Ferraro and Tammy Sutherland (1989: 202) combined the occupations of nurse practitioner and physician's assistant into a new category called physician extender (PE) and concluded that physicians thought of the physician extender "as useful, but limited." Ferraro and Sutherland concluded, "If PE's are recognized increasingly as aiding the practice of medicine without threatening the autonomy of the profession, we may well see the boundaries of the PE role extended." At the same time, should competition among physicians for practice intensify, PEs may "seem much less important."

Nursing is the most classic example of a medical satellite, and nurses represent "the largest, single health provider group." Predominantly a female occupation, nursing has been "subject to sex role stereotyping and sex discrimination in professional relationships and labor practices" (Aiken 1983:409). Developed as a helping hand to the physician, nursing originally emphasized dedication and service for the alleviation of suffering. Today the subservient role is offensive to nurses, and they are seeking to break loose of their orbit around the doctor.

Nurses' struggles to extricate themselves from the control of physicians and exert some autonomy over their work are played out within everyday medical settings and, according to L. Stein (1971), take the form of game playing. As Sharon J. Reeder and Hans Mauksch (1979: 219) explain, the physician expects communications to flow downward so that the nurse is simply the "obedient implementor of medical directives." At the same time, "the physician expects that the nurse will compensate for his shortcomings and mistakes.... [Consequently] day-to-day physician-nurse contacts are full of subtle, mutually understood games in which nurses surreptitiously infiltrate their inputs into the medical treatment plan." In this fashion, nurses are involved in diagnosis but they must pretend they are not. Similarly, physicians are constrained by this game playing to pretend nurses are not involved despite the attention they give to such inputs and the extent to which they incorporate them into their actions. Much of the chronic conflict between nurses and physicians derives from this doctor-nurse game. According to Linda H. Aiken (1983:415), "Clinical decision-making is the major source of continuing tension in the hospital context.... [It] could be reduced if better agreements regarding decision-making could be achieved which appropriately recognized nurses' levels of expertise."

The work settings for nurses vary widely, and within these settings there is considerable variation in physician-nurse relationships (Reeder and Mauksch 1979). Community health nurses, school nurses, and ambulatory care nurses practice independently of doctors. In contrast, office nurses are constantly at the call and under the direction of a physician. Between these two extremes is hospital nursing, in which nurses experience a wide range of autonomy vis-à-vis the physician. As members of nursing service departments, nurses are bureaucratic employees and the physician's deputy. As the head of nursing, a nurse acts as a hospital administrator. In this role, nurses exercise authority largely free of the physician, and their relationship is a sharply different one from the game playing one associates with patient care. At lower hierarchical levels, the patient-care nurse exercises considerable bureaucratic authority over licensed vocational nurses, nurses' aids, and clerks.

High technology has produced a growing number of clinical nursing specialties. Nurses are experts in such areas as coronary care, heart surgery, renal dialysis, and transplantation. Most of these specialists hold graduate degrees (M.S.) and formulate and carry out individual nursing-care plans for patients. These specialties provide nurses with opportunities to develop greater expertise than they can in other areas of nursing. As a result, clinical decision making has become a part of the nursing role. Clinical nursing "includes direct care of patients with complex needs, collaborative practice with physicians, and provision of clinical consultation to staff nurses" (Aiken 1983:412). Because these specialties are growing rapidly, they represent a prominent alteration in the typical physician-nurse pattern.

Other expanded occupations within nursing include the nurse practitioner, nurse clinician, nurse associate, and nurse administrator. Members of all of these occupations are attempting to devise a bundle of semiautonomous tasks for themselves that are different from those of other nursing specialists and physician's assistants. These efforts have not, however, altered appreciably typical doctor-nurse communications (Light 1983).

Overall, significant shifts have occurred that are slowly altering how physicians relate to nurses, but efforts to increase their educational requirements have met with mixed results. Donald Light (1983) reports that the long-standing debate between those nurses who advocate the need for more academic training and those who are in favor of more hands-on education continues. Although the American Nurses Association has lobbied vigorously for every nurse to have a B.S.N. degree, few states have such a requirement. Severe shortages of nurses have occurred periodically, and there are signs that physicians in general continue to hold deep-seated views that nurses "know what the proper relationship between a physician and an assistant ought to be" (Reeder and Mauksch 1979:220).

SUMMARY

Occupational subcultures adapt not only to managerial subcultures but to one another. Three prominent modes of adaptation are chronic clashes, accommodation, and assimilation. Chronic clashes are recurring conflicts between subcultures over occupational boundaries. They recur regularly over time and are resolved slowly, if at all, only when one or both of the occupations involved becomes licensed or otherwise acquires the right to perform certain tasks. Clashes can occur within the organization or in the surrounding community. Occupations often undertake symbolic acts of professionalism to gain a competitive advantage in such clashes. These acts include initiating credentialing programs by occupational associations, promulgating codes of ethics, and lobbying in state legislatures with the goal of preventing those who have not passed the occupation's prescribed tests from being licensed.

In contrast, other subcultures use adaptive modes of accommodation and assimilation. The accommodative mode is marked by regular contacts between occupations during which neither comes to dominate the other, while both make minor adjustments to accommodate each other. Craft unions in the building trades are an example.

In the assimilative mode, one occupation comes to take on the cultural elements of a dominant occupation and becomes one of its satellites. Prime examples of this case are the many health-care occupations that, in one way or another, have become absorbed into the physicians' culture.

9. CONCLUSIONS AND IMPLICATIONS
TOWARD A SUBCULTURAL ANALYSIS OF ORGANIZATIONAL CULTURE

RECALL THAT THREE MAJOR themes were set forth at the beginning of this book that guided our exploration of occupational cultures in the workplace. First, occupations, in and of themselves, can be viewed as cultures. Second, they can be thought of as subcultures since members typically practice their occupations inside a work organization. Other subcultures also function there, shifting the focus from the core culture to subcultures and their interrelations. Third, and finally, occupations can also be conceived as dynamic and volatile collectivities. Rarely are they fixed in their makeup over time. This feature pervades both their internal makeup and their external relations.

Relative to these themes, the previous chapters provide, *first*, a heightened awareness of the reality of occupational cultures, their ideologies, and the specific cultural forms that convey their beliefs. Although occupations have been analyzed using a cultural perspective (e.g. Van Maanen and Barley 1984; Gamst 1980), cultural studies of the workplace have typically confined themselves to organizational cultures, leaving out occupations (Hofstede et al. 1990). Compared with what we know about organizational cultures, the cultures of occupations have not been as carefully integrated and set forth in empirical detail. This shortcoming has been, at least in part, corrected by pulling together the hitherto scattered material in part I.

Occupations can no longer be viewed as simply statistical categories and census groupings. Rather, they are potent and shared belief systems held together by common emotional demands and by common myths, sagas, stories, symbols, songs, argot, rituals and taboos, and unique rites and ceremonies.

Comparatively speaking, "occupational consciousness and organizations play an unusually central role" (Lincoln and McBride 1987:297) in America. A culture grows in the process of the performance of a set of specific work tasks and the common roles that embrace them. Its distinctiveness depends on the strength of its ideologies and the vitality and clarity of the cultural forms that come to characterize it. In short, an autonomy comes to characterize many occupations, with the result that in America they cut across organizations and are relatively independent of them. Much the opposite pertains to Japanese organizations. Further, based on the accumulated empirical indicators of occupational cultures detailed in the previous chapters, one can conclude that the concept of culture can be applied not only to the traditional, established occupations but to those with lower occupational status. Lower status does not preclude the development of a viable and well-formed culture.

We have also seen evidence that occupations are not necessarily bent only on pursuing control over the content of their work (Sonnenstuhl and Trice 1991). This notion can now be refined in the light of our analysis. Occupational cultures vary by grid-group dimensions and are constructed and reconstructed as a result of their making ongoing adjustments to management's bureaucratic pressures. Moreover, like practically all modern cultures, occupational cultures have a potential for deep ambiguities (Keesing 1987; Meyerson 1991). Their ideologies and forms can be shot through with multiple meanings, contradictions, even paradoxes.

A *second conclusion* is that occupational cultures can be distinct subcultures inside organizations. They are an often overlooked element of an organization's culture, and their neglect has made for a blind spot in theorizing about organizations. To expand our understanding of organizational cultures, it is important that occupations be included because they can be a vital force.

The concepts being used in the recent revival of cultural analyses, described in the introduction to this book, are incomplete. As a result, their utility and fit with reality are impaired (Sonnenstuhl and Trice 1991). The inclusion of occupations would facilitate a more complete understanding of how organizations behave. Moreover, the inclusion of occupational subcultures would force students of organizations to frame their models and concepts with a variety of subcultures in mind, not just those spawned by occupations.

This observation leads to a *third conclusion:* organizations are primarily multicultural in nature. It is not sufficient merely to identify the core elements of an organization's overall culture (Martin, Sitkin, and Boehm 1985). It is clear from this analysis that this is only the first step in understanding the context in which subcultures emerge. It also seems clear that subcultures must interrelate and that the major dynamics of the organization may well arise in those interactions.

Thus, the *fourth conclusion* is that future studies of organizational cultures must increasingly grapple systematically with the nature of the relationships and adaptations of subcultures. Clearly, the study of organizational culture needs to refocus its attention so that the core culture of shared values is revealed but the complex and divergent ways in which meanings coinhabit the organization are highlighted.

We can further conclude that the patterns of interactions and adaptations that we have discerned between occupational subcultures and managerial/administrative subcultures, as well as between occupations themselves, are suggestive of the processes that characterize other interactions between subcultures. We will return to this point soon.

The *fifth conclusion* is that occupational cultures are typically in flux, often to the point of being not only unstable but actually disappearing. Moreover, this feature characterizes their internal evolution and change as well as their external adaptations to other prominent subcultures, such as ethnic groups, departments, and staff units. Apparently these adaptations can happen in a variety of modes. It is an open question which mode will emerge for specific relationships and under what conditions. It seems safe to say, however, that collectively these relationships will assume a discernable shape followed relatively soon by a different configuration.

Cultures, especially modern ones, continually change and are rarely if ever static. A variety of reasons explain this condition. Cultures depend on communications; these are usually imperfect. Individual differences abound, and persons often are not consciously aware of what their culture says about specific events or behaviors. Cultures rely on symbols, many of which have more than one meaning (Turner 1990). Finally, new demands, opportunities, and uncertainties inevitably arise. Occupational cultures react to all of these forces for change and are, beyond doubt, dynamic phenomena.

Our focus on occupational subcultures has led directly to a heightened awareness of the multiplicity of subcultures within an organization. Although numerous analysts have pointed out the multicultural nature of the workplace (Gregory 1983; Louis 1985; Jermier et al. 1991; O'Reilly, Chatman, and Caldwell 1991), few, if any, have suggested ways to express that observation conceptually. For example, Meyerson and Martin (1987), after studying the Peace Corps in Africa, concluded that consensus existed within organizational subcultures but not between them. Later, they and colleagues wrote that in this study they were "drawn to the relationship between various subcultures, such as the top management team in Africa, the staff and volunteers assigned to the various African nations and project assignments" (Frost et al. 1991:157). Also, Louis (1983) suggests that organizational subcultures can have positive, negative, or balanced relationships with each other. Unfortunately, their analyses seemed to stop at an acute awareness of subcultures. This analysis of occupational subcultures in organizations suggests how one might go beyond awareness of subcultures to an analysis of the relationships between them. That relationship, for example, is the focus of Cathy A. Enz's (1988:284) study of perceived departmental power and the extent to which departments in a quick-service restaurant chain appeared to share important organizational values with top management.

The question becomes, How can we devise a model of organizational cultures that is truly multicultural? In essence, the answer seems to be somewhat as follows: a multicultural model calls for a view of organizations as a collection of discrete subcultures held together by diverse modes of adjustment to one another; in sum, a multitude of subcultures interacting with one another. Further, the adjustments to one another seem to be impermanent adjustments that take on temporary shapes only to be replaced by other configurations as time goes by. This flux, combined with "temporary permanence," is the concept that seems to flow from our analysis of occupational subcultures operating within organizations.

OCCUPATIONAL SUBCULTURES AS MODELS FOR OTHER SUBCULTURES

One reason occupational subcultures could be viewed as models for other subcultures is that this book has already sketched out patterns of adaptation between both occupations themselves and between them and administrative/managerial subcultures. Thus, two adjustment modes have already been illustrated: accommodation and assimilation. These provide a beginning for exploring other modes of adaptation. For that matter, my detailed analysis of the internal dynamics of occupational cultures might form the basis for examining more closely the cultural features of other subcultures in organizations, which apparently have hardly been studied. Moreover, occupations are probably among the prime examples of subcultures. As a result, they could become the prototype subculture for future examinations of multiculturalism.

My analysis of occupations contains two additional features of subcultures that could facilitate the study of others. First, the inclusion of the grid dimension of culture makes for more realism. Although its inclusion complicates, it also adds to the realism of the study of subcultures. As we discovered in chapter 7, grid features can be an influential variable in assessing subcultures. Second, the occupational model emphasizes the dynamic nature of those subcultures' relationships. As we have seen, cultures and their contexts continually change; this point needs to be included in the study of all subcultures. Data in chapter 1 provide evidence of the distinct possibility of flux and change in the history of many, and probably most, occupations. On balance, then, the occupational model merits examination as the model to use in the study of other subcultures.

Six steps could make up a subcultural approach to organizations: (1) identification of the major locations of subcultures, including occupations; (2) the types of *acculturation* potentially available in subcultural interactions; (3) identification of high-density subcultural interactions; (4) assessment of the acculturation patterns of each interaction; (5) over time, a reassessment of flux in these patterns to get at the "kaleidoscope effect"; and (6) the interpretation of organizational behaviors such as decision making within the context of these shifting configurations.

MAJOR LOCATIONS OF SUBCULTURES

Observations by organizational scientists suggest that there are at least five prominent locations in organizations, in addition to occupations, where subcultures can arise: (1) cliques and coalitions (including those based on age, sex, and ethnicity), (2) technology and work flows, (3) departments, (4) top management, and (5) staff units (Trice and Morand 1991). Because of the recent widespread use of both hostile and friendly takeovers, a sixth could be added: sites of acquisitions. Apparently detailed materials and data to describe these locations culturally are not available or have not been integrated as thoroughly as they have for occupations. It seems reasonable to believe that they are largely unavailable. This seems especially to be the case vis-à-vis grid-group analysis or its equivalent. This does not preclude the collection of relevant data, however, and some of the major locations of subcultures can already be identified within the limits of the available literature. This is obviously a necessary first step in developing a subcultural approach to organizations. The next is to add cultural detail to our knowledge of each location.

CLIQUES AND COALITIONS

A clique is "a subset of members who are more closely identified with one another than the remaining members of the group and who exchange something among themselves" (Tichy 1973:197) (i.e., information, affection, friendship, favors, resources). Well-developed cliques can make decisions, control and transmit information, hide facts, avoid unpleasant situations, obtain privileges for members, and put members in a good light with supervisors (Lincoln and Miller 1979; Dalton 1959). Their face-to-face nature limits their size to relatively small groups, usually made up of employees of similar status, age, gender, and ethnicity.

Coalitions are clusters of cliques whose members discover they have common ideologies and definitions of situations (Druckman 1977). They are independent of the formal structure of the organization, issue oriented, and contrived deliberately (Stevenson, Pearce, and Porter 1985). In effect, they constitute "interest groups that are committed to achieving a common goal" (Bacharach and Lawler 1981:9) external to the coalition.

TECHNOLOGY AND WORK FLOWS

Subcultures may emerge as a result of the tools, machines, computers, and equipment used in work processes. Three technical features can encourage, or discourage, their growth: (1) the interdependence of tasks, (2) the similarity of tasks, and (3) physical nearness while performing tasks. When there is task interdependence, for example, workers depend on one another to finish particular assignments, thereby creating continuous interactions. Similar technical tasks, combined with freedom to move about, also encourage the growth of subcultures. Opportunities for interaction also occur in work that requires little concentration; in contrast, the content of some work requires practically all of an employee's attention.

Management frequently decides how workers should be grouped regarding technical tasks and how work should flow from one such group to another. The rationale is that such groups help facilitate administrative practices and supervision. Thus, workers are assigned to formal subunits, headed by managers, ranging in size from two or three to thirty. To the extent that the work has any, all, or none of the technical features that encourage interaction, subcultures form. This is especially the case when large formal units face high degrees of uncertainty. During World War I the famous Rainbow Division of the American expeditionary forces developed a myth, along with appropriate symbols, that a rainbow inevitably appeared and accompanied their attacks on the enemy. They painted, or otherwise attached, rainbow symbols to their equipment even though these symbols were formally forbidden (Linton 1924).

DEPARTMENTS

The department is a common administrative device. As a formal unit, it divides employees along various lines. The most typical divisions are by geographical location, function, and products or services produced. I and Janice M. Beyer (1992) have observed, however, that

> departments or other subunits based on function or geographical location are more likely to produce strong subcultures than product-based departments. ... Grouping workers by function puts people together who already have similar occupational interests, ongoing experiences, and educational backgrounds. A common supervisor, social interaction, shared identities and shared experiences facilitate elaboration of occupational ideologies already shared into unique departmental subcultures within organizations (see also Mintzberg 1979).

During the 1960s a study of industrial firms reported that "sales and production are 'natural enemies' of each other" (Perrow 1970:88). More recently, Donald Katz (1987) described in minute detail the vast and deep gulf between the sales divisions of Sears, Roebuck and the buyers and corporate staff. And employees in Silicon Valley computer firms distinguish between hardware and software departments as well as functional groupings in engineering and marketing (Gregory 1983).

Geographically isolated departments are more likely to produce sub-cultures since members must interact solely with other members of the department. The same is true of departments whose workers are mobile and dispersed. These conditions force workers to interact almost exclusively with others in the department and thus are likely to produce subcultures. For instance, the overhead department of a utility in a large metropolis was both geographically isolated from other departments and its members, of necessity, had to be highly mobile.

TOP MANAGEMENT

Managers—especially upper-level managers—constitute only a small percentage of any organization's labor force; nevertheless, as we have seen, they are a prominent subculture.

> They not only fashion bureaucratic rules they are also bound by them. . . . They are not only bosses, but bossed; they are not only the beneficiaries of the privileges and power that authority in bureaucracies bestow, but in most cases they are also subordinates who want to climb higher. . . . Their pivotal institutional position as a group not only gives their decisions great reach, but also links them to other important elites (Jackall 1988:13).

Some quite specific features mark management groups as powerful subcultures. In broad outline, these are as follows:

- They interact frequently with their own kind—both in informal face-to-face chance meetings and in relatively formal meetings. These interactions are characterized by their oral communications.
- These interactions tend to occur in physical isolation. Managers tend to become insulated from other employees, although they may be surrounded by a few co-workers who reassure them about their actions (Wright 1979; Kanter 1977).
- The most difficult and anxiety-producing problems are passed up the hierarchy to them. They wrestle with not only current uncertainties produced by their environment but future ones as well.
- They tend to come from very similar backgrounds, typically are male, and are likely to have finance or accounting training (Fligstein 1987). They often belong to social networks in their

communities that reinforce the values of their subcultures (Useem 1979).

● They embrace the administrative principle and the ideology of rationality and use these beliefs to justify the large power gap between those who manage and those who merely work in the organization.

● Because their role involves much uncertainty, they tend to recruit others like themselves. In essence, they value their similarities and often engage in what one observer called reproduction "in kind" (Kanter 1977:68).

● Many top managers are partially socialized in universities, typically in schools of business where they specialize in management education. Here they acquire the ideology that disorder and confusion can be reduced and organized by means of managerial techniques.

STAFF UNITS

Those units that produce the main outputs in an organization have typically been thought of as "line" departments (i.e., production, sales, and services in manufacturing organizations). In contrast, those units that provide specialized services for line personnel have traditionally been called staff (i.e., maintenance, personnel, purchasing, public relations, and internal accounting). Line managers are inclined to be skeptical and are often resistant to staff recommendations because they view staff as impractical and as representing a threat to their power and control (Dalton 1959). For instance, "street" police in New York City view themselves as a different breed from the computer specialists, personnel planners, and staff experts hired by headquarters to rationalize work procedures (Reuss-Janni 1983). Even though line police may be split among themselves into small factions, such as uniform and detective officers, senior and junior offices, blacks and white, and men and women, they nevertheless tend to close ranks against the personnel specialists and planners.

Staff specialists not only have many of the features of an occupational subculture but are positioned so that conflict with line managers is likely. This fact acts as a further stimulus to the establishment of their identity as a subculture. Often their role calls for them to devise both technical and organizational changes or to generate new rules such as safety and production directives. In addition, differences in age and education can symbolize the potential conflict. Even symbols such as dress, poise, fluency in speech, and personal grooming can exacerbate the potential for conflict (Dalton 1959; Wharton and Worthley 1981).

Observers of both friendly and hostile takeovers—instances in which one firm acquires and comes to control another—have consistently labeled them as cultural collisions (Sales and Mirvis 1984; Buono, Bowditch, and Lewis 1985; Walter 1985). These collisions happen because both organizations—the acquirer and the acquired—must interrelate in some fashion. Often hostile consequences result that turn the acquirer and its representatives into a powerful subculture opposed by many of the remaining segments of the acquired. The following two incidents illustrate this point.

> The top management of an acquired company had devised and implemented a policy of participative management, contrasting sharply with the elitist stance of the top management of the acquirer. During the year after the "friendly" sale of the acquired company, its top management continued to pursue vigorous efforts to retain its beliefs and practices about participative management, precipitating a series of confrontations and conflicts (Sales and Mirvis 1984).

> Two banks merged even though they had very different cultures. Researchers, after studying the merger, commented, "There is the possibility (even the probability) that subcultures, i.e., groups of people who share common systems of beliefs that distinguish them from the majority of organizational members, and countercultures, i.e., groups of people whose behavior rejects that of the dominant culture . . . evolve out of mergers and acquisitions" (Buono, Bowditch, and Lewis 1985:497).

Members of the acquired firm at all levels tend to feel exploited, plundered, and "occupied" and to react with hostility, anger, and fear toward the acquiring firm. Often the acquirer introduces scrupulous examinations at all levels and removes the acquired firm's entire top management (Pfeffer 1981). Takeovers are no longer thought of as questionable business practice, and, despite some diminution of their frequency in the 1990s, they have become rather common. As a result, their production of subcultures and countercultures in organizations is not an uncommon occurrence.

ACCULTURATION: ADJUSTMENTS BETWEEN SUBCULTURES

The above outline of some of the prominent locations of subcultures in organizations in no way exhausts the possible inventory. Thus, in several of the instances cited above, the subculture itself may produce distinct subcultures. Linda Smirich and Gareth Morgan (1982) reported, for example, that the top-management group in a large insurance company was fractured into two distinct subcultures.

The list of possible locations for subcultures makes manifest the notion that organizations are interacting multicultural phenomena. As we have seen, this notion is not new. But despite a growing awareness, there continues to be a lack of explicit focus on the interrelations between subcultures. What shape might they take with what consequences for the organization involved? One answer implied in the analyses of occupational and managerial interactions presented here lies in the anthropological concept of acculturation. Acculturation is "the phenomena which result when groups of individuals having different cultures come into firsthand contact" (Linton 1940:501). That is, there are a variety of modes whereby subcultures adapt to one another (Dohrenwend and Smith 1962). Some of these modes—such as assimilation—have already been introduced (see chaps. 7 and 8).

These modes have not been explicitly catalogued and expanded, however; nor have they been applied to subcultures other than occupations. Such an inventory needs to be in hand before a subcultural analysis of organizational cultures can be made more explicit. Further, such a cataloging would emphasize that the unit of analysis is the acculturation pattern between subcultures, not within the individual subculture itself. Since there are likely to be more than one or two subcultures in organizations, the analytical framework becomes truly complex. This point is made more cogent in that the grid dimension of a subculture probably will be present and must be included. In any event, some organizations may well contain within their boundaries all the modes of acculturation I will set forth. I have grouped these modes into three pairs, coupling together those modes that seem to have logical connections: accommodation/assimilation; chronic clashes/nativism, and alienation/reconstitution. It should be understood, however, that adjustment can take many forms. There seem to be few ways to predict explicitly what this form will be save when an adjustment is well under way.

ACCOMMODATION/ASSIMILATION

Both accommodation and assimilation were illustrated in chapter 7 relative to occupational subcultures and administrative/management subcultures. Accommodation can be thought of as biculturalism in that the pattern of adjustment is one in which a group retains much of its traditional culture but makes a few strategic changes to maintain an ongoing relationship with another subculture. Staff subcultures can be cited here as empirical examples. In the case of the metropolitan police force cited earlier, interrelations between "street cops" (line) and "management cops" (staff) were rather infrequent, but when they did occur the result was a reinforcement of the cultures of both groups along with ritualistic adherence to some basic formal rules promulgated by the staff group. When critical incidents occurred, however—the introduction of modern managerial techniques or a citywide blackout—the street cops (line) prevailed. The line police did not appear to assimilate the staff group into their culture, however. That is, the staff group did not replace basic elements of its culture with those of the dominant subculture.

An accommodative mode has also been reported in "symbiotic" takeovers (Haspeslagh and Jemison 1991:160). These, in effect, require "an adaptive attitude on behalf of both organizations." In such instances both cultures have continued to exist as both sides sort out what capabilities each has in the new organization.

Assimilation did not occur, however, in the clash of the top-management subcultures during the takeovers described earlier involving the two banks. There were extreme differences in the cultures of the two even though the merger was "friendly." A popular vice-president of the acquired bank resigned, informing all who were interested that he was disgruntled. Numerous others left and formed an ex-bank employees' newsletter that focused on the cultural differences between the two banks. They held informal meetings at which they talked and complained about the situation "back at the bank" and denounced the loss of commitment that occurred after the takeover (Buono, Bowditch, and Lewis 1985; Buono and Bowditch 1989). There were, in effect, three years of repeated tension and chronic clashes until the acquired bank became assimilated by its acquirer, and even then there were clear signs of militant opposition.

In the case of the two banks described above, there was a period of nativism in which members of the acquired bank vainly attempted to perpetuate and then to revive their native culture only to have it assimilated into the culture of the acquirer. Apparently, chronic clashes, both large and small, supported these efforts to keep the native culture alive.

In other instances, the chronic clashes appear to be of long standing and diminish only a little. A report from one industrial firm indicated that the sales and production departments were "natural enemies," as were the production, research, and development departments, whereas top management was highly critical of the production department (Perrow 1970:88). In another instance, a large-scale split in a nationwide department store fragmented the entire organization: "Two utterly conflicting large scale institutions within Sears had apparently coalesced around separate histories and ways of life. . . . On one side were the sellers. . . . On the other side were the buyers and corporate staff. . . . Each side had its own leaders, laws, language and long lists of epigrams and declarations from General Wood that were regarded as holy writ" (Katz 1987:198). And a well-known study of restaurants reported that status and other social differences created two chronically hostile cliques: the kitchen workers, on the one hand, and those who directly served customers—waiters and waitresses—on the other (Whyte 1948).

In yet another example, chronic clashes erupted in a hospital where a black technician had started a small laboratory when the hospital first opened. She hired six other technicians, most of whom were also black, who had high school degrees. Soon the hospital expanded and hired a young white woman to manage and expand the new laboratory. All the new hires were white and had college degrees; and they were technologists, whereas the "old guard were technicians." L. David Brown explains (1983:180): "the laboratory had expanded to a staff of fifteen, which was split into two antagonistic groups. One, led by the original supervisor, included the original staff and other minorities. . . . The other group [led by the white supervisor] included the five newly hired technologists."

The technologists reflected the dominant managerial culture, whereas the technicians came to be a very angry counterculture.

Chronic clashes ensued, marked over several years by insubordination and disciplinary actions. Lawsuits against the hospital's management culminated the clashes. They were soon settled out of court, setting the stage for much rejoicing among the old guard along with plans for a new attack.

Chronic clashes may eventually give way to accommodation. The interactions between staff purchasing agents and departments such as sales and personnel, for example, may be characterized by their running battles. Yet, in the midst of these clashes, negotiations and even exchange tactics may be used to achieve accommodation (Strauss 1964). In a case Strauss studied, these tactics included relying on favors, both past and future, to get managers to change their request and establishing formal rules providing for lead times. These rules were then ritualized by "going through the motions" with no expectation of actual delivery.

ALIENATION/RECONSTITUTION

Alienation constitutes "change on the part of members of one culture away from the rules governing their usual structured activities without internalizing the rules of the other cultures" (Dohrenwend and Smith 1962:33). Apathy and demoralization are the result. In sharp contrast, reconstitution takes place when one subculture, following tentative assimilation by a dominant subculture, devises new patterns by means of which it regains equity with the other.

Although research studies do not report an alienation pattern explicitly, in the case of the mergers of the two banks described above, it seems likely that some alienation occurred within some of the subcultures in the acquired bank. The merger forced many of them to abandon their traditional procedures, but, at the same time, they rejected the dominant culture's procedures and rules. Similarly, the constant conflict between the subculture of physicians and engineers, on the one hand, and of the managerial bureaucrats, on the other, reported in chapter 6, might well have led to alienation on the part of the physicians and engineers. Recall that a reorganization of a midwestern state Department of Health and Environment brought about a constant clash between the entrenched physicians and engineers and the newly created and potent top administrators (Maynard-Moody, Stull, and Mitchell 1986). These bureaucrats successfully dislodged and scattered the physicians and engineers. It seems likely that the physicians, especially, would have become alienated as they were forced to give up the rules and procedures that had guided their activities, yet they adamantly refused to take on the rules and procedures of the bureaucrats.

Descriptions of the reactions of some occupational subcultures to deskilling efforts by managerial subcultures illustrate the possibility of a pattern of reconstruction (Form 1987). In these instances, the occupation devised ways to accommodate rather than be assimilated, even destroyed, by a temporarily dominant management bureaucracy.

ACCULTURATION PATTERNS

Assuming that two or more subcultures (five, for instance) have been analyzed using the grid-group format, the stage is then set for assessing the relations between them. The analysis of single subcultures in the literature may be insufficient to permit such an analysis; additional data may be needed. In any event, the relations between subcultures in a given organization should be characterized by the mode of adjustment that appears to be functioning. In this manner a static portrait of the subcultural makeup of the organization is created.

Imagine that a staff subculture (the personnel occupations, for example) is in chronic conflict with a coalition that cuts across production and sales departments and with the specific cliques in them. This coalition, in turn, has been thoroughly assimilated by a higher management subculture. In addition, the coalition is in an assimilative mode with the sales department, is in an accommodative mode with top management, and is in constant clashes with personnel and sales. Sales, in turn, has come into repeated conflict with personnel but has been practically assimilated into a subculture of top managers. Top managers also operate in an accommodative mode with personnel and production. Although purely speculative, this hypothetical portrait suggests how a profile of the subcultures of an organization could be developed.

ROLE OF LEADERSHIP IN CULTURAL FLUX

So far this discussion has left out a basic ingredient: the role leaders can play in maintaining an ongoing pattern of adaptation or assimilation. Dynamic forces would work on our hypothetical configuration and alter it, but how quickly and with what consequences are practically impossible to predict. In any event, the choice of leadership style may be one of the influential forces in producing organizational integration. One such style has been labeled consensus leadership (Trice and Beyer 1991). Leaders who exhibit this style negotiate among groups in top-manager ranks with diverse values and interests using trade-offs, rewards and punishment, bargaining, and barter in an effort to incorporate these groups fully into overall decision making and action (Zaleznick and Kets de Vries 1975). As I and Beyer (1992:289) wrote: "Consensus leaders do not seek to homogenize diverse subcultures by changing or creating a single culture to embrace them all. Rather they use their influence to find workable compromises that allow subcultures to maintain their distinctiveness.... They are good communicators who can explain different subcultures to each other."

In our hypothetical case, a consensus leader might capriciously emerge, or one could be deliberately selected for his or her demonstrated capacity to maintain the organization's culture by reconciling diverse interests. Such a leader would probably operate "at a distance" rather than face to face and, because of his or her integrative function, would have to exercise influence across a variety of subcultures. Unlike face-to-face leaders, "[consensus leaders] must communicate their influence, ideas, and values across a far-flung group of followers . . . They must engage in dramatic, public acts" (Trice and Beyer 1992:289). Lee Iacocca of Chrysler Corporation, Mary Kay Ash of Mary Kay, Inc., and Thomas Watson, Jr., of IBM are well-known examples. Regardless of how such leaders emerge, they can help reduce a number of the constant clashes in an organization and possibly replace them, to a considerable degree at least, with an accommodative mode of interaction. One of the most obvious forces for change that might make the emergence of such leaders possible would be deaths, retirements, or resignations among leaders of top management and other subcultures.

By the same token, regardless of the leadership, turbulent forces in the environment can lead to the accentuation of top-management power and the increase in total assimilation into that subculture. This potential is ever present regardless of environmental conditions. Where constant clashes characterize a relationship, it is quite possible that many members of the less dominant subcultures will become alienated, in which case they will reject both the more dominant subculture and their own as well.

One simple but very basic point emerges from this book: the study of the cultures of work organizations inevitably involve *both* occupational and organizational dimensions. No longer can the examination of one proceed without a concomitant examination of the other. The inclusion of the intersection between the two is essential if studies of work life are to become more realistic than they have been in the past. The occupational dimensions of work have been repeatedly ignored, while organizational features have received almost exclusive attention. It is to this glaringly obvious omission in organizational theory, and the impact of this omission on the study of organizational cultures, that I have drawn attention. I hope this book will stimulate further efforts to integrate these two different but potent aspects of work life.

REFERENCES

Abbott, Andrew
  1988 *The system of professions.* Chicago: University of Chicago Press.
  1989 The new occupational structure: What are the questions? *Work and Occupations* 16:273–91.
Acheson, James M.
  1981 Anthropology of fishing. *Annual Review of Anthropology* 10:275–316.
Aiken, Linda H.
  1983 Nurses. In *Handbook of health, health care and health professionals,* ed. David Mechanic, 407–30. New York: Free Press.
Aiken, Michael, and Jerald Hage
  1968 Organizational interdependence and intraorganizational structure. *American Sociological Review* 33:912–29.
Akabas, Sheila H., and Paul A. Kurzman
  1982 *Work, workers and work organizations: A view from social work.* Englewood Cliffs, N.J.: Prentice-Hall.
Allen, Michael P., Sharon K. Panian, and Roy E. Lotz
  1979 Managerial succession and organizational performance: A recalcitrant problem revisited. *Administrative Science Quarterly* 24:167–80.
Angle, Harold, and James L. Perry
  1986 Dual commitment and labor-management relationship climates. *Academy of Management Journal* 29:31–50.
Applebaum, Herbert
  1981 *Royal blue: The culture of construction workers.* New York: Holt.
  1984a Introduction: Dangerous occupations—construction work, longshore work, fire fighting, mining. In *Work in market and industrial societies,* ed. Herbert Applebaum, 99–102. Albany: State University of New York Press.
  1984b Theoretical introduction: Work in market and industrial societies. In *Work in market and industrial societies,* ed. Herbert Applebaum, 1–32. Albany: State University of New York Press.

Arens, William
  1976   Professional football: An American symbol and ritual. In *The American dimension: Cultural myths and social realities,* ed. W. Arens and Susan P. Montague, 3–14. Port Washington, N.Y.: Alfred.
Arnold, David O.
  1970   *The sociology of subcultures.* Berkeley: Glendessary Press.
Arvey, Richard D., and James E. Campion
  1982   The employment interview: A summary and review of recent research. *Personnel Psychology* 35:281–322.
Ash, Mary Kay
  1981   *Mary Kay.* New York: Harper and Row.
Association of American Publishers (AAP)
  1977   *The accidental profession: Education, training and the people of publishing.* New York: AAP Education for Publishing Committee.
Aydin, Carolyn E.
  1989   Occupational adaptations to computerized medical information systems. *Journal of Health and Social Behavior* 30:163–79.
Baba, Marietta
  1988   The local knowledge content of technology-based firms: Rethinking informal organization. Paper presented at a conference, Managing the high technology firm, Jan. 13–15, University of Colorado, Boulder.
Bacharach, Samuel B., and Edward J. Lawler
  1981   *Bargaining power, tactics, and outcomes.* San Francisco: Jossey-Bass.
Bailyn, Lotte
  1977   Involvement and accommodation in technical careers: An inquiry into the relation to work at mid-career. In *Organizational careers: Some new perspectives,* ed. John Van Maanen, 109–32. New York: Wiley.
Baldridge, J. Victor
  1981   *Power and conflict in the university.* New York: Wiley.
Ball, Donald W., and John W. Loy
  1975   *Sport and social order: Contributions to the sociology of sport.* Reading, Mass.: Addison-Wesley.
Barley, Stephen R.
  1983a Semiotics and the study of occupational and organizational cultures. *Administrative Science Quarterly* 28:393–413.
  1983b The codes of the dead: The semiotics of funeral work. *Urban Life* 12: 3–31.
  1988   On technology, time, and social order: Technically induced change in the temporal organization of radiological work. In *Making time: Ethnographies of high technology organizations,* ed. F. A. Dubinskas, 123–69. Philadelphia: Temple University Press.
Barley, Stephen R., and Deborah Knight
  1988   Stress as a vocabulary of organizing. Paper presented at the 48th Academy of Management meetings, 15–19 Aug., Anaheim, Calif.

Barley, Stephen R., and Pamela S. Tolbert
  1991 Introduction: At the intersection of organizations and occupations. *Research in the Sociology of Occupations* 8:1–13.
Baron, George, and Asher Tropp
  1970 Teachers in England and America. In *Comparative perspectives in formal organizations*, ed. Henry A. Landsberger, 87–99. New York: Little, Brown.
Baron, James N., Frank R. Dobbins, and P. Deveraux Jennings
  1986 War and peace: The evolution of modern personnel administration in U.S. industry. *American Journal of Sociology* 92:350–83.
Barthes, Roland
  1972 *Mythologies*. London: Jonathan Cape.
Bartunek, Jean M., and Michael K. Moch
  1987 First order, second order and third order change and organizational development interventions: A cognitive approach. *Journal of Applied Behavioral Science* 23:483–500.
Bassis, Michael S., and William R. Rosengren
  1975 Socialization for occupational disengagement. *Sociology of Work and Occupations* 2:133–49.
Beck, Brenda E. F., and Larry F. Moore
  1985 Linking the host culture to organizational variables. In *Organizational cultures*, ed. Peter J, Frost, Larry F. Moore, Meryl R. Louis, Craig C. Lundberg, and Joanne Martin, 335–51. Beverly Hills: Sage.
Becker, Howard S.
  1951 The professional dance musician and his audience. *American Journal of Sociology* 57:136–44.
  1960 Notes on the concept of commitment. *American Journal of Sociology* 66:32–40.
  1963 *Outsiders: Studies in the sociology of deviance*. New York: Free Press.
  1982 *Art worlds*. Berkeley: University of California Press.
Becker, Howard S., and James Carper
  1956 The elements of identification with an occupation. *American Sociological Review* 21:341–48.
Becker, Howard S., B. Geer, E. C. Hughes, and A. M. Strauss
  1961 *Boys in white: Student cultures in medical school*. Chicago: University of Chicago Press.
Begun, James W., and Ronald C. Lippincott
  1987 The origins and resolution of interoccupational conflict. *Work and Occupations* 14:368–71.
Bell, Daniel
  1973 *The coming of post-industrial society*. New York: Basic Books.
Bell, Malinda
  1984 Teachings of the heart. *Journal of the American Medical Association* 252:2684
Bellah, Robert N., Richard Madsen, William M. Sullivan, Ann Swidler, and Steven M. Tipton
  1985 *Habits of the heart*. New York: Harper and Row.

Bendix, Reinhard
  1956   *Work and authority in industry.* New York: Harper and Row.
Bennis, Warren G.
  1966   *Changing organizations.* New York: McGraw-Hill.
Bensman, Joseph, and Israel Gerver
  1963   Crime and punishment in the factory: The function of deviancy in maintaining the social system. *American Sociological Review* 28:588–98.
Benson, Susan P.
  1986   *Counter-cultures: Saleswomen, managers, and customers in American department stores, 1890–1940.* Chicago: University of Illinois Press.
Berger, Peter L., and Thomas Luckman
  1966   *The social construction of reality.* New York: Anchor Books.
Bergren, Myrtle
  1966   *Tough timber: The loggers of the B.C.—their story.* Toronto: Progress Books.
Berry, John W.
  1980   Acculturation as varieties of adaptation. In *Acculturation: Theory, models, and some new findings,* ed. Amanda M. Padilla, 9–25. Boulder, Colo.: Westview Press.
Betcherman, Gordon, and Douglas Rebne
  1987   Technology and control of the labor process: Fifty years of longshoring on the U.S. West Coast. In *Workers, managers and technological change,* ed. Daniel B. Cornfield, 73–89. New York: Plenum Press.
Betz, Michael, and Lenahan O'Connell
  1983   Changing doctor-patient relationships and the rise in concern for accountability. *Social Problems* 31:84–95.
Beyer, Janice M.
  1981   Ideologies, values and decision-making in organizations. In *Handbook of organizational design,* vol. 2, ed. Paul Nystrom, and William H. Starbuck, 166–97. London: Oxford University Press.
Beyer, Janice, Roger L. Dunbar, and Alan D. Meyer
  1988   Comment: The concept of ideology in organizational analysis. *Academy of Management Review* 13:483–89.
Beyer, Janice M., and Harrison M. Trice
  1978   *Implementing change: Alcoholism policies in work organizations.* New York: Free Press.
  1979   A reexamination of the relation between size and various components of organizational complexity. *Administrative Science Quarterly* 24:48–63.
  1982   The utilization process: A conceptual framework and synthesis of empirical findings. *Administrative Science Quarterly* 27:591–622.
Billson, Janet M.
  1992   Wisconsin sociologists successfully challenge restrictive bill. *Footnotes* 19:2.
Birenbaum, Arnold
  1982   Reprofessionalization in pharmacy. *Social Science and Medicine* 16:871–78.

Blake, Joseph A.
1974 Occupational thrill, mystique, and the truck driver. *Urban Life and Culture* 3:205–21.
Blakelock, E.
1960 New look at old leisure. *Administrative Science Quarterly* 4:446–67.
Blase, Joseph J.
1986 Socialization as humanization: One side of becoming a teacher. *Sociology of Education* 59:100–113.
Blau, Judith R.
1984 *Architects and firms: A sociological perspective on architectural practice.* Cambridge: MIT Press.
Blau, Peter M., and Otis D. Duncan
1967 *The American occupational structure.* New York: Wiley.
Blau, Peter M., and Richard A. Schoenherr
1971 *The structure of organizations.* New York: Basic Books.
Blau, Peter M., and W. Richard Scott
1962 *Formal organizations.* San Francisco: Chandler.
Blauner, Robert
1964 *Alienation and freedom.* Chicago: University of Chicago Press.
Blumenfeld, Ruth
1965 Mohawks: Roundtrip to high steel. *Transaction* 3:19–21.
Boatright, Mody
1963 *Folklore of the oil industry.* Dallas: Southern Methodist Press.
Bocock, Robert
1974 *Ritual in industrial society.* London: Allen and Unwin.
Boland, Richard J.
1982 Myth and technology in the American accounting profession. *Journal of Management Studies* 19:109–27.
Boland, Richard J., and Raymond Hoffman
1983 Humor in a machine shop. In *Organizational symbolism,* ed. Louis R. Pondy, 187–98. Greenwich, Conn.: JAI Press.
Boles, Jacqueline, and A. P. Garbin
1977 Stripping for a living: An occupational study of the night club strippers. In *The social world of occupations,* ed. Bernard J. Gallagher, and Charles S. Palazzolo, 226–48. Chicago: Kendall/Hunt.
Boone, L. P.
1949 Patterns of innovation in the language of the oil field. *American Speech* 24:131–37.
Bosk, Charles L.
1979 *Forgive and remember.* Chicago: University of Chicago Press.
1980 Occupational rituals in patient management. *New England Journal of Medicine* 303:71–76.
Boudon, Raymond
1982 *The unintended consequences of social action.* New York: St. Martin's Press.
Boyer, Peter J.
1988 *Who killed CBS?* New York: Random House.

Braverman, Harry
  1974 *Labor and monopoly capital: The degradation of work in the twentieth century.* New York: Monthly Review Press.
Breer, Paul E., and Edwin A. Locke
  1965 *Task experience as a source of attitudes.* Homewood, Ill.: Dorsey Press.
Breslin, Jimmy.
  1986 *Table money.* New York: Ticknor & Fields
Brett, Jeanne M.
  1984 Job transitions and personal and role development. *Research in Personnel and Human Resource Management* 2:155–85.
Bright, James R.
  1958 Does automation raise skill requirements? *Harvard Business Review* 36:85–98.
Briloff, Abraham J.
  1972 *Unaccountable accounting.* New York: Harper and Row.
Brim, Orville
  1966 Socialization through the life cycle. In *Socialization after childhood,* ed. Orville Brim and Stanton Wheeler, 3–49. New York: Wiley.
Brinkerhoff, Merlin B., and David J. Corry
  1976 Structural prisons: Barriers to occupational goals in a society of "equal" opportunity. *International Journal of Comparative Sociology* 17:261–74.
Brint, Steven
  1984 New class and cumulative trend explanations of the liberal political attitudes of professionals. *American Journal of Sociology* 90:30–71.
  1985 The political attitudes of professionals. *American Review of Sociology* 11:389–414.
Brown, L. David
  1983 *Management conflict at organizational interfaces.* Reading, Mass.: Addison-Wesley.
Bryan, James H.
  1966 Occupational ideologies and individual attitudes of call girls. *Social Problems* 13:441–50.
Bryant, Clifford D.
  1972 Sawdust in their shoes: The carnival as a neglected complex organization and work culture. In *The social dimensions of work,* ed. Clifford D. Bryant, 112–39. Englewood Cliffs, N.J.: Prentice-Hall.
Bryant, Clifford D., and Kenneth B. Perkins
  1982 Containing work disaffection: The poultry processing worker. In *Varieties of work,* ed. Phyllis L. Stewart and Muriel G. Cantor, 199–212. Beverly Hills: Sage.
Bucher, Rue
  1962 Psychology: A study of social movements within a profession. *Social Problems* 10:40–51.
Bucher, Rue, and Joan Stelling
  1977 *Becoming professional.* Beverly Hills: Sage.

Bucher, Rue, and Anselm Strauss
1961 Professions in process. *American Journal of Sociology* 66:325–34.
Buono, Anthony F., and James L. Bowditch
1989 *The human side of mergers and acquisitions.* San Francisco: Jossey-Bass.
Buono, Anthony F., James L. Bowditch, and John W. Lewis
1985 When cultures collide: The anatomy of a merger. *Human Relations* 38: 477–500.
Burchell, S., C. Clubb, and A. G. Hopwood
1985 Accounting in its social context: Towards a history of value added in the United Kingdom. *Accounting, Organizations and Society* 10:381–413.
Burchell, S., C. Clubb, A. G. Hopwood, and J. Hughes
1980 The roles of accounting in organizations and society. *Accounting, Organizations and Society* 5:272–79.
Byington, Robert H.
1978 Strategies for collecting occupational folklife in contemporary urban/industrial contexts. *Western Folklore* 37 (special issue):185–212.
Calhoun, Craig
1982 *The question of class struggle.* Chicago: University of Chicago Press.
Calhoun, Craig, and Martha Copp
1988 Computerization in legal work. In *Research in the sociology of work,* vol. 4, ed. Richard L. Simpson and Ida Harper, 233–59. Greenwich, Conn.: JAI Press.
Calvert, Monte
1967 *The mechanical engineer in America, 1830–1910.* Baltimore: Johns Hopkins University Press.
Cameron, William B.
1954 Sociological notes on the jam session. *Social Forces* 33:177–82.
Campbell, Joseph
1949 *The hero with a thousand faces.* Princeton: Princeton University Press.
Caplow, Theodore
1954 *The sociology of work.* Minneapolis: University of Minnesota Press.
Carlton, Eric
1977 *Ideology and social order.* London: Routledge.
Carp, Robert, and Russell Wheeler
1972 Sink or swim: The socialization of a federal district judge. *Journal of Public Law* 21:359–97.
Carr-Saunders, Alexander, and P. A. Wilson
1941 *The professions.* Oxford: Clarendon Press.
Carroll, Jackson W.
1971 Structural effects of professional schools on professional socialization: The case of Protestant clergymen. *Social Forces* 50:61–74.
Carter, Reginald
1977 Are the work values of scientists and engineers different than managers? In *Work and technology,* ed. Marie R. Haug, 125–38. Beverly Hills: Sage.

Case, John, and R.C.R. Taylor, eds.
  1979 *Co-ops, communes and collectivities: Experiments in social change in the 1960s and 1970s.* New York: Pantheon.
Chambers, R. J.
  1980 The myths and the science of accounting. *Accounting, Organizations and Society* 5(1):167–80.
Chapple, Eliot D., and Charlton S. Coon
  1942 *Principles of anthropology.* New York: Holt.
Charles, Michael T.
  1982 The Yellowstone ranger: The social control and socialization of federal law enforcement officers. *Human Organization* 61:216–26.
Charnofsky, Harold
  1974 Ballplayers, occupational image and the maximization of profit. In *Varieties of work experience,* ed. Phyllis L. Stewart, and Muriel G. Cantor, 262–74. New York: Wiley.
Chatov, Robert
  1975 *Corporate financial reporting: Public or private control?* New York: Free Press.
Cherry, Mike
  1974 *On high steel.* New York: Ballantine Books.
Child, John R., and Janet Fulk
  1982 Maintenance of occupational control: The case of the professions. *Work and Occupations* 9:155–92.
Child, John R., J. Harvey Loveridge, and A. Spencer
  1984 Microelectronics and the quality of employment in services. In *New technology and the future of work and skills,* ed. Pauline Marstrand, 163–90. London: Pinter.
Child, John, and Chris Smith
  1987 The context and process of organizational transformation: Cadbury Limited in its sector. *Journal of Management Studies* 24:565–93.
Christensen, Barlow F.
  1980 The unauthorized practice of law: Do good fences really make good neighbors—or even sense? *American Bar Foundation Research Journal* 159:159–216.
Clark, Burton R.
  1970 *The distinctive college: Antioch, Reed and Swarthmore.* Chicago: Aldine.
Clark, R. E., and E. E. LaBeef
  1982 Death telling: Managing the delivery of bad news. *Journal of Health and Social Behavior* 23:366–80.
Clayman, Steven E.
  1988 Displaying neutrality in television news interviews. *Social Problems* 35:474–92.
Clearfield, Sidney
  1977 Professional self-image of the social worker: Implications for social work education. *Journal of Education for Social Work* 13:23–30.
Cleverley, Graham
  1973 *Managers and magic.* New York: Dutton.

Cohen, Marcia B., and David Wagner

    1982   Social work professionalism: Reality and illusion. In *Professionals as workers: Mental labor in advanced capitalism,* ed. Charles Derber, 141–53. Boston: Hall.

Cole, Robert E., and Kenichi Tominaga

    1976   Japan's changing occupational structure and its significance. In *Japanese industrialization and its social consequences,* ed. Patrick Hugh, 53–96. Berkeley: University of California Press.

Cornfield, Daniel, ed.

    1987   *Workers, managers, and technological change: Emerging patterns of labor relations.* New York: Plenum Press.

Corwin, Ronald G.

    1986   Organizational skills and the "deskilling hypothesis." In *Becoming a worker,* ed. Kathryn M. Borman and Jane Reisman, 221–43. Norwood, N.J.: Ablex.

Coser, Lewis A.

    1973   Servants: The obsolescence of an occupational role. *Social Forces* 52: 31–40.

Cottrell, W. Fred

    1940   *The railroader.* Stanford: Stanford University Press.

Couto, Richard A.

    1987   Changing technologies and consequences for labor in coal mining. In *Workers, managers, and technological change: Emerging patterns of labor relations,* ed. Daniel B. Cornfield, 175–202. New York: Plenum Press.

Cowie, James B., and Julian Roebuck

    1975   *An ethnography of a chiropractic clinic.* New York: Free Press.

Cressey, Paul G.

    1932   *The taxi-dance hall.* Chicago: University of Chicago Press.

Crompton, Rosemary, and Gareth Jones

    1984   *White collar proletariat: Deskilling and gender in clerical work.* Philadelphia: Temple University Press.

Crozier, Michael

    1964   *The bureaucratic phenomenon.* Chicago: University of Chicago Press.

Cullen, John B.

    1978   *The structure of professionalism.* New York/Princeton: Petrocelli Books.

Dalton, Melville

    1959   *Men who manage.* New York: Wiley.

Daniels, Arlene K.

    1969   The captive professional: Bureaucratic limitations in the practice of military psychiatry. *Journal of Health and Social Behavior* 10:255–65.

Davies, C.

    1983   Professionals in bureaucracies: The conflict thesis revisited. In *The sociology of the professions,* ed. R. Dingwell, and P. Lewis, 189–201. London: Macmillan.

Davis, Stanley M.

    1984   *Managing corporate culture.* Cambridge, Mass.: Ballinger.

Deal, Terrence E., and Allan A. Kennedy
  1982   *Corporate cultures: The rites and rituals of corporate life.* Reading, Mass.: Addison-Wesley.
DeCamp, L. Sprague
  1960   *The ancient engineers.* New York: Ballantine Books.
Deetz, S., and A. Kersten
  1983   Critical models of interpretive research. In *Communication and organization: An interpretive approach,* ed. L. Putnam and M. Pacanowsky, 147–72. Beverly Hills: Sage.
Dellheim, Charles
  1987   The creation of a company culture. *American History Review* 92:13–44.
Denzin, Norman
  1968   Incomplete professionalization: The case of pharmacy. *Social Forces* 46: 375–81.
Derber, Charles
  1982   Professionals as new workers. In *Professionals as workers: Mental labor in advanced capitalism,* ed. Charles Derber, 3–10. Boston: G. K. Hall.
DiFazio, William
  1985   *Longshoreman: Community and resistance on the Brooklyn waterfront.* South Hadley, Mass.: Bergin and Garvey.
DiMaggio, Paul, and Walter Powell
  1983   The iron cage revisited: Institutional isomorphism and collective rationality in organizational fields. *American Sociological Review* 48:147–60.
Dingwall, Robert
  1977   Atrocity stories and professional relationships. *Sociology of Work and Occupations* 4:372–95.
Dohrenwend, Bruce P., and Robert J. Smith
  1962   Toward a theory of acculturation. *Southwest Journal of Anthropology* 18: 30–39.
Donovan, F. R.
  1920   *The woman who waits.* Chicago: University of Chicago Press.
  1931   *The saleslady.* Chicago: University of Chicago Press.
  1938   *The school ma'am.* New York: Winton House.
Dorson, Richard M.
  1973   *America in legend: Folklore from the colonial period to the present.* New York: Pantheon.
Douglas, Mary
  1970   *Natural symbols.* London: Crescent Press.
  1975   *Implicit meanings: Essays in anthropology.* London: Routledge.
  1978   *Cultural bias.* London: Royal Anthropological Institute of Great Britain and Ireland.
  1982   Introduction to grid/group analysis. In *Essays in the sociology of perception,* ed. Mary Douglas, London: Routledge.
Druckman, Daniel, ed.
  1977   *Negotiations.* Beverly Hills: Sage.

Dubin, Robert
  1951   Organization fictions. In *Human relations in administration*, ed. Robert Dubin, New York: Prentice-Hall.
Dulles, Foster Rhea, and Melvyn Dubofsky
  1984   *Labor in America: A history*. 4th ed. Arlington Heights, Ill.: Harlan Davidson.
Duncan, Otis D., and Robert W. Hodge
  1963   Education and occupational mobility. *American Journal of Sociology* 67: 629–44.
Durkheim, Emile
  1964a [1893]   *The division of labor in society*. Trans. George Simpson. Glencoe, Ill.: Free Press.
  1964b [1897]   *Suicide*. Glencoe, Ill.: Free Press.
Dyer, Gwynne
  1985   *War*. New York: Crown.
Eckholm, Erik
  1986   Rocket engineers tell of pressure for launching. *New York Times*, Feb. 26, 137.
Edwards, P. K., and Hugh Scullion
  1982   *The social organization of industrial conflict: Control and resistance in the workplace*. Oxford: Basil Blackwell.
Edwards, R.
  1979   *Contested terrain*. New York: Basic Books.
Eilbert, Henry
  1959   The development of personnel management in the United States. *Business History Review* 33:345–64.
Eisenhower, David
  1986   *Eisenhower at war: 1943–1945*. New York: Random House.
Eitzen, D. Stanley
  1981   The structure of sports and society. In *The social world*, ed. Ian Robertson, 59–62. New York: Worth.
Eitzen, D. Stanley, and Norman R. Yetman
  1972   Managerial change, longevity, and organizational effectiveness. *Administrative Science Quarterly* 17:110–16.
England, G. W., and R. Lee
  1974   Organizational goals and expected behaviors among American, Japanese, and Korean managers: A comparative study. *Academy of Management Journal* 14:425–38.
Enz, Cathy A.
  1988   The role of value congruity in intraorganizational power. *Administrative Science Quarterly* 33:284–304.
Erikson, Kai T.
  1962   Notes on the sociology of deviance. *Social Problems* 9:307–14.
Everstine, Louis, and Diana S. Everstine
  1986   Preface. In *Psychotherapy and the law*, ed. Louis Everstine and Diana S. Everstine, xi–xii. New York: Grune and Stratton.

Faulkner, Robert R.
   1973   Orchestra interaction. *Sociological Quarterly* 14:147–57.
   1974a Making us sound bad: Performer compliance and interaction in the
          symphony orchestra. In *Varieties of work experience,* ed. Phyllis L. Stew-
          art and Muriel G. Cantor, 238–48. New York: Wiley.
   1974b Coming of age in organizations: A comparative study of career con-
          tingencies and adult socialization. *Sociology of Work and Occupations* 1:
          131–73.
Fayol, Henri
   1949 [1919]   *General and industrial management.* Trans. Constance Stours.
          London: Pitman.
Federico, Ronald C.
   1974   Recruitment, training and performance: The case of ballet. In *Varieties
          of Work Experience,* ed. Phyllis Stewart and Muriel G. Cantor, 249–61.
          New York: Wiley.
Feldman, Steven P.
   1987   The crossroads of interpretation: Administration in professional or-
          ganizations. *Human Organization* 46:95–102.
Ferraro, Kenneth F., and Tammy Sutherland
   1989   Domains of medical practice: Physicians' assessment of the role of
          physician extenders. *Journal of Health and Social Behavior* 30:192–205.
Fidel, Ken, and Roberta Garner
   1987   Computer workers: Career lines and professional identity. Paper pre-
          sented at the annual meeting of the Society for the Study of Social
          Problems, Aug. 9–11, Chicago.
Filippelli, Ronald L.
   1984   *Labor in the U.S.A.: A History.* New York: Knopf.
Fine, Gary A.
   1987   Working cooks: The dynamics of professional kitchens. In *Current re-
          search on occupations and professions,* vol. 4, ed. Helena Z. Lopata, 141–
          58. Greenwich, Conn.: JAI Press.
   1988   Letting off steam? Redefining a restaurant's work environment. In
          Inside organizations: Understanding the human dimension, ed. Michael O.
          Jones, Michael D. Moore, and Richard Snyder, 119–27. Beverly Hills:
          Sage.
Fine, Gary A., and Sherryl Kleinman
   1979   Rethinking subculture: An interactionist analysis. *American Journal of
          Sociology* 85:1–20.
Fineman, Stephen
   1985   The skills of getting by. In *The symbolics of skill,* ed. Antonio Strati, 18–
          28. Trento, Italy: Tipolitografia TEMPI.
Finholt, Tom, and Lee S. Sproull
   1990   Electronic groups at work. *Organization Science* 1:41–64.
Firth, Raymond
   1930   A dart match in Tikopia: A study in the sociology of primitive sport.
          Oceania 1:64–96.

Fitzpatrick, John S.
  1980 Adapting to danger: A participant observation study of an underground mine. *Sociology of Work and Occupations* 7:131–58.
Fligstein, Neil
  1987 The intraorganizational power struggle: Rise of finance personnel to top leadership in large corporations, 1919–1979. *American Sociological Review* 52:44–58.
Form, William
  1987 On the degradation of skills. *Annual Review of Sociology* 13:29–47.
Freidman, Lawrence
  1965 Freedom of contract and occupational licensing, 1890–1910: A legal social study. *California Law Review* 53:494–95.
Freidson, Eliot
  1973 Professions and the occupational principle. In *Professions and their prospects,* ed. Eliot Freidson, 19–33. Beverly Hills: Sage.
  1976 The division of labor as social interaction. *Social Problems* 23:304–13.
  1977 The future of professionalization. In *Health and the division of labor,* ed. Margaret Stacey, 14–38. London: Croom Helm.
  1982 Occupational autonomy and labor market shelters. In *Varieties of work,* ed. Phyllis L. Stewart and Muriel G. Cantor 39–54. Beverly Hills: Sage.
  1984 The changing nature of professional control. *Annual Review of Sociology* 10:1–20.
  1985 Foreword. In *The making of rehabilitation,* by Glenn Gritzer, and Arnold Arluke, xi–xxii. Berkeley: University of California Press.
  1986 *A study of the institutionalization of formal knowledge.* Chicago: University of Chicago Press.
Freund, Julien
  1969 *The sociology of Max Weber.* New York: Vintage Press.
Friedmaan, Albert B.
  1968 The scatological rites of burglars. *Western Folklore* 27:171–79.
Friedman, Andy
  1977 Responsible autonomy versus direct control over the labor process. *Capital and Class* 1:43–57.
Frost, Peter J., Larry F. Moore, Meryl R. Louis, Craig C. Lundberg, and Joanne Martin, eds.
  1985 *Organizational culture.* Beverly Hills: Sage.
  1991 *Reframing organizational culture.* Newbury Park, Calif.: Sage.
Fukami, Cynthia V., and E. Larsen
  1984 Commitment to company and union: Parallel models. *Journal of Applied Psychology* 69:367–71.
Gagliardi, Pasquale
  1989 Culture and management training: Closed minds and change in managers belonging to organizational and occupational communities. In *Organizational symbolism,* ed. Barry A. Turner, 159–71. New York: de Gruyter.

Galante, Mary Ann
   1986   California bar attorneys end strike. *National Law Journal,* June 2, 8.
Gambling, Trevor
   1977   Magic, accounting and morale. *Accounting Organizations and Society* 2:
          141–51.
Gamst, Frederick C.
   1977   An integrating view of the underlying premises of an industrial eth-
          nology in the United States and Canada. *Anthropology Quarterly* 50:1–
          9.
   1980   *The hoghead: An industrial ethnology of the locomotive engineer.* New York:
          Holt.
   1990   *Highballing with flimsies: Working under train orders.* Crete, New Bruns-
          wick: J-B Publishing.
Gans, Herbert J.
   1982   Values in the news. In *The social world,* ed. Ian Robertson, 40–48. New
          York: Worth.
Gardner, Burleigh B.
   1946   The factory as a social system. In *Industry and society,* ed. William F.
          Whyte, 4–20. New York: McGraw-Hill.
Garson, Barbara
   1988   *The electronic sweatshop: How computers are transforming the office of the
          future into the factory of the past.* New York: Simon and Schuster.
Geertz, Clifford
   1964   Ideology as a cultural system. In *Ideology and discontent,* ed. David E.
          Apter, 47–76. New York: Free Press.
   1970   The impact of the concept of culture on the concept of man. In *Man
          makes sense,* ed. Eugene A. Hammal and William S. Simmons, 47–65.
          Boston: Little, Brown.
   1972   Deep play: notes on the Balinese cockfight. *Daedalus* 101:1–37.
   1973   *The interpretation of cultures: Selected essays.* New York: Basic Books.
   1975   Common sense as a cultural system. *Antioch Review* 33:5–26.
   1979   From the native's point of view: On the nature of anthropological
          understanding. In *Interpretive social science: A reader,* ed. Paul Rabinow,
          225–367. Berkeley: University of California Press.
   1983   *Local knowledge: Further essays in interpretive anthropology.* New York:
          Basic Books.
Gephart, Robert J.
   1978   Status degradation and organizational succession: An ethnometho-
          dological approach. *Administrative Science Quarterly* 23:553–81.
Gerrity, Martha S., et al.
   1992   Uncertainty and professional work: Perceptions of physicians in clin-
          ical practice. *American Journal of Sociology* 97:1022–51.
Gerstl, Joel E.
   1961   Determinants of occupational community in high status occupations.
          Sociological Quarterly 2:37–40.
Gieryn, Thomas F.
   1983   Boundary-work and the demarcation of science from nonscience:

Strains and interests in professional ideologies of scientists. *American Sociological Review* 48:781–95.

Gilder, Joshua
1982   The rage for cowboy art. *Saturday Review*, Jan., 32–35.

Gillespie, Angus K.
1984   Narrative of the Jersey Shore lifeguards. *New Jersey Folklore* 9:1–5.

Gilmore, Samuel
1987   Coordination and convention: The organization of the concert world. *Symbolic Interaction* 10:209–27.

Ginzberg, Eli
1984   The monetarization of medical care. *New England Journal of Medicine* 310:1162–65.

Glaser, Barney G., and Anselm L. Strauss
1971   *Status passage.* Chicago: Aldine-Atherton.

Gluckman, Max
1962   Les rites de passage. In *Essays on the ritual of social relations,* ed. Max Gluckman, 1–53. Manchester, Eng.: University Press.

Gmelch, George
1971   Baseball magic. *Trans-Action* 8:39–42.

Goffman, Erving
1959   *The presentation of self in everyday life.* Garden City, N.Y.: Anchor Books.
1961a *Asylums.* Garden City, N.J.: Anchor Books.
1961b *Encounters.* Indianapolis: Bobbs-Merrill.
1967   *Interaction ritual: Essays in face-to-face behavior.* New York: Anchor Books.

Gold, Raymond L.
1964   In the basement: The apartment building janitor. In *The human shape of work: Studies in the sociology of occupations,* ed. Peter L. Berger, 1–51. Macmillan.

Goldner, Fred H.
1961   Industrial relations and the organization of management. Ph.D. diss., University of California, Berkeley.
1970   The division of labor: Process and power. In *Power in organizations,* ed. Mayer N. Zald, 97–143. Nashville: Vanderbilt University Press.

Goode, William J.
1961   The librarian: From occupation to profession. *Library Quarterly* 31:306–20.

Goodenough, Ward H.
1978   Multiculturalism as the normal human experience. In *Applied anthropology in America,* ed. Elizabeth Eddy and William L. Partidge, 113–32. New York: Columbia University Press.

Gouldner, Alvin
1957   Cosmopolitans and locals: Toward an analysis of latent social roles. *Administrative Science Quarterly* 2:281–306.

Gowler, Dan, and Karen Legge
1983   The meaning of management and the management of meaning: A

view from social anthropology. In *Perspectives on management: An interdisciplinary approach,* ed. M. J. Earl, 197–233. London: Oxford University Press.

Graham, Frank, Jr.
1989 Taming the wild blueberry. *Audubon,* July 4, 48–69.

Granovetter, Mark S.
1973 The strength of weak ties. *American Journal of Sociology* 78:1360–80.

Graves, Bennie
1958 Breaking out: An apprenticeship system among pipeline construction workers. *Human Organization* 17:9–14.
1985 A note on the argot of pipeline construction. *Anthropology of Work Review* 6:30–31.
1989 Informal aspects of apprenticeship in selected American occupations. In *Apprenticeship: From theory to method and back again,* ed. Michael W. Coy, 51–64. Albany: State University of New York Press.

Green, Archie
1965 American labor lore: Its meanings and uses. *Industrial Relations* 4:51–68.
1972 *Only a miner.* Urbana: University of Illinois Press.
1978 Industrial lore: A bibliographic-semantic query. In *Working Americans: Contemporary approaches to occupational folklore,* ed. Robert H. Byington, 71–101. Smithsonian Folklore Studies no. 3. Washington, D.C.: Smithsonian Institution Press.

Greenberger, David B., and Stephen Strasser
1986 Development and application of a model of personal control in organizations. *Academy of Management Review* 11:164–77.

Greenwood, Davydd
1988 Egalitarianism or solidarity in Basque industrial cooperatives: The FAGOR group of Mondragón. In *Rules, decisions, and inequality in egalitarian societies,* ed. James G. Flanagan and Steve Rayner, 43–69. Brookfield, Vt.: Gower.

Gregory, Kathleen L.
1983 Native view paradigms: Multiple cultures and culture conflict in organizations. *Administrative Science Quarterly* 28:359–76.

Gritzer, Glenn, and Arnold Arluke
1985 *The making of rehabilitation.* Berkeley: University of California Press.

Gross, James A.
1988 *Teachers on trial: Values, standards, and equity in judging conduct and competence.* Ithaca, N.Y.: ILR Press.

Gulick, Luther, and Lyndall Urwick
1937 *Papers on the science of administration.* New York: Columbia University Institute of Public Administration.

Gusfield, Joseph R.
1963 *Symbolic crusade: Status politics and the American temperance movement.* Urbana: University of Illinois Press.
1975 *Community: A critical response.* New York: Harper and Row.

Gusfield, Joseph R., and Jerzy Michalowicz
1984   Secular symbolism: Studies of ritual, ceremony, and symbolic order in modern life. *Annual Review of Sociology* 10:417–35.

Guth, W. D., and R. Taniuri
1965   Personal values and corporate strategies. *Harvard University Review* 43:123–32.

Guy, Mary Ellen
1985   *Professionals in organizations: Debunking a myth.* New York. Praeger.

Haas, Jack
1972   Binging: Educational control among high steel iron workers. *American Behavioral Scientist* 16:27–34.
1974   The stages of the high-steel ironworker apprentice career. *Sociological Quarterly* 15:93–108.
1977   Learning real feelings: A study of high-steel ironworkers' reaction to fear and danger. *Sociology of Work and Occupations* 4:147–69.

Haas, Jack, and William Shaffir
1982a   Ritual evaluation of competence. *Work and Occupations* 9:131–54.
1982b   Taking on the role of doctor: A dramaturgical analysis of professionalization. *Symbolic Interaction* 5:187–203.

Hackman, J. Richard
1984   The transition that hasn't happened. In *New futures: The challenge of managing corporate transitions* ed. John R. Kimberly and Robert E. Quinn, 29–59. Homewood, Ill.: Dow Jones-Irwin.

Haerle, R.
1975   Career patterns and career contingencies of professional baseball players: An occupational analysis. In *Sport and social order,* ed. Donald Ball and John Loy, 457–519. Reading, Mass.: Addison-Wesley.

Hage, Jerald, and Michael Aiken
1967   Relationship of centralization to other structural properties. *Administrative Science Quarterly* 12:79–84.

Haldeman, Scott
1992   Is chiropractic treatment valuable for back pain? *Executive Health Report* 28:1, 4.

Hall, Douglas T., and Benjamin Schneider
1973   *Organizational climates and careers: The work lives of priests.* New York: Seminar Press.

Hall, K., and I. Miller
1975   *Retraining and tradition: The skilled worker in an era of change.* London: Allen and Unwin.

Hall, Richard H.
1969   *Occupations and the social structure.* Englewood Cliffs, N.J.: Prentice-Hall.
1975   *Occupations and the social structure.* 2d ed. Englewood Cliffs, N.J.: Prentice-Hall.
1983   Theoretical trends in the sociology of occupations. *Sociological Quarterly* 87:5–23.

Hall, Richard H., and Gloria V. Engel
   1974   Autonomy and expertise: Threats and barriers to occupational auton-
          omy. In *Varieties of work experience,* ed. Phyllis L. Stewart and Muriel
          G. Cantor, New York: Wiley.
Harris, Richard
   1973   *The police academy: An inside view.* New York: Wiley.
Haspeslagh, Phillippe C., and David B. Jemison
   1991   *Managing acquisitions: Creating value through corporate renewal.* New
          York: Free Press.
Hathaway, Barbara, and Harrison M. Trice
   1992   Becoming an EAP worker. Working paper #24, Program on Alcohol-
          ism and Occupational Workers, School of Industrial and Labor Rela-
          tions, Cornell University.
Haug, Marie R.
   1975   The deprofessionalization of everyone? *Sociological Forces* 8:197–213.
   1977   Computer technology and the obsolescence of the concept of profes-
          sion. In *Work and technology,* ed. Marie R. Haug and Jacques Dofny,
          215–28. Beverly Hills: Sage.
Haug, Marie R., and M. B. Sussman
   1969   Professional autonomy and the revolt of the client. *Social Problems* 17:
          153–60.
   1971   Professionalization and unionization. *American Behavioral Scientist* 14:
          525–40.
Hearn, H. L., and Patricia Stoll
   1975   Continuance commitment in low-status occupations: The cocktail
          waitress. *Sociological Quarterly* 16:105–14.
Hebden, J. E.
   1975   Patterns of work identification. *Sociology of Work and Occupations* 2:
          107–32.
Heinz, J. P. and E. O. Laumann
   1982   *Chicago lawyers: The social structure of the bar.* New York: Russell Sage
          Foundation and the American Bar Association.
Henslin, J. M.
   1973   Trust and the cab driver. In *Bureaucracy and the public,* ed. Elihu Katz
          and Brenda Danet, 338–56. New York: Basic Books.
Hinrichs, J. R.
   1972   Value adaptation of new Ph.D.s to academic and industrial environ-
          ments. *Personnel Psychology* 25:545–65.
Hochschild, Arlie R.
   1983   *The managed heart: The commercialization of human feelings.* Berkeley:
          University of California Press.
Hofstede, Geert, Bran Neuijen, Denise D. Ohayv, and Geert Sanders
   1990   Measuring organizational cultures: A qualitative and quantitative
          study across twenty cases. *Administrative Science Quarterly* 35:286–316.
Hogan, Daniel B.
   1979   *The regulation of psychotherapists.* Vol. 2. Cambridge, Mass.: Ballinger.

Holbrook, S. H.
  1962   *The American lumberjack.* New York: Collier.
Holleb, Gordon P., and Walter H. Abrams
  1975   *Alternatives in community mental health.* Boston: Beacon Press.
Holloway, S.W.F., N. Jewson, and D. Mason
  1986   Reprofessionalism or occupational imperialism? Some reflections on pharmacy in Britain. *Social Science and Medicine* 23:323–32.
Holmes, T. S., and R. H. Rahe
  1967   The social readjustment rating scale. *Journal of Psychosomatic Research* 11:213–18.
Homans, George C.
  1946   The small warship. *American Sociological Review* 11:294–300.
  1950   *The human group.* New York: Harcourt, Brace.
Hood, Jane C.
  1988   From night to day: Timing and the management of custodial work. *Journal of Contemporary Ethnography* 17:96–116.
Horn, J. L. and P. D. Knott
  1971   Activist youth of the 1960s. *Science* 171:977–85.
Hornosty, Roy W.
  1989   The development of idealism in pharmacy school. *Symbolic Interaction* 12:121–37.
Hornum, Finn
  1968   The executioner: His role and status in Scandinavian society. In *Sociology and everyday life,* ed. Marcello Truzzik, 125–37. Englewood Cliffs, N.J.: Prentice-Hall.
Hughes, Everett C.
  1958   *Men and their work.* Glencoe, Ill.: Free Press.
Huntington, Richard, and Allan Metcalf
  1979   *Celebrations of death: The anthropology of mortuary ritual.* New York: Cambridge University Press.
Ingle, Grant
  1980   Keeping alternative institutions alternative. Ph.D. diss. University of Massachusetts, Amherst.
Jackall, Robert
  1988   *Moral mazes.* New York: Oxford University Press.
Jackall, Robert, and Joseph Crain
  1984   The shapes of the small worker cooperative movement. In *Worker cooperatives in America,* ed. Robert Jackall and Henry M. Levin, 88–104. Berkeley: University of California Press.
Jackall, Robert, and Henry M. Levin, eds.
  1984   *Worker cooperatives in America.* Berkeley: University of California Press.
Jackman, N. R., R. O'Toole, and G. Geis
  1963   The self image of the prostitute. *Sociological Quarterly* 4:150–61.
Jackson, R. M.
  1984   *The formation of crafts markets.* New York: Academic Press.

Jacobs, P.
  1962   Dead horse and the featherbird: The specters of useless work. *Harper's*
         225:47–54.
Janowitz, Morris
  1960   *The professional soldier.* Glencoe, Ill.: Free Press.
  1977   The journalistic profession and the mass media. In *Culture and its cre-
         ators: Essays in honor of Edward Shils,* ed. Joseph Ben-David and Terry
         N. Clark, 72–96. Chicago: University of Chicago Press.
Jermier, John M.
  1982   Ecological hazards and organizational behavior: A study of dangerous
         urban space-time zones. *Human Organizations* 41:198–207.
Jermier, John M., John W. Slocum, Jr., Louis W. Fry, and Jeannie Gaines
  1991   Organizational subcultures in a soft bureaucracy: Resistance behind
         the myth and facade of an official culture. *Organization Science* 2:170–
         95.
Johnson, Harry M.
  1968   Ideology and the social system. In *International encyclopedia of the social
         sciences,* 7:76–85. New York: Macmillan.
Jones, Bryn
  1982   Destruction or redistribution of engineering skills: The case of nu-
         merical control. In *The degradation of work: Skill, deskilling and the labor
         process,* ed. S. Wood, 179–200. London: Hutchinson.
Joseph, Nathan, and Nicholas Alex
  1972   The uniform: A sociological perspective. *American Journal of Sociology*
         77:719–30.
Kalleberg, Arne L., Michael Wallace, Karyn A. Loscoco, Kevin T. Leicht, and
Hans-Helmut Ehm
  1987   The eclipse of craft: The changing face of labor in the newspaper in-
         dustry. In *Workers, managers, and technological change,* ed. Daniel Corn-
         field, 47–71. New York: Plenum Press.
Kanter, Rosabeth M.
  1977   *Men and women of the corporation.* New York: Basic Books.
  1989   *When giants learn to dance.* New York: Simon and Schuster.
Katz, Donald
  1987   *The big store.* New York: Viking.
Katz, Fred E.
  1958   Occupational contact networks. *Social Forces* 37:52–55.
  1969   Nurses. In *The semi-professions and their organization,* ed. Amitai Etzioni,
         54–78. New York: Free Press.
Katz, Fred E., and Harry W. Martin
  1962   Career choice processes. *Social Forces* 149–54.
Katzenstein, Peter J.
  1975   International interdependence: Some long-term trends and recent
         changes. *International Organization* 29:1021–34.
Katzman, D. M.
  1981   *Seven days a week: Women and domestic service in industrializing America.*
         Chicago: University of Illinois Press.

Kaufman, Herbert

1976   *The forest ranger*. Baltimore: Johns Hopkins University Press.

Keesing, Roger M.

1974   Theories of culture. *Annual Review of Anthropology* 3:73–97.

1987   Anthropology as interpretive quest. *Current Anthropology* 28:161–76.

Keidel, Robert W.

1984   Baseball, football, and basketball: Models for business. *Organizational Dynamics* 12:5–18.

1985   *Game plans: Sports strategies for business*. New York: Dutton.

Kemnitzer, Luis S.

1973   Language, learning and socialization on the railroad. *Urban Life and Culture* 1:363–78.

1977   Another view of time and the railroader. *Anthropological Quarterly* 59: 25–31.

Kenyon, K.

1982   A pink-collar worker's blues. *Newsweek*, Oct. 4, 15.

Kiechel, W.

1981   Beyond the liberated secretary. *Fortune*, Dec. 14, 173–74.

Kilmann, Ralph H.

1984   *Beyond the quick fix: Managing five tracks to organizational success*. San Francisco: Jossey-Bass.

Kilmann, Ralph H., Mary J. Saxton, Roy Serpa, and Associates, eds.

1985   *Gaining control of the corporate culture*. San Francisco: Jossey-Bass.

Klott, Gary

1985   Accounting roles seen in jeopardy. *New York Times*, Feb. 21, D22–23.

Kluckhohn, Clyde

1942   Myths and rituals: A general theory. *Harvard Theological Review* 35:45–79.

Kluger, Richard, with the assistance of Phyllis Kluger

1986   *The paper*. New York: Knopf.

Kochan, Thomas, Harry C. Katz, and Robert B. McKersie

1986   *The transformation of American industrial relations*. New York: Basic Books.

Kohn, Melvin L., and Carmi Schooler

1978   The effects of the substantive complexity of the job on intellectual flexibility: A longitudinal assessment. *American Journal of Sociology* 84: 24–52.

1983   *Work and personality*. Norwood, N.J.: Ablex.

Kornhauser, William

1962   *Scientists in industry: Conflict and accommodation*. Berkeley: University of California Press.

Korson, George

1965   *Coal dust on the fiddle: Songs and stories of the bituminous industry*. Hatboro, Penn: Folklore Associates.

Kraft, Phillip

1979   The routinizing of computer programming. *Sociology of Work and Occupations* 6:139–55.

Kranzberg, M. and J. Gies
1975 *By the sweat of thy brow.* New York: Putnam.
Kroeber, Alfred L., and Talcott Parsons
1970 The concepts of culture and social systems. In *Man makes sense,* ed. Eugene A. Hammel and William S. Simon, 85–87. Boston: Little, Brown.
Kronus, Carol L.
1976a Occupational versus organizational influences on reference group identification. *Sociology of Work and Occupations* 3:303–30.
1976b The evolution of occupational power: A historical study of task boundaries between physicians and pharmacists. *Sociology of Work and Occupations* 3:3–37.
Kunda, Gideon
1991 *Engineering culture.* Philadelphia: Temple University Press.
Lachman, R., and N. Aranya
1986 Job attitudes and turnover intentions among professionals in different work settings. *Organizational Studies* 7:279–93.
Langton, Phyllis A.
1991 Competing occupational ideologies, identities, and the practice of nurse-midwifery. *Current Research on Occupations and Professions* 6: 149–77.
Larkin, G. V.
1983 *Occupational monopoly and modern medicine.* London: Tavistock.
Larson, Magali Sarfatti
1977 *The rise of professionalism.* Berkeley: University of California Press.
Lasson, K.
1971 *The workers: Portrait of nine American job holders.* New York: Grossman.
Lawrence, Elizabeth A.
1982 *Rodeo: An anthropologist looks at the wild and the tame.* Knoxville: University of Tennessee Press.
Lawrence, Paul R., and J. W. Lorsch
1967 *Organization and environment.* Cambridge: Harvard University Press.
Layton, E.
1971 *The revolt of the engineers.* Cleveland: Case Western University Press.
Lazarsfeld, Paul F.
1949 The American soldier: An expository review. *Public Opinion Quarterly* 13:377–404.
Leach, Edmund
1968 Ritual. *International Encyclopedia of the Social Sciences* 13:520–26. New York: Free Press.
1976 Social anthropology: A natural science of society? In *Proceedings of the British Academy of Science* 62:157–80. London: Oxford University Press.
Leary, James P.
1978 Strategies and stories of the Omaha stockyards. *Folklore Forum* 11:29–41.
Lee, Alfred McClung
1937 *The daily newspaper in America.* New York: Macmillan.

Lembright, Muriel F., and Jeffrey W. Riemer
  1982   Women truckers' problems and the impact of sponsorship. *Work and Occupations* 9:457–74.
Leonard, George B.
  1973   Winning isn't everything: It's nothing. *Intellectual Digest*, Oct., 41–47.
Letkemann, Peter
  1973   *Crime as work*. Englewood Cliffs, N.J.: Prentice-Hall.
Lett, James
  1987   An anthropological view of television journalism. *Human Organization* 26:356–59.
Levinson, Daniel J.
  1978   *The seasons of a man's life*. New York: Ballantine.
Light, Donald
  1980   *Becoming psychiatrists: The professional transformation of self*. New York: Norton.
  1983   Medical and nursing education: Surface behavior and deep structure. In *Handbook of health, health care and health professionals*, ed. David Mechanic, 455–78. New York: Free Press.
Lincoln, James R., and Kerry McBride
  1987   Japanese industrial organization in comparative perspective. *Annual Review of Sociology* 13:289–312.
Lincoln, James R., and Jon Miller
  1979   Work and friendship ties in organizations: A comparative analysis of relational networks. *Administrative Science Quarterly* 24:181–99.
Linton, Ralph
  1924   Totemism and the A.E.F. *American Anthropologist* 26:296–300.
  1940   *Acculturation in seven American Indian tribes*. New York: Appleton-Century.
Lipset, Seymour M., Martin A. Trow, and James S. Coleman
  1956   *Union democracy*. New York: Free Press.
Littler, Craig
  1982   Deskilling and changing structures of control. In *The Degradation of work: Skill, deskilling and the labor process*, ed. S. Wood, 122–45. London: Hutchison.
Lodahl, Janice B., and Gerald Gordon
  1972   The structure of scientific fields and the functioning of university graduate departments. *American Sociological Review* 37:57–72.
Loeske, Donileen, and Spencer E. Cahill
  1986   Actors in search of a character: Student workers' quest for professional identity. *Symbolic Interaction* 9:245–58.
Long, J. Scott, Paul Allison, and Robert McGinnis
  1979   Entrance into the academic career. *American Sociological Review* 44:816–30.
Lopata, Helena Z., ed.
  1987   *Current research on occupations and professions*. Greenwich, Conn.: JAI Press. Annual.

Lortie, Dan C.
  1968 Shared ordeal and induction to work. In *Institutions and the person*, ed. Howard Becker, Blanche Geer, David Riesman, and Robert S. Weiss, 252–64. Chicago: Aldine.
  1975 *School teacher: A sociological study*. Chicago: University of Chicago Press.
Louis, Meryl R.
  1980 Surprise and sense making: What newcomers experience in entering unfamiliar organizational settings. *Administrative Science Quarterly* 25: 226–51.
  1983 Culture: yes; organization: no. Paper presented at the annual meeting of the Academy of Management, Aug. 13–15, Dallas.
  1985 An investigator's guide to workplace culture. In *Organizational culture*, ed. Peter Frost, Larry F. Moore, Meryl R. Louis, and Craig C. Lundberg, 73–94. Beverly Hills: Sage.
Louis, Meryl R., and Robert I. Sutton
  1991 Switching cognitive gears: From habits of mind to active thinking. *Human Relations* 44:55–76.
Lurie, Elinore E.
  1981 Nurse practitioners: Issues in professionalization. *Journal of Health and Social Behavior* 22:21–48.
Luschen, Guuther
  1967 The interdependence of sports and culture. *International Review of Sport Sociology* 2:127–39.
Lyall, Sarah
  1988 Police-fire feud is set off again by copter death. *New York Times*, May 3, A1.
McCarl, Robert S.
  1974 The production welder: Product, process, and industrial craftsman. *New York Folklore Quarterly* 30:244–53.
  1976 Smoke jumper initiation: Ritualized communication in a modern occupation. *Journal of American Folklore* 81:49–67.
  1980 *Good fire/bad night*. Washington, D.C.: National Endowment for the Arts, Folk Arts Program, and Columbia Fire Fighters, Local 36.
  1984 You've come a long way and now this is your retirement. *Journal of American Folklore* 97:393–422.
McClenahen, Lachlan, and John Lofland
  1976 Bearing bad news. *Sociology of Work and Occupations* 3:251–72.
McHugh, Peter
  1969 Structured uncertainty and its resolution: The case of the professional actor. In *Changing perspectives in mental illness*, ed. Stanley C. Plog, and Robert B. Edgerton, 539–55. New York: Holt.
Mack, R. W., and A. P. Merriam
  1960 The jazz community. *Social Forces* 35:211–22.
McKinlay, John B.
  1982 Toward the proletarianization of physicians. In *Professionals as workers:*

Mental labor in advanced capitalism, ed. Charles Derber, 109–21. London: Hutchison.

McKinney, J. C.
1966 *Construction typology and social theory.* New York: Appleton-Century-Crofts.

Magenan, J. W., J. E. Martin, and M. M. Peterson
1988 Dual and unilateral commitment among stewards and rank-and-file union members. *Academy of Management Journal* 31:359–76.

Manning, Peter K.
1977 *Police work: The social organization of policing.* Cambridge: MIT Press.

March, James, and Johan Olsen
1976 *Ambiguity and choice in organizations.* Bergen, Germany: Universitetsforlaget.

March, J. B., and Herbert A. Simon
1958 *Organizations.* New York: Wiley.

Marcson, Simon
1960 *The scientist in American industry.* Princeton: Industrial Relations Section, Princeton University.

Marglin, Stephen A.
1976 *Value and price in the labour surplus economy.* Oxford: Clarendon Press.

Mars, Gerald
1982 *Cheats at work: An anthropology of workplace crime.* Boston: Allen and Unwin.
1987 Longshore drinking, economic security, and union politics in Newfoundland. In *Constructive drinking,* ed. Mary Douglas, 15–28. Cambridge, Eng.: Cambridge University Press.

Mars, Gerald, and Michael Nicod
1984 *The world of waiters.* London: Allen and Unwin.

Martin, Joanne, and Debra Meyerson
1988 Organizational cultures and the denial, channelling and acknowledgment of ambiguity. In *Managing ambiguity and change,* ed. Louis R. Pondy, Richard Boland, Jr., and Howard Thomas, 93–125. New York: Wiley.

Martin, Joanne, Sim B. Sitkins, and Michael Boehm
1985 Founders and the elusiveness of a cultural legacy. In *Organizational cultures,* ed. Peter J. Frost, Larry F. Moore, Meryl R. Louis, Craig C. Lundberg, and Joanne Martin, 99–124. Beverly Hills: Sage.

Martin, Susan E.
1982 Equal versus equitable treatment: Policewomen and patrol work. In *Varieties of work,* ed. Phyllis L. Stewart and Muriel G. Cantor, 101–21. Beverly Hills: Sage.

Mayer, John E., and Aaron Rosenblatt
1975 Encounters with danger: Social workers in the ghetto. *Sociology of Work and Occupations* 2:227–45.

Maynard-Moody, Steven, Donald D. Stull, and Jerry Mitchell
1986 Reorganization as status drama: Building, maintaining, and dis-

placing dominant subcultures. *Public Administration Review* 46:301–12.

Mead, George H.
1934 *Mind, self, and society.* Chicago: University of Chicago Press.

Meara, Hannah
1974 Honor in dirty work: The case of American meatcutters and Turkish butchers. *Sociology of Work and Occupations* 1:259–82.

Meissner, Martin
1976 The language of work. In *Handbook of work, organizations, and society,* ed. Robert Dubin, 205–79. Chicago: Rand McNally.

Melbin, Murray
1978 Night as frontier. *American Sociological Review* 43:3–22.
1987 *Night as frontier: Colonizing the world after dark.* New York: Free Press.

Melosh, Barbara
1982 *The physician's hand: Work culture and conflict in American nursing.* Philadephia: Temple University Press.

Merton, Robert K.
1936 The unanticipated consequences of purposive social action. *American Sociological Review* 1:894–904.

Merton, Robert K., George Reader, and Patrica Kendall
1957 *The student physician.* Cambridge: Harvard University Press.

Meyer, Alan D.
1982 How ideologies supplant formal structures and shape responses to environments. *Journal of Management Studies* 19:45–61.

Meyer, Marshal W.
1968 Two authority structures of bureaucratic organization. *Administrative Science Quarterly* 13:216–21.

Meyer, John W., and Brian Rowan
1977 Institutionalized organizations: Formal structure, myth, and ceremony. *American Journal of Sociology* 83:340–61.

Meyerhoff, Barbara
1982 Rites of passage: Process and paradox. In *Celebration, studies in festivity and ritual,* ed. Victor Turner, 109–35. Washington, D.C.: Smithsonian Institution Press.

Meyerson, Debra
1988 On studying ambiguities in cultures. Paper presented at annual meeting of Academy of Management, Aug. 13–15, Anaheim, Calif.
1991 "Normal ambiguity"? A glimpse of an occupational culture. In *Reframing organizational culture,* ed. Peter Frost, Larry F. Moore, Meryl R. Louis, Craig Lundberg, and Joanne Martin, 131–44. Newbury Park, Calif.: Sage.

Meyerson, Debra, and Joanne Martin
1987 Culture change: An integration of three different views. *Journal of Management Studies* 24:623–47.

Michels, Robert
1949 [1915] *Political parties.* Glencoe, Ill: Free Press.

Milkman, Ruth, and Cydney Pullman
    1991   Technological change in an auto assembly plant. *Work and Occupations* 18:123–47.
Miller, Delbert C., and William H. Form
    1980   *Industrial sociology: Work in organizational life.* 3d ed. New York: Harper and Row.
Miller, Frank B., and Mary Ann Coghill
    1961   *Historical sources of personnel work: An annotated bibliography of developments to 1923.* Bibliography Series no. 5. Ithaca, N.Y.: New York State School of Industrial and Labor Relations, Cornell University.
Miller, M., and J. Van Maanen
    1979   Boats don't fish; people do: Some ethnographic notes on federal management of fisheries. *Human Organization* 38:377–85.
    1982   Getting into fishing: Social identities among fishermen. *Urban Life* 11: 27–54.
Mintzberg, Henry
    1979   *The structure of organizations.* Englewood Cliffs, N.J.: Prentice-Hall.
Mitford, Jessica
    1963   *The American way of death.* New York: Simon and Schuster.
Molloy, John T.
    1975   *Dress for success.* New York: Wyden.
Molstad, Clark
    1988   Control strategies used by industrial brewery workers: Work avoidance, impression management, and solidarity. *Human Organization* 47: 354–60.
Montagna, Paul D.
    1968   Professionalization and bureaucratization in large professional organizations. *American Journal of Sociology* 74:138–45.
    1973   The public accounting profession. In *The professions and their prospects,* ed. Eliot Freidson, 135–51. Beverly Hills: Sage.
    1974   *Certified public accounting.* Houston: Scholars.
Montague, Susan P., and Robert Morais
    1976   Football games and rock concerts: The ritual enactment of American success models. In *The American dimension: Cultural myths and social realities,* ed. W. Arens and S. P. Montague, 33–51. Port Washington, N.Y.: Alfred.
Moore, David G.
    1982   The Committee on Human Relations in Industry. In *Academy of Management proceedings,* ed. Kae H. Chung, 117–21. New York: Academy of Management.
Moore, Sally F.
    1975   Epilogue: Uncertainties in situations, indeterminacies in culture. In *Symbols and politics in communal ideology,* ed. Sally F. Moore and Barbara G. Myerhoff, 211–39. Ithaca, N.Y.: Cornell University Press.
Moore, Sally F., and Barbara G. Myerhoff
    1977   Secular ritual: Forms and meaning. In *Secular ritual,* ed. Sally F. Moore

and Barbara G. Myerhoff, 3–25. Amsterdam, the Netherlands: Van Gorcum.

Moore, Wilbert E.
  1969   Occupational socialization. In *Handbook of socialization theory and research,* ed. David A. Goslin, 861–82. Chicago: Rand McNally.

Morales, Armando, and Bradford Sheafor
  1983   *Social work: A profession of many faces.* 3d ed. Boston: Allyn and Bacon.

Morison, Elting
  1982   Gunfire at sea: A case study of innovation. In *Readings in the management of innovation,* ed. Michael L. Tushman and William L. Moore, 84–95. Boston: Pittman.

Mosk, Stanley
  1986   Forward. In *Psychotherapy and the law,* ed. Louis Everstine and Diana S. Everstine, ix–x. New York: Grune and Stratton.

Myerhoff, Barbara G.
  1982   Rites of passage: Process and paradox. In *Celebration,* ed. Victor Turner, 109–35. Washington, D.C.: Smithsonian Institution Press.

Myers, Richard C.
  1952   Myth and status systems in industry. *Social Forces* 26:331–37.

Nathanson, C. A.
  1971   Peer surveillance and patient orientation on a pediatric out-patient clinic. *Human Organization* 30:255–65.

Nelson, R. L.
  1988   *Partners with power: The social transformation of the large law firm.* Berkeley: University of California Press.

Newman, Katherine
  1980   Incipient bureaucracy: The development of hierarchies in egalitarian organizations. In *Hierarchy and society: Anthropological perspectives on bureaucracy,* ed. Gerald M. Britan and Ronald Cohen, 143–63. Philadelphia: Institute for Studies on Human Issues.

Nicholson, Nigel, and Michael West
  1989   Transitions, work histories, and careers. In *Handbook of career theory,* ed. Michael B. Arthur, Douglas T. Hall, and Barbara S. Lawrence, 181–210. New York: Cambridge University Press.

Nielsen, Georgia P.
  1982   *From sky girl to flight attendant.* Ithaca, N.Y.: ILR Press.

Noble, David F.
  1977   *America by design.* New York: Oxford University Press.
  1979   Social choice in machine design: The case of automatically controlled machine tools. In *Case studies in the labor process,* ed. A. Zimbalest, 18–50. New York: Monthly Review Press.

Nussbaum, Bruce, and Alex Beam
  1986   Remaking the Harvard Business School. *Business Week,* March 24, 54–58.

O'Brien, Michael
  1987   *Vince: A personal biography of Vince Lombardi.* New York: Morrow.

Olesen, Virginia L., and Elvi W. Whittaker
  1968   *The silent dialogue: A study in the social psychology of professional social-ization.* San Francisco: Jossey-Bass.
Orbach, Michael
  1977   *Hunters, seamen and entrepreneurs,* Berkeley: University of California Press.
O'Reilly, Charles A., Jennifer Chatman, and David F. Caldwell
  1991   People and organizational culture: A profile comparison approach to assessing person-organization fit. *Academy of Management Journal* 34: 487–516.
Orlikowski, Wanda J.
  1988   The data processing occupation: Professionalization or proletar-ianization. In *Research in the sociology of work,* vol. 4, ed. Richard L. Simpson and Ida Harper Simpson, 95–124. Greenwich, Conn.: JAI Press.
Ouchi, William G.
  1981   *Theory Z: How American business can meet the Japanese challenge.* Reading, Mass.: Addison-Wesley.
Ouchi, William G., and Allan L. Wilkins
  1985   Organizational culture. *Annual Review of Sociology* 11:457–83.
Padgett, J. F.
  1980   Managing garbage can hierarchies. *Administrative Science Quarterly* 25: 583–604.
Padilla, Amado M.
  1980   Introduction. In *Acculturation: Theory, models, and some new findings,* ed. Amado M. Padilla, 1–8. Boulder, Colo. Westview Press.
Parkes, Henry Bamford
  1947   *The American experience.* New York: Knopf.
Parsons, Talcott
  1939   The professions and social structure. *Social Forces* 17:457–67.
Pascale, Richard
  1984   Fitting new employees into the company culture. *Fortune,* May 28, 28–40.
Patry, Bill
  1978   Taylorism comes to the social service. *Monthly Review* 30:30–37.
Pavalko, Ronald M.
  1971   *Sociology of occupations and professions.* Itasca, Ill.: Peacock.
  1988   *Sociology of occupations and professions.* 2d ed. Itasca, Ill.: Peacock.
Pawluch, Dorothy
  1983   Transitions in pediatrics: A segmented analysis. *Social Problems* 30: 449–65.
Penn, R.
  1982   Skilled manual workers in the labour process: 1956–1964. In *The degradation of labor,* ed. S. Wood, 90–108. London: Hutchison.
Perrow, Charles
  1970   Departmental power and perspective in industrial firms. In *Power in*

organizations, ed. Mayer H. Zald, 59–89. Nashville: Vanderbilt University Press.

1986   *Complex organizations*. 3d ed. New York: Random House.

Perrucci, Robert, and Joel Gerstl

1969   *Profession without community: Engineers in American society*. New York: Random House.

Peters, Thomas J., and Robert H. Waterman

1982   *In search of excellence: Lessons from America's best run companies*. New York: Harper and Row.

Peterson, Kent D.

1987   Computerized instruction, information systems, and school teachers: Labor relations in education. In *Workers, managers, and technological change: Emerging patterns of labor relations*, ed. Daniel B. Cornfield, 135–51. New York: Plenum Press.

Pettigrew, Andrew W.

1973   *The politics of organizational decision-making*. London: Tavistock.

Pfeffer, Jeffrey

1974   Administrative regulations and licensing: Social problems or solution? *Social Problems* 21:468–79.

1981   Management as symbolic action: The creation and maintenance of organizational paradigms. In *Research in organizational behavior*, vol. 3, ed. L. L. Cummings and Barry Staw, 1–52. Greenwich, Conn: JAI Press.

Pfeffer, Jeffrey, and Alison Davis-Blake

1986   Administrative succession and organizational performance: How administrator experience mediates the succession effect. *Academy of Management Journal* 29:72–83.

Pierce, Joe E.

1977   Culture: A collection of fuzzy sets. *Human Organization* 36:197–200.

Pilcher, William W.

1972   *The Portland longshoremen*. New York: Holt.

Polsky, Ned

1969   *Hustlers, beats, and others*. Garden City, N.Y.: Anchor Books.

Pondy, Louis R.

1978   Leadership is a language game. In *Leadership: Where else do we go?* ed. Morgan McCall and M. Lombardo, 103–21. Durham, N.C.: Duke University Press.

1983   Union of rationality and intuition in management action. In *The executive mind*, ed. Suhesh Srivasta, 169–89. San Francisco: Jossey-Bass.

Pondy, Louis R., Peter J. Frost, Gareth Morgan, and Thomas C. Dandridge, eds.

1983   *Organizational symbolism*. Greenwich, Conn.: JAI Press.

Pondy, Louis R., and Ian I. Mitroff

1979   Beyond open system models of organization. In *Research in organizational behavior*, vol. 1, ed. Barry M. Staw, 3–39. Greenwich, Conn.: JAI Press.

Pople, Harry E.

1984   CADUCENS: An experimental expert system for medical diagnosis.

In *The AI business,* ed. P. H. Winston and K. A. Prendergast, 110–27. Cambridge: MIT Press.

Prange, Gordon W.
1982.   *Miracle at Midway.* New York: McGraw-Hill.

Previtz, Gary J., and Barbara D. Merino
1979   *A history of accounting in America.* New York: Wiley.

Price, James L.
1968   The impact of departmentalization on interoccupational cooperation. *Human Organization* 27:362–67.

Prus, Robert, and Styllianoss Irini
1980   *Hookers, rounders, and desk clerks: The Social organization of the hotel community.* Toronto: Gage.

Purdum, Elizabeth D.
1985   Subculture of deputy court clerks: Implications for access and reform. *Human Organization* 44:353–59.

Quick, R. C., W. J. Sonnenstuhl, and H. M. Trice
1987   Educating the employee assistance professional: Cornell University's employee assistance education and research program. *Public Personnel Management* 16:333–43.

Radcliffe-Brown, A. R.
1964   *The Andaman islanders.* Glencoe, Ill.: Free Press.

Raelin, Joseph A.
1985   *The clash of cultures: Managers and professionals.* Boston: Harvard Business School Press.
1987   The '60s kids in the corporation: More than just daydream believers. *Executive Magazine* 1:21–30.

Rafaeli, Anat, and Robert I. Sutton
1987   Expression of emotion as part of the work role. *Academy of Management Review* 12:23–37.

Record, J. C., and M. R. Greenlick
1975   New health professions and the physician's role. *Public Health Reports* 90:241–46.

Reeder, Sharon J., and Hans Mauksch
1979   Nursing: Continuing change. In *Handbook of medical sociology,* ed. Howard Freeman, 209–29. Englewood Cliffs, N.J.: Prentice-Hall.

Reeves, W. J.
1980   *Librarians as professionals: The occupation's impact on library work arrangements.* Lexington, Mass.: Lexington Books.

Reuss, Richard A.
1983   Songs of American labor, industrialization, and the urban work experience: A discography. Ann Arbor: Labor Studies Center, Institute of Labor and Industrial Relations, University of Michigan.

Reuss-Janni, Elizabeth
1983   *Two cultures of policing: Street cops and management cops.* New Brunswick, N.J.: Transaction Books.

Riemer, Jeffrey W.
1977   Becoming a journeyman electrician. *Sociology of Work and Occupations* 4:87–98.

1979   Hard hats: The work world of construction workers. Beverly Hills: Sage.

Riley, Patricia
1983   A structurationist account of political culture. *Administrative Science Quarterly* 28:414–37.

Ritchey, F. J. and M. R. Raney
1981   Medical role-task boundary maintenance: Physician's opinion on clinical pharmacy. *Medical Care* 19:90–103.

Ritzer, George
1975   Professionalization, bureaucratization and rationalization: The views of Max Weber. *Social Forces* 53:627–34.

Ritzer, George, and Harrison M. Trice
1969a   *An occupation in conflict: A study in conflict.* Ithaca, N.Y.: School of Industrial and Labor Relations, Cornell University.
1969b   An empirical study of Howard Becker's side-bet theory. *Social Forces* 47:475–78.

Ritzer, George, and David Walczak
1986   *Working: Conflict and change.* 3d ed. Englewood Cliffs, N.J.: Prentice-Hall.

Roberts, Steven V.
1983   House censors Crane and Studds for sexual relations with pages. *New York Times,* July 21, A1, B22.

Robin, Gerald D.
1964   The executioner: His place in English society. *British Journal of Sociology* 15:234–53.

Roethlisberger, F. J., and William J. Dickson
1946   *Management and the worker.* Cambridge: Harvard University Press.

Roman, Paul, and Terry Blum
1988   The core technology of employee assistance programs: A reaffirmation. *ALMACAN,* Aug., 17–22.

Romero, Mary
1988   Chicanas modernize domestic service. *Qualitative Sociology* 11:319–34.

Rorbaugh, W. J.
1986   *The craft apprentice: From Franklin to the Machine Age in America.* New York: Oxford University Press.

Rosen, Michael
1985   Breakfasts at Spiro's: Dramaturgy and dominance. *Journal of Management* 11:31–48.

Rosenbaum, James E.
1979   Tournament mobility: Career patterns in a corporation. *Administrative Science Quarterly* 24:220–41.
1984   *Career mobility in a corporate hierarchy.* New York: Academic Press.
1989   Organizational career systems and employee misconceptions. In *Handbook of career theory,* ed. Michael B. Arthur, Douglas T. Hall, and Barbara S. Lawrence, 329–53. New York: Cambridge University Press.

Rosenberg, M.
1957   *Occupations and values.* New York: Free Press.

Rosenstein, David, Lireka P. Joseph, Leslie Mackenzie, and Ron Wyden
1980   Professional encroachment: A comparison of the emergence of den-
        turists in Canada and Oregon. *American Journal of Public Health* 70:
        614–18.
Rothman, Robert A.
1979   Occupational roles: Power and negotiation in the division of labor.
        Sociological Quarterly 20:495–515.
1984   Deprofessionalization: The case of law in America. *Work and Occupa-
        tions* 11:183–206.
1987   *Working: Sociological perspectives.* Englewood Cliffs, N.J.: Prentice-Hall.
Rothschild, Joyce
1986   Alternatives to bureaucracy: Democratic participation in the economy.
        Annual Review of Sociology 12:307–28.
Rothschild, Joyce, and A. Allen Whitt
1986   *The cooperative workplace: Potentials and dilemmas of organizational de-
        mocracy and participation.* New York: Cambridge University Press.
Rothschild-Whitt, Joyce
1979   The collectivist organization: An alternative to rational bureaucratic
        models. *American Sociological Review* 44:509–27.
Rothstein, William G.
1969   Engineers and the functionalist model of professions. In *The engineer
        and the social system,* ed. Robert Perrucci and Joel E. Gerstl, 73–99. New
        York: Wiley.
Roy, Donald
1952   Quota restrictions and gold bricking in a machine shop. *American Jour-
        nal of Sociology* 57:427–42.
1953   Work satisfaction and social reward in quota achievement. *American
        Sociological Review* 18:507–14.
1954   Efficiency and the fix: Informal intergroup relations in a piece-work
        machine shop. *American Journal of Sociology* 60:255–66.
1960   Banana time: Job satisfaction and informal interaction. *Human Organ-
        ization* 18:158.
Rubinstein, Jonathan
1973   *City police.* New York: Farrar, Straus, and Giroux.
Runcie, John F.
1974   Occupational communication as a boundary mechanism. *Sociology of
        Work and Occupations* 11:419–41.
Sabel, C. F.
1982   *Work and politics.* New York: Cambridge University Press.
Sahlins, Marshall
1972   *Stone Age economics.* Chicago: Aldine.
Salaman, Graeme
1974   *Community and occupation: An exploration of the work/leisure relationship.*
        London: Cambridge University Press.
1986   *Working.* London: Tavistock.
Sales, Amy, and Phillip H. Mirvis
1984   When cultures collide: Issues in acquisition. In *Managing organizational*

transitions, ed. John Kimberly and Robert Quinn, 107–32. Homewood, Ill.: Irwin.

Samuel, Yitzhak, and Noah Lewin-Epstein
  1979   The occupational situs as a predictor of work values. *American Journal of Sociology* 85:625–39.

Santino, Jack
  1978   Characteristics of occupational narratives. *Western Folklore* 37:199–243.

Sapir, Edward
  1966 [1915]   The social organization of the West Coast tribes. In *Indians of the North Pacific coast,* ed. Tom McFeat, 26–57. Seattle: University of Washington Press.

Sassoon, Joseph
  1990   Color, artifacts and ideologies. In *Symbols and artifacts: Views of the corporate landscape,* ed. Pasquale Gagliardi, 169–84. New York: de Gruyter.

Schein, Edgar H.
  1985   *Organizational culture and leadership.* San Francisco: Jossey-Bass.

Schneller, Eugene S.
  1978   *The physician's assistant.* Lexington, Mass.: Lexington Books.

Schon, D. A.
  1971   *Beyond the stable state.* New York: Norton.

Schor, Juliet B.
  1991   *The Overworked American.* New York: Basic Books.

Schrier, D. A., and F. D. Mulcahy
  1988   Middle-management and union realities: Coercion and anti-structure in a public corporation. *Human Organization* 47:146–50.

Schwartzman, Helen B.
  1981   Hidden agendas and formal organizations or how to dance at a meeting. *Social Analysis* 9:77–88.
  1984   Stories of work: Play in organizational context. In *Proceedings of the American Ethnological Society,* ed. E. Bruner, 80–93. Washington, D.C.: American Ethnological Society.

Schwartzman, Helen B., Anita Kneifel, and Merton Krause
  1978   Culture conflict in a community mental health center. *Journal of Social Issues* 34:93–110.

Scott, Donald M.
  1983   Public lecturing in mid-nineteenth century America. In *Professions and professional ideologies in America,* ed. Gerald L. Geiuson, 12–38. Chapel Hill: University of North Carolina Press.

Scott, W. Richard
  1965   Reactions to supervision in a heteronomous professional organization. *Administrative Science Quarterly* 10:65–81.
  1981   *Organizations: Rational, natural, and open systems.* Englewood Cliffs, N.J.: Prentice-Hall.
  1987   *Organizations: Rational, natural, and open systems.* 2d ed. Englewood Cliffs, N.J.: Prentice-Hall.

Scott, William G., and David K. Hart
  1979   *Organizational America.* Boston: Houghton Mifflin.
Sewell, William H.
  1969   The educational and early occupational attainment process. *American Sociological Behavior* 34:82–92.
Shaiken, Harley A.
  1984   *Work transformed.* New York: Holt.
Shapiro, David, and Joan E. Crowley
  1982   Aspirations and expectations of the youth in the United States: Past employment activity. *Youth and Society* 14:33–58.
Shils, Edward
  1975   *Center and periphery: Essays in macro-sociology.* Chicago: University of Chicago Press.
Shostak, Arthur B.
  1987   Technology, air traffic control, and labor management relations. In *Workers, managers, and technological change,* ed. Daniel B. Cornfield, 153–72. New York: Plenum Press.
Shuman, Todd M.
  1988   Hospital computerization and the politics of medical decision making. In *Research in the sociology of work,* vol. 4, ed. Richard L. Simpson and Ida H. Simpson, 261–87. Greenwich, Conn.: JAI Press.
Silver, Marc L.
  1986   *Under construction: Work and alienation in the building trades.* Albany: State University of New York Press.
Simmel, George
  1971   *On individuality and social forms.* Chicago: University of Chicago Press.
Simon, Herbert A.
  1957   *Administrative behavior.* 2d ed. New York: Macmillan.
Simpson, Ida H.
  1967   Patterns of socialization into professions: The case of student nurses. *Sociological Inquiry* 37:47–54.
  1979   *From student to nurse: A longitudinal study of socialization.* New York: Cambridge University Press.
  1989   The sociology of work: Where have the workers gone? *Social Forces* 67:563–81.
Simpson, Ida H., and Richard L. Simpson, eds.
  1981– *Research in the sociology of work.* Greenwich, Conn.: JAI Press. Annual.
Simpson, Richard L.
  1985   Social control of occupations and work. *Annual Review of Sociology* 11: 415–36.
Simpson, Richard L., and Ida H. Simpson
  1959   The psychiatric attendant: Development of an occupational self image in a low status occupation. *American Sociological Review* 24:389–92.
Sitkin, Sim, and Kathleen Sutcliffe
  1989   Dispensing legitimacy: Professional, organizational, and legal influ-

ences on pharmacist behavior. Paper presented at the annual
meeting of the Academy of Management, Aug. 13–15, Washington,
D.C.

1991   Dispensing legitimacy: Professional, organizational, and legal influences on pharmacist behavior. *Research in the Sociology of Organizations*
8:269–95.

Sloane, Arthur A., and Fred Witney
1985   *Labor relations.* 5th ed. Englewood Cliffs, N.J.: Prentice-Hall.

Smigel, Erwin O.
1964   *The Wall Street lawyer.* New York: Free Press.

Smircich, Linda, and Gareth Morgan
1982   Leadership: The management of meaning. *Journal of Applied Behavioral
Science* 18:257–73.

Smith, Allen C., III, and Sherryl Kleinman
1989   Managing emotions in medical school: Students' contacts with the living and the dead. *Social Psychology Quarterly* 52:56–69.

Smith, Charles W.
1989   *Auctions: The social construction of value.* New York: Free Press.

Smith, Harvey L.
1962   Contingencies of professional differentiation. In *Man, work, and society,*
ed. Sigmund Nosow and William Form, 219–25. New York: Basic
Books.

Sokol, Marc, and Meryl R. Louis
1984   Career transitions and life event adaptations: Integrating alternative
perspectives on role transitions. In *Role transitions: Explorations and
explanations,* ed. Allen Vermont and Evert va de Vliert, 81–93. New
York: Plenum Press.

Sonnenstuhl, William J., and Harrison M. Trice
1987   Social construction of alcohol problems in a union's peer counseling
program. *Journal of Drug Issues* 17:223–54.

1991   Organizations and types of occupational communities: Grid-group
analysis in the linkage of organizational and occupational theory. *Research in the Sociology of Organizations* 9:295–318.

Sorensen, J., and T. Sorensen
1974   The conflict of professionals in bureaucratic organizations. *Administrative Science Quarterly* 19:98–106.

Spangler, Eve
1986   *Lawyers for hire.* New Haven: Yale University Press.

Spangler, Eve, and Peter M. Lehman
1982   Lawyering as work. In *Professionals as workers: Mental labor in advanced
capitalism,* ed. Charles Derber, 63–99. Boston: Hall.

Sperber, A. M.
1986   *Murrow: His life and times.* New York: Freundlich Books.

Spenner, Kenneth I.
1979   Temporal changes in work content. *American Sociological Review* 44:
968–75.

Spradley, James P., and Brenda J. Mann
  1975   *The cocktail waitress: Woman's work in a man's world.* New York: Wiley.
Sprey, Jetse
  1962   Six differences in occupational choice patterns among Negro adolescents. *Social Problems* 10:11–22.
Sproull, Lee
  1981   Beliefs in organizations. In *Handbook of organizational design,* ed. Paul C. Nystrom, and William H. Starbuck, 203–23. New York: Oxford University Press.
Sproull, Lee, Stephen Weiner, and David Wolf
  1978   *Organizing an anarchy: Belief, bureaucracy, and politics in the National Institute of Education.* Chicago: University of Chicago Press.
Starr, Paul
  1982   *The social transformation of American medicine.* New York: Basic Books.
Steffens, Robert A.
  1972   Class, status, and power among jazz and commercial musicians. In *The social dimensions of work,* ed. Clifford D. Bryant, 206–21. Englewood, N.J.: Prentice-Hall.
Steiger, Thomas L., and William Form
  1991   The labor process in construction: Control without bureaucratic and technological means? *Work and Occupations* 18:251–70.
Stein, L.
  1971   The doctor-nurse game. In *New directions for nurses,* ed. B. Bullough and V. Bullough, New York: Springer.
Stein, Margot
  1978   The meaning of skill: The case of the French engine drivers, 1837–1917. *Politics and Society* 8:339–428.
Stenross, Barbara, and Sherryl Kleinman
  1989   The highs and lows of emotional labor: Detectives' encounters with criminals and victims. *Journal of Contemporary Ethnography* 17:435–52.
Stevenson, William B., Jane L. Pearce, and Lyman W. Porter
  1985   Concept of coalition in organizational theory and research. *Academy of Management Review* 10:256–68.
Stewart, Phyllis L., and Muriel G. Cantor, eds.
  1982   *Varieties of work.* Beverly Hills: Sage.
Stinchcombe, Arthur L.
  1959   Bureaucratic and craft administration of production. *Administrative Science Quarterly* 4:168–87.
Stodtbeck, Fred L., and Marvin B. Sussman
  1956   Of time, the city, and the "one-year guarantee": The relations between watch owners and repairers. *American Journal of Sociology* 61:602–9.
Stone, K.
  1979   The origin of job structures in the steel industry. *Review of Radical Political Economy* 6:113–73.
Strachey, Lytton
  1918   *Eminent Victorians: Cardinal Manning, Florence Nightingale, Dr. Arnold, General Gordon.* New York: Putnam.

Straus, Robert
  1991   Seldon D. Bacon as a teacher, colleague, scholar and founder of modern alcohol studies. In *Alcohol: The development of sociological perspectives on use and abuse,* ed. Paul M. Roman, 113–23. Brunswick, N.J.: Rutgers Center of Alcohol Studies.
Strauss, Anselm, Leonard Schatzman, Rue Bucher, Danuta Ehrlich, and Melvin Sabshin
  1964   *Psychiatric ideologies and institutions.* New York: Free Press.
Strauss, George
  1964   Work flow frictions, interfunctional rivalry, and professionalism: A case study of purchasing agents. *Human Organization* 23:137–49.
  1972   Professionalism and occupational associations. In *The social dimensions of work,* ed. Clifford Bryant, 236–53. Englewood Cliffs, N.J.: Prentice-Hall.
Sullivan, Teresa A., and Daniel B. Cornfield
  1979   Downgrading computer workers: Evidence from occupational and industrial redistribution. *Sociology of Work and Occupations* 6:184–203.
Sutherland, E. H.
  1937   *The professional thief.* Chicago: University of Chicago Press.
Sutton, Robert I.
  1991   Maintaining norms about expressed emotions: The case of bill collectors. *Administrative Science Quarterly* 36:245–68.
Sutton, Robert I., and Anat Rafaeli
  1988   Untangling the relationship between displayed emotions and organizational sales. *Academy of Management Journal* 31:461–87.
Swidler, Ann
  1979   *Organization without authority: Dilemmas of social control in free schools.* Cambridge: Harvard University Press.
  1986   Culture in action: symbols and strategies. *American Sociological Review* 51:273–86.
Swieringa, Robert J., and Karl E. Weick
  1981   Interfaces between management accounting and organizational behavior. *Exchange: The Organizational Behavior Teaching Journal* 6:25–33.
Taylor, F. W.
  1967   [1911] *The principles of scientific management.* New York: Norton.
Tead, Ordway
  1933   *Personnel administration: Its principles and practice.* New York: McGraw-Hill.
Terkel, Studs
  1972   *Working.* Chicago: Avon.
Terry, W. C.
  1981   Police stress: The empirical evidence. *Journal of Police Science and Administration* 9:61–75.
Thompson, James D.
  1967   *Organizations in action.* New York: McGraw-Hill.

Thompson, Lawrence C.
1947   The customs of the chapel. *Journal of American Folklore* 60:329–44.
Thompson, Stith
1946   *The folktale.* New York: Holt.
Tichy, Noel M.
1973   An analysis of clique formation and structure in organizations. *Administrative Science Quarterly* 18:194–208.
Tolbert, Pamela S.
1985   Institutional sources of organizational culture in major law firms. In *Culture and environment,* ed. Lynne Zucker, 101–14. Cambridge, Mass.: Ballinger.
Tolbert, Pamela S., and Robert N. Stern
1988   Organizations and professions: Governance structures in large law firms. Working paper no. 6. School of Industrial and Labor Relations, Cornell University.
Tolbert, Pamela S., and Lynne Zucker
1983   Institutional sources of change in organizational structure: The diffusion of civil service reform, 1880–1930. *Administrative Science Quarterly* 28:22–39.
Toren, Nino
1975   Deprofessionalization and its sources: A preliminary analysis. *Sociology of Work and Occupations* 2:323–37.
Triandis, Harry C.
1973   Work and nonwork: Intercultural perspectives. In *Work and nonwork in the Year 2001,* ed. Marvin D. Dunnette, 29–68. Monterey, Calif.: Brooks/Cole.
Trice, Harrison M.
1964   The nightwatchman: A study of an isolated occupation. *ILR Research* 10:3–11.
1985   Rites and ceremonials in organizational cultures. *Research in the Sociology of Organizations* 4:221–70.
1991   Comments and discussion. In *Reframing organizational culture,* ed. Peter J. Frost et al., 298–309. Newbury Park, Calif.: Sage Publications.
Trice, Harrison M., James Belasco, and Joseph A. Alutto
1969   The role of ceremonials in organizational behavior. *Industrial and Labor Relations Review* 23:40–51.
1988   Critical factors operating among university students in their occupational choices. Working paper no. 26. School of Industrial and Labor Relations, Cornell University.
Trice, Harrison M., and Janice M. Beyer
1984   Studying organizational cultures through rites and ceremonials. *Academy of Management Review* 9:653–69.
1986   Charisma and its routinization in two social movement organizations. In *Research in organizational behavior,* vol. 8, ed. Barry M. Staw and L. L. Cummings, 113–64. Greenwich, Conn.: JAI Press.
1991   Cultural leadership in organizations. *Organizational Science* 2:149–69.
1992   *The cultures of work organizations.* Englewood Cliffs, N.J.: Prentice-Hall.

Trice, Harrison M., and David Morand
1989 Rites of passage in work careers. In *Handbook of career theory*, ed. Michael Arthur, Douglas T. Hall, and Barbara Lawrence, 397–417. New York: Cambridge University Press.
1991 Cultural diversity: Organizational subcultures and countercultures. *Studies in Organizational Sociology: Essays in Honor of Charles K. Warriner* 10:69–105.
Trice, Harrison M., and George Ritzer
1972 The personnel manager and his self image. *Personnel Administrator* 35: 46–51.
Tuchman, Gaye
1972 Objectivity as strategic ritual: An examination of newsmen's notions of objectivity. *American Journal of Sociology* 77:660–79.
1978 *Making news: A study in the construction of reality*. New York: Free Press.
Tunstall, W. Brooke
1983 Cultural transition at A.T.&T. *Sloan Management Review* 25:15–26.
Turnbull, Colin
1984 Interview with Colin Turnbull. *Omni*, June, 87–90, 124–34.
Turner, Barry
1971 *Exploring the industrial subculture*. London: Macmillan.
1990 The rise of organizational symbolism. In *Organizations: Critical issues and new perspectives*, ed. John Hazzard and Dennis Pym, 83–96. London: Routledge.
Turner, Ralph H.
1969 The theme of contemporary social movements. *British Journal of Sociology* 20:390–405.
Turner, Terence S.
1977 Transformation, hierarchy, and transcendence. In *Secular ritual*, ed. Sally F. Moore and Barbara G. Myerhoff, 57–69. Amsterdam, The Netherlands: Van Gorcum.
Turner, Victor W.
1969 *The ritual process*. Chicago: Aldine.
1970 Betwixt and between: The liminal period in rites of passage. In *Man makes sense*, ed. Eugene A. Hammel and William S. Simons, 354–69. Boston: Little, Brown.
1977 Symbols in African ritual. In *Symbolic anthropology*, ed. David Kemnitzer and David M. Schneider, 183–94. New York: Columbia University Press.
Turnstall, Jeremy
1971 *Journalists at work*. London: Constable.
Turow, Scott
1977 *One L*. New York: Putnam.
Tushman, Michael L.
1977 A political approach to organizations: A review and rationale. *Academy of Management Review* 2:206–16.
Useem, Michael
1979 The social organization of the American business elite and participa-

tion of corporate directors in the governance of American institutions. *American Sociological Review* 44:553–72.

Van Gennep, Arnold

1960 [1909]   *Rites of passage*. Chicago: University of Chicago Press.

Van Maanen, John

1973   Observations on the making of policemen. *Human Organization* 32: 407–17.

1977   Summary: Toward a theory of career. In *Organizational careers: Some new perspectives*, ed. John Van Maanen, 161–79. New York: Wiley.

1978   People processing: Strategies of organizational socialization. *Organizational Dynamics*, Summer, 19–36.

1986   Power in the bottle: Informal interactions and formal authority. In *Executive power*, ed. S. Srivastva and Associates, 204–38. San Francisco: Jossey-Bass.

Van Maanen, John, and Stephen R. Barley

1984   Occupational communities: Control in organizations. In *Research in organizational behavior*, vol. 6, ed. Barry M. Staw and Larry Cummings, 287–365. Greenwich, Conn.: JAI Press.

1985   Cultural organization: Fragments of a theory. In *Organizational culture*, ed. Peter M. Frost, Meryl R. Louis, Craig C. Lundberg, Larry Moore, and Joanne Martin, 31–44. Beverly Hills: Sage.

Van Maanen, John, and Gideon Kunda

1989   "Real feelings": Emotional expression and organizational culture. *Research in Organizational Behavior* 11:43–103.

Van Maanen, John, and Edgar H. Schein

1979   Toward a theory of organizational socialization. In *Research in organizational behavior*, vol. 1, ed. Barry M. Staw, 209–59. Greenwich, Conn.: JAI Press.

Vaught, Charles, and David L. Smith

1980   Incorporation and mechanical solidarity in an underground coal mine. *Sociology of Work and Occupations* 7:159–67.

Veblen, T.

1921   *The engineers and the price system*. New York: Viking.

Wald, Matthew L.

1989   A hitch in plans for nuclear posterity. *New York Times*, Feb. 12, C2.

Waldman, Barry

1980   The reactions of the dental profession to changes in the 1970's. *American Journal of Public Health* 70:619–24.

Waldman, Peter

1986   More doctors and lawyers joining unions to fight large institutions. *Wall Street Journal*, May 23, 21.

Wall, Jim.

1986.   *Bosses*. Lexington, Mass.: Lexington Books.

Wallace, Linda

1989   The image and what you can do about it in the year of the librarian. *American Librarian*, Jan, 22–25.

Wallace, Michael
    1989   Brave new workplace: Technology and work in the new economy. *Work and Occupations* 16:363–92.
Wallace, Michael, and Kalleberg, Arne L.
    1982   Industrial transportation and the decline of craft: The decomposition of skill in the printing industry, 1931–1978. *American Sociological Review* 47:307–14.
Walsh, Diana C.
    1986   Divided loyalties in medicine: The ambivalence of occupational medical practice. *Society, Science, and Medicine* 23:789–96.
Walsh, Edward J., and Marylee C. Taylor
    1980   Occupational correlates of multidimensional self esteem: Comparisons among garbage collectors, bartenders, professors, and other workers. Paper presented at the annual meeting of the American Sociological Association, Aug. 21–26, Toronto.
Walsh, John P.
    1987   Skill and deskilling in retail meat. Paper presented at the annual meeting of the American Sociological Association, Aug. 18–23, Chicago.
    1989   Technological change and the division of labor: The case of retail meatcutters. *Work and Organizations* 16:165–83.
Walter, Gordon A.
    1985   Culture collisions in mergers and acquisitions. In *Organizational Culture,* ed. Peter Frost, Larry Moore, Meryl R. Louis, Craig Lundberg, and Joanne Martin, 301–14. Beverly Hills: Sage.
Walters, Vivian
    1982   Company doctors' perception of and responses to conflicting pressures from labor and management. *Social Problems* 30(1):1–12.
Wardwell, Walter
    1979   Limited and marginal practitioners. In *Medical sociology,* 3d ed., ed. Howard E. Freeman, 230–50. Englewood Cliffs, N.J.: Prentice-Hall.
Warner, W. Lloyd
    1937   *A black civilization.* New York: Harper and Brothers.
Warner, W. Lloyd, and O. J. Low
    1947   *The social system of the modern factory.* New Haven: Yale University Press.
Warren, Richard L.
    1975   Context and isolation: The teaching experience in an elementary school. *Human Organization* 34:139–48.
Watson, Tony J.
    1978   *The personnel manager: A study of the sociology of work and employment.* Boston: Routledge.
Wayne, Leslie
    1982   The year of the accountant. *New York Times,* Jan. 3, F1, 15.
    1989   Where were the accountants? CPA's come under attack as the search widens for culprits in the savings and loan crisis. *New York Times,* March 12, business section, 1–3, 11–13.

Weber, Max
1947 *The theory of social and economic organization,* ed. and trans. A. M. Henderson and T. Parsons. Glencoe, Ill.: Free Press.
1949 *The methodology of the social sciences,* ed. and trans. E. A. Shils and H. A. Finch. Glencoe, Ill.: Free Press.

Weick, Karl E.
1979 Cognitive processes in organizations. In *Research in organizational behavior,* vol. 1, ed. Barry M. Staw, 41–74. Greenwich, Conn.: JAI Press.

Weinberg, S. Kirson, and Henry Arond
1952 The occupational culture of the boxer. *American Journal of Sociology* 58 (March): 460–70.

Wharton, Joseph W., and John A. Worthley
1981 A perspective on the challenge of public management: Environmental paradox and organizational culture. *Academy of Management Review* 6: 357–61.

Whipp, Richard, Robert Rosenfeld, and Andrew Pettigrew
1989 Culture and competitiveness: Evidence from two mature U.K. industries. *Journal of Management Studies* 26:561–85.

Whittaker, Elvi, and Virginia Olesen
1964 The faces of Florence Nightingale: Functions of the heroine legend in an occupational sub-culture. *Human Organization* 23:123–30.

Whyte, William F.
1948 *Human relations in the restaurant industry.* New York: McGraw-Hill.
1956 Engineers and workers: A case study. *Human Organization* 14:3–12.
1978 Organizational behavior research. In *Applied anthropology in America,* ed. Elizabeth M. Eddy and William L. Partridge, 129–46. New York: Columbia University Press.

Whyte, William F., and Kathleen King Whyte
1988 *Making Mondragón: The growth and dynamics of the worker cooperative complex.* Ithaca, N.Y.: ILR Press.

Whyte, William F., Tove Helland Hammer, Christopher B. Meek, Reed Nelson, and Robert N. Stern
1983 *Worker participation and ownership.* Ithaca, N.Y.: ILR Press.

Wilensky, Harold L.
1964a The professionalization of everyone. *American Journal of Sociology* 70: 137–58.
1964b Varieties of work experience. In *Man in a world at work,* ed. Henry Borow, 125–54. Boston: Houghton Mifflin.
1967 *Organizational intelligence: Knowledge and policy in government and industry.* New York: Basic Books.

Williams, Robin M., Jr.
1960 *American society: A sociological interpretation.* 2d ed. New York: Knopf.
1970 *American society.* 3d ed. New York: Knopf.
1977 *Mutual accommodation: Ethnic conflict and cooperation.* Minneapolis: University of Minnesota Press.

Wilson, Robert N.
  1982   Team work in the operating room. In *The social world*, ed. Ian Robert-
         son, 100–106. New York: Worth.
Wilson, William A.
  1981   *On being human: The folklore of Mormon missionaries.* Logan: Utah State
         University Press.
Winston, D.
  1984   Scut work. *Working Woman*, Jan., 26.
Wister, Owen
  1902   *The Virginian: A horseman of the plains.* New York: Grosset and Dunlap.
Wolkomir, Richard
  1985   For many truckers, life on the road is an uphill struggle. *Smithsonian*
         16:91–96.
Woods, Clyde M.
  1972   Students without teachers: Student culture at a barber college. In
         Learning to work, ed. Blanche Geer, 19–30. Beverly Hills: Sage.
Wright, J. Patrick
  1979   *On a clear day you can see General Motors.* Grosse Pointe, Mich.: Wright
         Enterprises.
Wuthnow, Robert
  1987   *Meaning and moral order.* Berkeley: University of California Press.
Wuthnow, Robert, and Marsha Witten
  1988   New directions in the study of culture. *Annual Review of Sociology* 14:
         49–67.
Yinger, J. Milton
  1978   Countercultures and social change. In *Major social issues: A multidis-
         ciplinary view*, ed. J. Milton Yinger and Stephen J. Cutler, 476–97. New
         York: Free Press.
  1982   *Countercultures.* New York: Free Press.
Young, Frank W.
  1965   *Initiation ceremonies: A cross-cultural study of status dramatization.* New
         York: Bobbs-Merrill.
Young, Wesley O., and Louis D. Cohen
  1979   The nature and organization of dental practice. In *Handbook of medical
         sociology*, 3d ed. Howard Freeman, 193–208. Englewood Cliffs, N.J.:
         Prentice-Hall.
Zahn, Gordon
  1969   *The military chaplaincy: A study of role tenision in the Royal Air Force.*
         Buffalo, N.Y.: University of Toronto Press.
Zaleznik, Abraham, and M.F.R. Kets de Vries
  1975   *Power and the corporate mind.* Boston: Houghton Mifflin.
Zerubavel, Eviatar
  1981   *Hidden rhythms: Schedules and calendars in social life.* Chicago: Univer-
         sity of Chicago Press.

Zuboff, Shoshana
    1988   *In the age of the smart machine: The future of work and power.* New York: Basic Books.
Zuckerman, L. T., and R. A. Savedra
    1972   Professional licensing legislation in the United States with an emphasis on social work statistics in California. Venice, Calif. Typescript.
Zussman, R.
    1985   *Mechanics of the middle class.* Berkeley: University of California Press.

INDEX

Abbott, Andrew, 8–9, 14–15, 133, 197
Abrams, Walter H., 179
Academic researchers, 83
Academics. *See* Professors; Universities
Academy of Management, xv
Accommodation: between occupational and managerial cultures, 44, 162–66, 182–84, 185, 215; between occupational cultures, 186, 198–204, 211, 215; between subcultures, 222, 223–24
Accountants: assimilation of, 168–69; Census Bureau classification of, 13; code of ethics of, 194; conflict with lawyers, 7; control of tasks by, 153; development of, 5; group solidarity among, 41, 44; ideology of, 48–49, 67–68, 168–69; job boundaries of, 171–72, 195; as metaphor in organizations, 76; midcareer changes for, 134; myths held by, 84, 87–90; peer review for, 11; stereotype of, 73; stories about, 93
Acculturation, between subcultures, 222–26
Acquisitions, 216, 221–22, 223, 225
Actors, 50, 135
Addams, Jane, 6
Administrative principle. *See* Managerial (administrative) principle
Administrative subcultures: adaptations with occupational subcultures, 44, 161–85; conflicts with occupational subcultures, 152–55, 159, 160–61; description of, 149–51
Advertising agents, 50, 73
Aiken, Linda H., 209
Air Line Pilots Association, 194
Air traffic controllers, 18, 38, 181

Alienation, of subcultures, 225–26
Alutto, Joseph A., 86
American Association of Social Workers, 73
American Bar Association, 60, 195
American Medical Association, 72, 194
American Newspaper Guild, 61
American Nurses Association, 210
American Society of Newspaper Editors, 60
Anarchies, organized, 175
Andaman Islanders, 126
Anesthesiologists, 17
Applebaum, Herbert, 31, 99, 198
Applied occupations: development compared to craft occupations, 10; formal training in, 9; occupational associations compared to craft occupations, 10
Apprenticeships, 9, 12, 32, 42, 53, 55, 84, 121, 124, 128, 130, 194; medieval, 51–52
Aranya, N., 169
Architects: ancient, 5; code of ethics of, 194; control of tasks by, 153; distinctive set of tasks associated with, 7; heroes among, 6; lifestyle of, 33; socialization of, 136; symbolism in uniforms of, 99
Argot. *See* Language and argot
Arluke, Arnold, 205
Artists, in police organizations, 145
Ash, Mary Kay, 29, 227
Assimilation: between occupational and managerial cultures, 44, 166–70, 180–81, 185, 215; between

occupational cultures, 186, 204–10, 211, 215; between subcultures, 222, 223–24

Astronauts, 70, 135

Athletes: leadership for, 72; as metaphors in management, 77–80; mistake management among, 11; myths about, 92; occupational age of, 135; rituals practiced by, 103; specialized gestures used by, 102; stories about, 97; symbolism in uniforms of, 98; taboos of, 103

Athletic coaches: ancient, 5; and emotional attachment to winning, 24, 71; heroes and leaders among, 6, 71–72, 97; job boundaries of, 190; stories about, 97

Attorneys. See Lawyers

Auctioneers, 94

Authors. See Journalists; Writers

Automobile workers, 95

Bakers, 8

Bali, cockfighting in, 77

Ballet dancers, 116

Bank tellers, 29

Bank-wiring assembly room, in Hawthorne studies, xiv

Barbers: as distinct from hairdressers, 97; licensing of, 56, 193; self-image of, 37; socialization of, 116

Barley, Steven R., 4n, 19, 86, 114, 141, 145

Baron, George, 11

Bartenders, 37, 104, 130

Baseball players. See Athletes

Beck, Brenda E. F., 47

Becker, Howard S., 27, 37, 148

Belasco, James, 86

Beyer, Janice M., 218, 227

Bill collectors, 29, 49

Biologists, 187

Blacksmithing, 5, 193

Blaik, Earl, 71

Blake, Joseph A., 28

Blakelock, E., 35

Blau, Judith R., 136

Blau, Peter M., 157

Blauner, Robert, 156

Boland, Richard J., 87, 88

Boles, Jacqueline, 49

Bosk, Charles L., 109

Boudon, Raymond, 146

Boxers. See Athletes

Braverman, Harry, 17, 18

Brewery workers, 41, 51

Bricklayers, 84–85

Briloff, Abraham J., 88

Brint, Steven, 75

Broun, Heywood, 61

Brown, L. David, 224

Buffalo Bill's Wild West shows, 90

Building Trades Council, 199

Building tradesmen. See Construction workers

Bureaucracy, xiv–xv, 151, 154, 162, 225–26

Burnout, 86

Businesspersons: political beliefs of, 75; stereotype of, 73; symbolism in uniforms of, 99

Business Week, xv

Butchers, 28, 32, 163–64

California Bar Association, 57

Calvert, Monte, 168

Campbell, Joseph, 84

Cantor, Muriel G., 147

Capitalism, 54, 55, 151, 168

Carlton, Eric, 47

Carnival workers, 33, 35

Carpenters, 8, 51, 84, 98

Carper, J., 27

Carter, Reginald, 167–68

Cartoonists, 73

Cattle brokers, 101

CBS news (television), 70–71

Ceremonies. See Rites and ceremonies

Certification: of employee assistance program (EAP) workers, 136; and legitimization of an occupation, 10, 86

Certified public accountants, 48. See also Accountants

Challenger spacecraft, 153–54, 159

Chambers, R. J., 87

Chandlers, 51

Charisma, 69, 82

Chase, David B., 93

Check-out clerks, 29

Chemists, 75

Chicago Cubs, 97

Child, John, 182

Child, Julia, 6

Chiropractors, 102, 188, 207

Christensen, Barlow F., 194

Chrysler Corporation, 227

Church of the Afterlife, 15

Civil engineers, 8. See also Engineers

Clark, R. E., 30

Clayman, Steven E., 61

Clergy: in conflict with biologists, 187;

defrocking of, 107; forms of address for, 99; job boundaries of, 188, 190; as a profession, 55; symbolism in uniforms of, 98; task demands on, 30

Clerical workers. *See* Secretaries

Clinical psychologists. *See* Psychologists

Cliques and coalitions, 216, 217

Clowns, 98

Coalitions, 216, 217, 226

Coal miners. *See* Miners

Cockfighting, in Bali, 77

Cocktail waitresses: lifestyle of, 34, 36; rites of conflict reduction of, 109; selection of occupation by, 113; taboos of, 104

Code of ethics, 9, 10, 86, 194, 210

Cole, R. E., 6

Collective bargaining, 53, 54, 57

Colleges, adaptation between subcultures within, 203

Collingwood, Charles, 70

Committee on Human Relations in Industry, xiv

Committees, 109

Communication interlocks, 143–44, 158–59

Computer coders, 14

Computer data processors, 39, 40

Computer programmers: allegiance to occupational subculture of, 156; assimilation of, 170, 181; emergence of, 205; job boundaries of, 14; myths and fictions held by, 92; socialization by investiture of, 135–36; special language of, 101

Computers: in accounting, 88; and deprofessionalization, 57; and deskilling of office workers, 18; and satellite occupations, 205

Computer software compilers, 14

Computer systems analysts, 14, 156, 170

Computer workers, 27–28, 41, 156, 170. *See also names of individual specialities*

Concert musicians, 201–3

Conflict: within communities, 187–89; from countercultures, 147; and emergence of occupations, 7–8; between emerging and established occupations, 190–93; and ethnocentrism, 40, 41; leadership in, 69; between occupational and managerial cultures, 43, 152–55, 159; between occupational cultures, 186, 187–98, 210–11; within organizations, 189–90; and rites of conflict reduction, 109–10, 147, 192, 193–94

Congress of Industrial Organizations (CIO), 37

Construction workers: accommodations with management, 164; commitment to occupation among, 164; ideology of, 49; job boundaries of, 198–201; lifestyle of, 33; mistake management among, 11, 200; myths held by, 84–85; responsible autonomy of, 24, 49; socialization of, 122, 127, 130, 131; special language of, 100; and strong grid dimensions, 43, 164; symbolism in uniforms of, 98. *See also names of individual trades*

Contingency theory, 151

Cooks and chefs, xiv, 6, 28

Cornfield, Daniel, 181, 183

Corporate Cultures: The Rites and Rituals of Corporate Life (Deal and Kennedy), xv

Corwin, Ronald G., 181

Counselors, 35, 86, 197–98

Countercultures, 141, 143, 146–49, 158, 159, 221–22

Court clerks, 41

Cowboys: as metaphor in organizations, 76–77; myths about, 90–92; rites of renewal of, 108; specialized gestures used by, 102; in stockbrokers' imagery, 101; symbolism in uniforms of, 98; taboos of, 104

Craft occupations: apprenticeships in, 9, 12, 42, 53, 55, 84, 121, 124, 128, 130, 194; control of tasks in, 12; deskilling of, 18; development of, 10; grid dimensions of, 42–43; occupational associations in, 10; rites of renewal in, 108; socialization into, 127–28

Craft unionism, 53, 152

Crain, J., 178–79

Creationism, 187

Criminals, 4, 100, 103

Cryptographers, 6

Cultural anthropology, xiv

Cultural forms: definition of, 20, 21, 82–83; as dysfunctional, 25; symbols as, 23, 82, 97–99

Culture: ambiguity in, 21–22, 82; as approach to occupations, xiii–xvi, 213; core vs. periphery/subcultures, xi, xii, 22, 142, 143, 158; and countercultures, 141, 143, 146–49, 158, 159, 221; definition of, 20–21; as dysfunctional, 25; emergence and dynamism of, 22–23; and emotion, 24; features of, 21–26; grid dimension of, 25–26, 42–44, 161, 216; group dimension of, 25–41, 43–44, 161; multiplicity of, xvi, 22, 141;

relation to subcultures, xi–xii, 141–44;
and social relations, 25–26, 143
Custodians. *See* Janitors

Dalton, Melville, 68, 89
Dancers, 116, 135
Daniels, Arlene K., 166
Darrow, Clarence, 6
Deal, Terrence E., 70
Deauthorization, 146–47
Degradation, rites of, 107–8, 124
Dentists, 50, 196, 206
Departments, 216, 218–19
Depersonalization, 125
Deprofessionalization, 56–57, 147, 167,
179, 183–84
Derber, Charles, 57
Deskilling: due to new technology, 17–19,
27, 167, 182; by management, 7, 10, 18,
19, 27, 181–82, 226; process of, 17–19;
through assimilation, 167, 181–82
DiFazio, William, 102
Differentiation model (of culture), xvi, 22
Disney, Walt, 85
Doctors: affective neutrality of, 24, 30,
50, 104, 120; code of ethics of, 194;
commitment to occupation of, 131–32;
control of tasks by, 153; cultural forms
for, 39; deprofessionalization of, 183–
84; as dominating occupational
subculture, 184–85; emergence of, 8;
forms of address for, 99; heroes among,
39; ideology of, 50; job boundaries of,
7–8, 17, 188, 195–96; licensing of, 56;
121; myths held by, 85; and new
technology, 28; occupational association
for, 39; within organizations, 44, 139,
145, 162–63; peer review for, 11; as a
profession, 55; rites of passage for, 39;
satellite occupations around, 205–10;
selection of occupation by, 118–19;
socialization of, 115, 116, 118–19, 120–
21, 122, 137; social value of, 38;
specialized language of, 119, 120;
symbolic costumes of, 119; taboos of,
104; task demands on, 30. *See also*
Chiropractors; Pediatricians; Surgeons
Domestic servants, 15, 98
Domination, of occupational culture by
group features, 44, 170–74, 184–85
Douglas, Mary, 20, 43
Draftsmen, 13
Dry cleaners, 153
DuPont, Pierre S., 6
DuPont Company, 6, 8
Durkheim, Émile, 4

Editors, 113
Education: in alternative schools, 44, 174,
176; and emergence of occupations, 9;
of lawyers, 173; for nurses, 64–65; and
professionalism, 57; vocational
emphasis of, 6. *See also* Apprenticeships;
School teachers; Training programs
Egalitarianism, of occupational and
administrative subcultures, 44, 174–80,
185
Eisenhower, Dwight D., 6
Electricians: accommodation of, 183;
control of tasks by, 12, 152; emergence
of, 8; specialized language of, 128;
symbolism in uniforms of, 98; tools of,
128
Embalmers, 56, 190
Employee assistance program (EAP)
workers: and countercultures, 147; job
boundaries of, 191–92; shared cultural
forms of, 39; socialization by
investiture of, 136
Employers. *See* Organizations
Engineers: ancient, 5; assimilation of,
167–68, 181; code of ethics of, 194; in
conflict with geologists, 189; control of
tasks by, 153; emergence of, 8; group
solidarity among, 44; heroes among, 6;
myths held by, 85; occupational age of,
135; stereotype of, 73
Enhancement, rites of, 107
Enz, Cathy A., 215
Ethnocentrism: development of, 40–41,
44; encouragement of, 20, 24, 145; and
rituals, 102
Evans, Daniel, 107
Everstine, Diana S., 189
Everstine, Louis, 189
Examinations, and legitimization of an
occupation, 9
Executioners, demise of, 15
Exotic dancers, 67

Factory workers, 73, 131, 183
Fashion models, 135
Faulkner, Robert R., 135, 201
Federal Aviation Authority (FAA), 18
Feldman, Steven P., 173
Feminist health cooperatives, 44, 174,
176
Ferraro, Kenneth F., 208
Fervand School of Nursing (Detroit), 65
Fictions. *See* Myths and fictions
Fiddling, 130–31
Fidel, Ken, 156
Fine, Gary A., 28, 143

Fineman, Stephen, 72
Firefighters: athlete analogy for, 79; in conflict with police, 187; socialization of, 115, 122–23, 129; social value of, 38; stories about, 93, 96; task demands on, 31, 32
Fishermen, commercial: ethnocentrism among, 40; ideology of, 50, 67; job boundaries of, 13–14; lifestyle of, 35; midcareer changes for, 134; socialization of, 119, 120, 127
Fitzpatrick, John S., 31
Flight attendants: ideology of, 49, 67; stories about, 95–96; symbolism in uniforms of, 98; task demands on, 29
Football players. *See* Athletes
Forest rangers. *See* Park and forest rangers
Form, William H., 49, 84, 182, 186
Fortune, xv, 76
Franklin, Benjamin, 6
Freidson, Eliot, 41, 153, 190, 205
Funeral directors: control of tasks in, 12; job boundaries of, 188, 190; symbolism in uniforms of, 99; taboos of, 104; task demands on, 30. *See also* Embalmers; Grave diggers

Game analogies, 77–80
Gamst, Frederick C., 12
Gans, Herbert J., 62
Garbage collectors. *See* Sanitation workers
Garbin, A. P., 49
Gardner, Burleigh B., xiv
Garner, Roberta, 156
Garson, Barbara, 18
Geertz, Clifford, 46, 66, 77, 141
General Electric, 8
General Motors, 183
Geologists, 6, 100, 189
Gerstl, Joel, 167
Gestures, symbolic, 101–2
Gieryn, Thomas F., 187
Gilmore, Samuel, 201–2
Glaser, Barney G., 134
Goffman, Erving, 36, 77
Goodenough, Ward H., 141
Gouldner, Alvin, 156
Government regulatory agencies, 57
Gowler, Dan, 48
Grave diggers, 38
Greeley, Horace, 59
Green, Archie, 93
Green Bay Packers, 71–72
Greenwood, Davydd, 180
Gregory, Kathleen L., 142

Gritzer, Glenn, 205
Guilds, 51–52, 171

Haas, Jack, 121
Haight-Asbury Free Clinic, 176–77
Hairdressers, 97
Hall, K., 19
Hangmen. *See* Executioners
Hawthorne studies, xiv, 151
Health care workers, 85, 109. *See also names of individual occupations*
Hearn, H. L., 104
Hearst, William Randolph, 60
Henslin, J. M., 36
Heroes, 70
Hewlett-Packard, 6
High Noon (film), 91
Hinrichs, J. R., 75
Hispanics, in domestic service, 15
Hochschild, Arlie R., 49
Hogan, Daniel B., 72–73
Holleb, Gordon P., 179
Homans, George C., 142
Hood, Jane C., 35
Hoover, Herbert, 6
Horseshoers, 56
Hospitals, chronic clashes in, 224–25
Hospital ward attendants, 38
House painters, 98
Hughes, Everett C., 3, 10–11, 12–13, 73, 112
Human relations theory, 150–51

Iacocca, Lee, 227
IBM Corporation, 6, 227
Ideologies: and culture, xi, xii, 20, 21; definition of, 46–48, 80; dominant, 51–58; as dysfunctional, 25, 66–69, 81; and emotions, 24; evolution of, 58–66; examples of, 48–50; and models for organizations, 75–80; and personal values, 73–75; purveyors of, 69–73, 81; renewal of, 108–9; of subcultures, 143
Imenhotep (Egyptian engineer), 5
Incorporation, rites of, 117, 118, 121–25, 126–28, 137
Indoctrination, 117
Industrialization, and leisure time, 4
Industrial relations specialists, 92
Industrial Revolution, 51, 151
Industrial unionism, 53
In Search of Excellence (Peters and Waterman), xv
Insurance agents, 195
Integration, rites of, 110
Interest theory, 66–67

International Typographers Union, 167
Investigative reporters, 14. *See also*
    Journalists
Investment counselors, 153
Iron workers, high-steel: socialization of,
    120, 127; specialized gestures used by,
    102; stories about, 94; taboos of, 104;
    task demands on, 31, 32; training for,
    27
Italy, management in, 157

Jackall, Robert, 77, 78, 178–79
Janitors, 35–36, 38, 50
Janowitz, Morris, 33
Japan, 137, 213
Jargon. *See* Language and argot
Jazz musicians: as counterculture, 148;
    lifestyle of, 33, 35, 36; mistake
    management among, 11; primary
    reference group for, 39; self-image of,
    37; stories about, 96
Job titles, 6, 13, 27
Johnson, Harry M., 66
Joking relationships, and conflict
    reduction, 109
Joser (Egyptian king), 5
Journalists: code of ethics for, 61; control
    of tasks by, 12, 152; counterculture
    among, 147–48; emergence of, 7; heroes
    and leaders among, 6, 70–71; ideologies
    of, 59–62, 66, 67, 81; job boundaries of,
    14; rituals practiced by, 103; unionism
    among, 61. *See also* Writers
Judges, 39, 98

Kalleberg, Arne L., 18
Kanter, Rosabeth M., 3, 76, 130, 149
Katz, Donald, 218
Katz, Fred E., 113, 144
Keidel, Robert W., 80
Kennedy, Alan A., 70
Kennedy, John F., 72
Kiddy, John, 84–85
Kleinman, Sherryl, 143
Kluger, Richard, 59
Kneifel, Anita, 178
Kohn, M. L., 73
Krause, Merton, 178

LaBeef, E. E., 30
Lachman, R., 169
Language and argot, 82, 83, 99–102
Lawyers: code of ethics of, 194; collective
    of, 177, 178; conflict with accountants,
    7; in conflict with psychotherapists,
    189–90; education of, 173; emergence

of, 8; forms of address for, 99; heroes
    among, 6; job boundaries of, 13, 57,
    171–72, 194–95; licensing of, 165, 178;
    myths held by, 85; occupational age of,
    135; peer review for, 11; and personal
    values, 73; in police organizations, 145;
    political beliefs of, 75; as a profession,
    55; rituals practiced by, 103; role in
    organizations, 145, 164–66; satellite
    occupations around, 205; socialization
    of, 115, 129, 172–73; stereotype of, 73;
    symbolism in uniforms of, 99; training
    for, 27; unionism among, 57
Layton, E., 168
Leadership: and cultural flux, 226–27; and
    ideologies, 69–73, 81
Leahy, Frank, 71
Legge, Karen, 48
Leisure time, amount of, 3–4
Lembright, Muriel F., 130
Lett, James, 62
Levinson, Daniel J., 113
Lewin-Epstein, Noah, 74
Librarians: control of tasks by, 12;
    ethnocentrism among, 40–41; ideology
    of, 50; job boundaries of, 13; as
    professionals, 55
Licensing: of apprentices, 52; and
    legitimization of an occupation, 9, 10;
    and professionalism, 56, 193, 211
Light, Donald, 210
Liminality, during socialization, 119–20
Lincoln, Abraham, 54
Lincoln, James R., 6
Locomotive engineers. *See* Railroad
    engineers
Loggers, 99–100, 104
Lombardi, Vince, 6, 24, 71–72, 81, 97
Longshoremen: and counterculture, 148–
    49; deskilling of, 181–82; ethnocentrism
    among, 40; ideology of, 50; lifestyle of,
    33, 34; specialized gestures used by,
    102; special language of, 100, 128;
    taboos of, 104; task demands on, 31,
    32
Louis, Meryl R., 118, 215

McBride, Kerry, 6
McCarl, Robert S., 96, 115
McCarthy, Joseph, 70
Machinists: accommodation of, 183; as
    counterculture, 148; deskilling of, 17,
    18, 181; rites of conflict, reduction of,
    110; socialization of, 125; task demands
    on, 32
Maintenance workers, 92. *See also* Janitors

Management: athlete metaphors in, 77–80; control of tasks by, 145–46, 150, 159; cowboy metaphor in, 76–77; deskilling of occupations by, 7, 10, 18, 19, 27, 181–82, 226; functions of, 151; midcareer movement into, 134–35; stories about dealing with, 95; as a subculture, xii, 149–55, 159; work hours of, 3. *See also* Scientific management

Managerial (administrative) principle, 41, 145–46, 149, 150, 151, 159, 161, 220

Managers: as job title, 13; as location of subcultures, 216, 219–20, 226

Mann, Brenda J., 37

Mars, Gerald, 148, 174

Marshall, S. L. A., 32

Martin, Harry W., 113

Martin, Joanne, xvi, 22, 215

Martin, Susan E., 117

Mary Kay, Inc., 29, 227

Mason, Mr., 154

Mauksch, Hans, 209

Meara, Hannah, 32

Meat cutters. *See* Butchers

Mechanics, 73

Medical professions: conflict between, 7–8, 195–98, 204. *See also* Doctors; Nurses; Pharmacists; Psychiatrists; Veterinarians

Melbin, Murray, 120

Mental hospitals, adaptation between subcultures within, 204

Mentors, 129–31

Mergers, 216, 221–22, 223, 224

Merrill Lynch, 18

Metalworkers, 8

Meteorologists, 6

Meyer, Alan D., 68

Meyerson, Debra, xvi, 22, 72, 215

Midwest Community Mental Health Center, 175, 177, 178

Midwives, 7–8, 49, 190

Military history: and emergence of rehabilitation therapists, 8; non-military occupations' impact on, 6; and professionalization of nurses, 62–64

Military professions, 142–43. *See also* Sailors; Soldiers

Miller, Delbert C., 84

Miller, I., 19

Miners: accommodation of, 183; ancient, 5; control of tasks in, 12; decline of numbers of, 15; lifestyle of, 34; socialization of, 123–24, 127; songs about, 93; task demands on, 31; uniform of, 123

"Mines of Avondale, The" (song), 93

Mingus, Charles, 96

Mintzberg, Henry, 117

Missionaries, 94

Mitroff, Jan I., 69

Mondragón, Spain, 180

Montague, Susan P., 78

Moore, Larry F., 47

Moore, Wilbert E., 73

Morais, Robert, 78

Morgan, Gareth, 222

Mormon missionaries, 94

Mosk, Stanley, 189

Moyers, Bill, 70

Mulcahy, F. D., 135

Murrow, Edward R., 6, 70–71, 81

Musicians. *See* Concert musicians; Jazz musicians; Orchestra musicians

Mutual Aid Society (for psychological mediums), 15

Myerhoff, Barbara G., 137

Myths and fictions, 82, 83–92, 110

National Association for the Advancement of Colored People, 195

National Football League (NFL), 72

National Organization of Spiritualists, 15

Neophytes. *See* Socialization of newcomers

Newman, Katherine, 177

New York Giants, 72

New York Times, xv

New York World Board of Accuracy and Fair Play, 60

Nicholson, Nigel, 133

Nightingale, Florence, 6, 63–64, 65–66, 69, 81

Nightingale Training School for Nurses, 65

Nightwatchmen, 38

Night workers, 35–36, 45, 51, 120

Noble, David F., 168

Novices. *See* Socialization of newcomers

Nurses: allegience to occupational subculture of, 157; code of ethics for, 65, 194; and counterculture, 148; education for, 64–65; heroes among, 6; ideologies of, 62–66, 67–68, 81; job boundaries of, 17, 64–65, 208–10; myths held by, 86, 87; primary reference group for, 39; rituals practiced by, 103; selection of occupation by, 113; socialization of, 125, 126, 129; social value of, 38; specialized gestures used by, 102; symbolism in uniforms of, 97–98; task demands on, 30, 31, 32

O'Brien, Michael, 97
Occupational associations: impact of
    specialization on, 57; and legitimization
    of an occupation, 8, 9–10, 86, 194, 210;
    meetings as rites of integration for, 110;
    for secretaries, 155
Occupational community, 26
Occupational countercultures, 146–49,
    159, 221–22
Occupational cultures: accommodations
    between, 186, 198–204, 211, 215;
    assimilation between, 186, 204–10, 211,
    215; attraction to, 112–14, 137; chronic
    clashes between, 186, 187–98, 210–11;
    grid dimension of, 42–44, 161–79
    passim; group dimension of, 26–41, 43–
    44, 161–79 passim
Occupational principle, 41, 145, 153–55,
    159
Occupational subcultures: adaptations
    with administrative subcultures, 161–
    85; allegience to, 156; chronic clashes
    between, 224–25; conflicts with
    administrative subcultures, 152–55,
    159, 160–61; core culture of, xii, 141;
    and cultural forms, 46–48, 82–111
    passim; description of, 144–49; effects
    on organizations, 155–58, 213; and
    ideologies, xii, 46–81 passim; as models
    for other subcultures, 215–16; potency
    of, 158
Occupations: commitment to, 131–32,
    144; conflict between emerging and
    established, 190–93; consciousness of
    kind in, 32–33; and control over tasks,
    7, 10–13, 145–46, 160, 213; cultural
    forms of, 33, 39, 212; decline and
    demise of, 14–16; and deskilling, 17–19;
    development of, 7–10; distinctive set of
    tasks associated with, 7–10; expertise
    in, 26–28, 45, 55; language and argot in,
    82, 83, 99–102; midcareer changes
    between, 133–35, 137; myths and
    fictions about, 82, 83–92, 110; and
    personal/social identity, 3, 36–38, 45,
    145; pervasiveness of, 33–36, 45; as
    primary reference group, 38–39, 145;
    revivals of, 16–17; and right to define
    mistakes, 10–11; rites and ceremonies
    in, 82, 83, 104–10, 111; rituals and
    taboos in, 82, 83, 102–4; role of, 4–7;
    selection of, 112–14; stories and songs
    about, 82–83, 92–97, 110; task demands
    of, 28–32, 45
Office workers. See Secretaries
Oil industry, 6, 100

Olesen,Virginia L., 66, 129
Oligarchy, Iron Law of, 177
O'Neill, Thomas P., 108
"Only a Miner" (song), 93
Ophthalmologists, 188
Optometrists, 188–89, 206, 207
Orchestra musicians, 135
Organizations: acculturation within,
    222–26; attachment to, 6, 156–57;
    bureaucratic model of, xiv–xv, 151;
    chronic clashes within, 189–90, 224–25;
    cultural model of, xiii–xvi, 213–15;
    effects of occupational subcultures on,
    155–58; as focus of research, 4–5, 212;
    leadership of, 226–27; location of
    subcultures in, 216–22; occupations
    as ideological models for, 75–80, 81
Osteopaths, 207
Ouchi, William G., 6

Packard, David, 6
Padgett, J. F., 175
Painters. See House painters
Park and forest rangers, 38, 99, 116
Pascale, Richard, 126
Passage. See Rites of passage
Pathologists, 68
Pavalko, Ronald M., 4, 110
Peace Corps, 215
Pearl Harbor, attack on, 142–43
Pediatricians, 68
Perrucci, Robert, 167
Personality, and occupations, 73–75
Personnel administrators: allegience to
    occupational subculture of, 157;
    assimilation of, 169–70; group
    solidarity among, 44; job boundaries
    of, 190–91; myths and fictions held
    by, 85, 86, 92
Pharmacists: allegience to occupational
    subculture of, 157; job boundaries of,
    16–17, 155, 195–96; licensing of, 56, 193;
    revival among, 16; rituals practiced by,
    103
Philostratus, 5
Physicians. See Doctors
Physician's assistants (PAs), 208
Pilcher, William W., 128, 148
Pimps, 49–50
Plasterers, 98
Plumbers: control of tasks by, 12, 152;
    development of, 5; emergence of, 8;
    licensing of, 56, 193; symbolism in
    uniforms of, 98
Podiatrists, 206–7
Police detectives, 28

Police officers: and administration, 173; in conflict with firefighters, 187; dominating group dimensions among, 44; ethnocentrism of, 21; lifestyle of, 35; myths held by, 87; rites of passage for, 107; selection of occupation by, 114; socialization of, 115, 117, 124–25, 129–30, 131; specialized gestures used by, 102; subcultures of, 220, 223; symbolism in uniforms of, 98; task demands on, 30, 31; training for, 27
Political beliefs, and occupations, 75
Polsky, Ned, 29
Pondy, Louis, 48, 69, 76, 99
Pool hustlers, 29
Post office employees, 120
Printers and typographers: allegience to occupational subculture of, 156; deskilling of, 18, 27, 167, 181; heroes among, 6; lifestyle of, 33, 34, 35, 36; socialization of, 120; special language of, 99; unionism among, 61, 167
Prison inmates, as hired workers, 52
Producer cooperatives, 44, 176
Professional Air Traffic Controllers Organization, 18
Professionalization: and deprofessionalization, 56–57, 147, 167, 179, 183–84; history of, 51, 54–58, 80–81; and legitimization of an occupation, 10, 153, 193; myths about, 85–90; of pharmacists, 16–17; of police officers, 125; as a rite of conflict reduction, 193–94; and traits of professionals, 54–55, 85
Professions: definition of, 55; expertise questioned, 147; as focus of study, 12–13; job boundaries of, 14, 101; and job title proliferation, 6; and political beliefs, 75; specialization within, 57, 155; unionism in, 57
Professors: ceremonies of, 105, 107; commitment to occupation of, 131–32; conflicting occupational subcultures of, 156; control of tasks by, 153; forms of address for, 99; rites of conflict reduction about, 109; self-image of, 37; symbolism in uniforms of, 98, 99. *See also* Universities
Project teams, 109
Prostitutes: group solidarity among, 41; ideology of, 49–50, 67; socialization of, 131; taboos of, 104
Psychiatrists: emergence of, 10; job boundaries of, 15–16, 197–98; in military, 166
Psychological mediums, demise of, 15–16

Psychologists: job boundaries of, 197–98; licensing of, 197; myths held by, 86; in police organizations, 145; role in organizations, 145
Psychotherapists, 189–90, 197–98, 204. *See also* Counselors; Psychiatrists; Psychologists
Publicity agents, 7
Public lecturers, demise of, 16
Public relations, 14
Pulitzer, Joseph, 60
Purchasing agents, 110, 189, 225

Radcliffe-Brown, A. R., 126
Radiologists, 27
Raelin, Joseph A., 147
Rafaeli, Anat, 31
Railroad engineers: deskilling of, 18; lifestyle of, 33, 34; social value of, 38; stories about, 95
Railroad mechanics, 95
Railroad workers: lifestyle of, 33, 34, 36; socialization of, 127; special language of, 99, 100, 128; stories about, 95
Rather, Dan, 71
Rationality, 149–50, 159, 177, 220
Realtors, 57, 195
Reconstitution, of subcultures, 225–26
Reeder, Sharon J., 209
Rehabilitation therapists, 88
Renewal, rites of, 108–9, 147
Restaurant employees, xiv, 224. *See also* Bartenders; Cocktail waitresses; Cooks and chefs; Waitpersons
Reynolds, Burt, 70
Riemer, Jeffrey W., 130, 199
Rites and ceremonies: of conflict reduction, 109–10, 147, 192, 193–94; of degradation, 107–8, 124; description of, 82, 83, 104–10, 111; of enhancement, 107; graduations, 121–22, 126; of integration, 110; of renewal, 108–9, 147. *See also* Rites of passage
Rites of passage: definition of, 105–7; incomplete, 125, 126–28; of incorporation, 117, 118, 121–25, 126–28, 137; individualized, 133–37; and role commitment, 131–33; of separation, 117, 118–19, 122–25, 126–28, 137; socialization of newcomers through, 105, 106–7, 111, 112, 117–28; of transition, 117, 118, 119–21, 122–25, 126–28, 137
Rituals and taboos, 82, 83, 102–4
Ritzer, George, 4, 47, 155, 157
Rockwell, Norman, 85

Role models, 70
Role reversals, 108, 109
Rookies. See Socialization of newcomers
Rosenbaum, James E., 134–35
Rosenstein, David, 196
Rothman, Robert A., 4, 8, 114, 195–96
Rothschild, Joyce, 176, 178
Rothschild-Whitt, Joyce, 177
Roy, Donald, 125, 148
Royal Canadian Mounted Police, 91
Ruth, Babe, 97

Sagas. See Myths and fictions
Sailors, 100, 102
Salespersons: ideology of, 49, 67;
    socialization of, 130; sociological study
    of, 4; special language of, 101; task
    demands on, 29
Samuel, Yitzak, 74
Sandhogs, 31, 34–35, 36–37
Sanitation workers, 37–38
Santino, Jack, 95
Sassoon, Joseph, 98
Savedra, R. A., 198
Savings and loan banking crisis, 88–89
Sawmill workers, 102
Schein, Edgar H., 40, 69, 125, 129, 134
Schneller, Eugene S., 208
Schooler, C., 73
School teachers: commitment to
    occupation of, 131, 132; control of
    tasks by, 11–12; dominating group
    dimensions among, 44; as professionals,
    55; rituals practiced by, 103; and school
    administration, 173; socialization of,
    116, 132–33; sociological study of, 4;
    stereotype of, 73
Schrier, D. A., 135
Schwartzman, Helen B., 109, 175, 178
Scientific management, 17, 150–51
Scientists: control of tasks by, 152;
    ideology of, 67; myths held by, 85;
    occupational age of, 135. See also
    Biologists; Chemists; Geologists
Scott, Donald M., 16
Scott, W. Richard, 150, 157
Sears, Roebuck and Co., 218, 224
Secretaries: control of tasks by, 154–55;
    and countercultures, 149; deskilling
    of, 17, 181; ethnocentrism of, 155;
    occupational associations for, 155
Self-employment, and licensing, 56
Sensationalism, ideology of, 59–60
Separation, rites of, 117, 118–19, 122–25,
    126–28, 137
Septic tank cleaners, 153

Serial socialization, 129
Shaffir, William, 121
Shakespeare, William, 82
Shearson Lehman, 18
Shipbuilders, 95
Silicon Valley, 41, 218
Silver, Marc L., 130, 200
Simmel, George, 77
Simpson, Ida Harper, 18–19
Simpson, Richard, 205
Sitkin, Sim, 157
60 Minutes (television magazine), 137
Slang. See Language and argot
Smirich, Linda, 222
Smith, David L., 123
Smoke jumpers, 98, 122
Socialization of children, 116, 117
Socialization of newcomers: informal,
    128–29; by investiture, 135–36; by
    mentors, 129–31; and occupational
    community, 26–27; through education,
    9, 12; through rites of passage, 105,
    106–7, 111, 112, 117–28
Social workers: and administration, 173;
    allegience to occupational subculture
    of, 157; commitment to occupation
    of, 131–32; compared to health care
    workers, 85; deskilling of, 18;
    dominating group dimensions among,
    44; heroes among, 6; ideology of, 47,
    49, 67; job boundaries of, 72–73, 187–88,
    197–98; licensing of, 72–73; myths held
    by, 85, 86; as professionals, 55; rites of
    conflict reduction of, 109; socialization
    of, 132–32, 136; task demands on, 32
Sociologists, 187–88, 194
Soldiers: and military lifestyle, 33, 35;
    rites of degradation of, 107; rituals
    practiced by, 103; socialization of,
    115; stories about, 95; symbolism in
    uniforms of, 98; task demands on, 31–
    32
Songs. See Stories and songs
Sonnenstuhl, William J., 160, 185n
Sorensen, J., 169
Sorensen, T., 169
Spangler, Eve, 172
Spenner, Kenneth I., 19
Spiritualists. See Psychological mediums
Sports. See Athletes; Athletic coaches
Spradley, James P., 37
Staff units, 216, 220–21, 226
Statisticians, police, 145
Steelworkers, 27. See also Iron workers,
    high-steel
Steiger, Thomas L., 49

Stein, L., 209
Stereotypes, 68, 73
Stern, Robert N., 172–73
Stewardesses. *See* Flight attendants
Stewart, Phyllis, 147
Stinchcombe, Arthur, L., 164
Stockbrokers, 18, 100–101
Stoll, Patricia, 104
Stories and songs, 82–83, 92–97, 110
Strain theory, 66–67
Strauss, Anselm L., 134, 204, 225
Striptease artists: Census Bureau
    classification of, 13; ideology of, 49;
    lifestyle of, 36; occupational age of, 135;
    socialization of, 116; taboos of, 104
Studds, Gerry, 107
Subcultures, definition of, 141–44. *See also*
    Occupational subcultures
Sunbelt Savings Bank (Dallas), 89
Surgeons, 102, 108–9
Sutcliffe, Kathleen, 157
Sutherland, Tammy, 208
Sutton, Robert I., 31
Swieringa, Robert J., 90
Symbols: as expression of culture, 23, 39,
    82, 97–99; imprecision of, 23, 82

Taboos. *See* Rituals and taboos
Takeovers. *See* Acquisitions
Tangu ethnic group (New Guinea), 77
Task forces, 109
Taxi-dancers, 4
Taxi drivers, 36, 130
Taylor, F. W., 150
Taylor, Marylee C., 37
Taylorism. *See* Scientific management
Teachers. *See* School teachers
Technology: and accommodation, 182–83;
    and deprofessionalization, 57; and
    deskilling, 17–19, 27, 167, 182; and
    location of subcultures, 216, 217–18;
    and satellite occupations, 205
Theory Z (Ouchi), xv
Timbira ethnic group (Brazil), 77
Title insurers, 57, 195
Tolbert, Pamela S., 172–73
Tominaga, K., 6
Trade unions. *See* Unions
Train dispatchers, 99
Training programs: and acquisition of
    expertise, 27; and legitimization of an
    occupation, 9; and socialization of
    newcomers, 117
Transition, rites of, 117, 118, 119–21, 122–
    25, 126–28, 137. *See also* Rites of passage
Trice, Harrison M., 86, 157

Trice, William M., 160
Tropp, Asher, 11
Truck drivers: midcareer changes for,
    134; self-images of, 28–29; socialization
    of, 130; task demands on, 28
Tuchman, Gaye, 61
Tunnel and Construction Workers Union,
    36
Turner, Ralph, 146
Turner, Terence S., 125
Turner, Victor W., 120
Turow, Scott, 73
Tymms, Mr. (an accountant), 5

Uniforms, 97–99
Unions: administrative role of, 152;
    allegience to, 157; history of, 51, 52–54,
    80; and job title proliferation, 6; and
    legitimization of an occupation, 10, 193;
    and study of organizational behavior, 5
United States Census Bureau, job
    classification by, 13
United States House of Representatives,
    107–8
United States Marine Corps, 23
United States marshals, 30–31
Universities, adaptation between
    subcultures within, 203

Values, personal, 73–75
Van Gennep, Arnold, 105, 112, 122, 125
Van Maanen, John, 4n, 19, 21, 86, 106–7,
    114, 125, 129, 134, 141, 145
Vaught, Charles, 123
Veterinarians, 99
Victoria (queen of England), 63
Village Gate (New York), 96
Virginian, The (Wister), 91
Vocation vs. profession, 64

Wagner Act of 1935, 53, 54
Waitpersons: ethnographic study of, xiv;
    ideology of, 49, 67; midcareer changes
    for, 134; rites of conflict reduction of,
    109; rites of renewal of, 108; and role of
    bartenders, 37; socialization of, 130;
    sociological study of, 4. *See also*
    Cocktail waitresses
Walczak, David, 4, 47
Wall, Jim, 50
Wallace, Mike, 6, 70
Wall Street Journal, xv, 3
Walsh, Edward J., 37
Walsh, John P., 164
Wardwell, Walter, 206, 207
Warner, W. Lloyd, xiv–xv

Index

Warren, Richard L., 12
Watch repairers, demise of, 14
Watson, Thomas, Jr., 6, 227
Wayne, John, 70
Wayne, Leslie, 87–88
Weber, Max, 149, 151
Weick, Karl E., 90
Welders, 94, 119, 121, 122, 137
West, Michael, 133
Whitt, A. Allen, 176, 178
Whittaker, Elvi W., 66, 129
Whyte, William F., xiv, 37
Wilensky, Harold L., 9–10, 142
Williams, Robin M., Jr., 193

Wister, Owen, 91
Witten, Marsha, 58
Work hours, 3–4
Wright, Frank Lloyd, 6
Writers, 13, 14. *See also* Journalists
Western Electric, 101
Wuthnow, Robert, 46, 58, 62

Yinger, Milton J., 147

Zuboff, Shoshana, 181
Zuckerman, L. T., 198
Zussman, R., 168

HARRISON M. TRICE is a professor emeritus in the Department of Organizational Behavior, School of Industrial and Labor Relations, Cornell University. His longstanding interest in applying the concept of culture to work organizations began when he was a graduate student in the Department of Sociology/Anthropology at the University of Wisconsin, where he received his Ph.D. His research interests include equal employment opportunity policy, the implementation of innovation in organizations, cultural leadership in work organizations, and employee assistance programs. His many publications include *The Cultures of Work Organizations*, written with Janice M. Beyer; *Strategies for Employee Assistance Programs: The Crucial Balance*, written with William J. Sonnenstuhl; and *Spirits and Demons at Work: Alcohol and Other Drugs on the Job*, written with Paul Roman.